travelwithme365
An Unexpected Match

travelwithme365
An Unexpected Match

A JOURNEY OF LUST, LOVE AND INTIMATE LETTERS

CAROL MURRAY

For more information, email: carolmurraywriter@gmail.com

ISBN: paperback - 979-8-9878658-9-7

ISBN: eBook - 979-8-9893076-0-9

ISBN: hardback - 979-8-9893076-1-6

Author Bio

Carol Murray has always enjoyed writing. Although this is her first published novel, she has always journaled and connected with family and friends through crafty emails and handwritten notes. Carol has said for years that she wanted to chronicle her journey with her Captain, share her gratitude for him, and let others know of his kindness, unselfishness, and compassion.

Carol lives in Shelby Township, Michigan, with her husband, Paul, who is retired. During the day, while she works as a Realtor®, her husband day trades.

Carol's love for this project has left the door open to future writing. She feels that by sharing the simple act of gratefulness with her readers, they may be inspired to share their gratitude with others, acknowledging them with the spoken or written word. With that in mind, writing this book would be a success in and of itself.

TABLE OF CONTENTS

DEDICATION

This book is written for my Captain, Paul Benjamin Murray, for without you and the letters you saved, this book would not have been possible. My love for you goes beyond the spoken word. You give unconditionally and never ask for or need accolades. As a divorced mother of three, I never dreamed it would be possible to live the life you have given me. May you continue to realize how grateful I am for you and the depth of my admiration for you. We have always said that it is about the journey and not the destination; well, love of my life, our journey has been phenomenal.

To my dearly departed friend, Tom K., may you be smiling down now, knowing this book has been written for all to read. You were not only my real estate mentor but a true friend. This story would have ended differently without your suggestion to go online and encouragement to step out of my comfort zone with Captain.

ACKNOWLEDGMENTS

Thank you to our children, Sara, Diana, Erica, Madeline, Joseph, and Charles, and their spouses or significant others, Nick, Kevin, Isaiah, Cody, Margie, and our grandbabies, who have traveled this journey with us. May they learn even more about our love story and commitment.

Thank you to my former spouse, Ludovico, for the graciousness you have always provided to Paul and me and for making my travel possible when our children were younger. I am grateful for the relationship we have.

Thank you to Sue, Paul's former spouse, for the kindness you've shown me, especially when I was missing my children. You and Paul have raised three amazing daughters.

Mom and Dad, I am so grateful you got to know Paul and his heart before you left this world.

To my siblings, Cindy and Doug, and their partners, Leon and Monika, thank you for welcoming Captain into the fold and the newly formed cigar and bourbon club. We have all shared some truly unique experiences.

There have been many friends who have witnessed our love story. Elaine, from the beginning, you have been there every step of the way. Thank you for talking me off the cliff at times. Thank you to my longtime friend, Anne Marie, for your countless support and belief in me. To our friends: Russ and Cara, Rob and Tina, Barb and Joe, Bruce and Sue, Joe and Nancy, Rob and Val, Tom (RIP) and Lynda, Jack and Margie, and everyone who came on this journey with us. The memories we've made with all of you can only be described as epic and legendary.

Lastly, I would like to thank Match.com for having the platform for Paul and me to meet and an algorithm that matched us—as my Captain was out of my geographic location requirements by fifteen miles!

And I would be remiss if I didn't recognize and thank Gabrielle White, my editor, for all the hours she dedicated to my labor of love. Thank you for the support you've given me and your professionalism when my manuscript may have been difficult to read. Although you are an adult, I'll never forget that precious little girl in cowboy boots. I want to thank my other editor, Lara C. from the UK, who also assisted with editing and formatting.

INTRODUCTION

I did not think I was looking for the "one." After a crummy date, I thought I would go online to see what was out there. I wanted to have fun, yet I didn't want to love and leave them, or vice versa. After being married for fifteen years, divorced for three, and dating a few men off and on, I figured I would dig a little deeper in the "pond." I felt it was important to attract someone that had the qualities I was looking for.

What does one do to attract someone? Send out that positive energy! I compiled a list of qualities I was looking for in a man. I wrote it, typed it up, and carried it around with me. One of my previous boyfriends, Michael, used to say to me, "Ask for one-hundred percent of what you want. If the answer is 'no,' be willing to negotiate." Some of my matches were not a perfect fit for me; however, I did get close with some, and others were downright crazy—as I am sure many of you can attest to in the online dating realm. There was one, though… One exceptional one caught my eye.

This is a true story of my journey with my "match" and the extraordinary relationship I was not expecting. Read on if you want to hear about a girl who never dreamed this could happen to her— being swept off her feet while being wined and dined and traveling the country! I have included numerous letters and correspondence from Paul and me—thank you, Captain, for saving them—to demonstrate that it is possible to find your "one" and embark on your own journey. If you're already in a great relationship, read on anyway for enjoyment or a hint at how we managed to sustain a ten-year-long distance relationship.

This book is not for the cynical or people who refuse to believe fairy tales can happen to them. But if a tiny space is open to the possibility, keep reading.

Please also note that this book contains some adult content. Therefore, it is not suitable for persons under eighteen years of age.

Many people have wondered how Paul and I made it work and have asked what our secret was. Well, within these pages, you will find the answers. It all started with a click...

May 25, 2015

"I pray one day that I can do something so wonderful for you to show all of my appreciation. In the meantime, you have my heart and all of its love."
Your Princess; 4Ever & A Day!

CHAPTER ONE

Click, Respond, Meet

Friday, January 1, 2010

It was New Year's Day, and the previous night had been a crushing disappointment in the realm of romance. But such is the unpredictable nature of dating—it can swing either way. On this particular occasion, my date had turned out to be a dud.

John and I initially crossed paths through a mutual friend, and later, he asked me what I was doing on New Year's Eve. So, when my dear friend Cara and her husband Russ extended an invitation for me and a plus one to join them for New Year's Eve cocktails, followed by a delightful evening of dining and dancing at the nearby boat harbor and event center, I naturally asked John to be my date. It was a fun night overall, and on the surface, John seemed nice. He was an ambitious entrepreneur, wore a genuine smile, and had a laid-back demeanor—admirable qualities but truthfully, I felt my energy wane whenever I was around him. An unsettling feeling gnawed at my stomach as he drove me home later that night. You see, there is always a percentage of men who expect something more at the end of a date, and unsure if John had picked up on my lack of interest, I knew saying goodbye would probably not go smoothly. When we eventually pulled up outside my house, I genuinely thanked him for a good evening and went to leave, only to have my suspicions confirmed when he stopped me.

"*Wait, aren't you going to invite me in?*" he asked.

I tried to stay congenial despite the awkwardness of the moment.

"*No, I don't think this is going to work,*" I replied.

"*But it's New Year's Eve. Come on…*" he persisted.

I shook my head, increasingly annoyed by his refusal to accept my answer.

Nice guy, my ass.

"*Nope. In fact, I think it's best if you leave now,*" I stated firmly before making my way into the sanctuary of my home.

The following morning, I realized I had to expand my dating horizon. The time had come to take the plunge, venture into the pond and check out the fish. If you want groceries, you go to the grocery store, and if you want to meet someone go to where they are gathered, virtually that is, online.

Ironically, a few weeks prior, my beloved friend and mentor, Tom—who I deeply miss since his passing—had playfully joked during our office holiday gift exchange that I had won a subscription to Match.com. Tom was well aware of my dating history. While the men I'd dated were kind-hearted, they simply did not meet my expectations. In light of this revelation, I decided to compile a list of qualities I desired in a partner. If I was going to put myself out there, I resolved to seek a reciprocal connection with "quality" men. In the end, my list consisted of over forty criteria that I hoped to attract into my life. The irony lay in that I wasn't looking for a serious relationship. It was more about exploring the vast pool and embracing the unknown. After all, as the saying goes, "Girls just want to have fun!" Yet, deep down, I knew I wasn't a "love and leave 'em" kind of gal who engaged in casual flings. I was never one to take advantage of another person's emotions.

As fate would have it, Tom's joke turned into reality. On January second, my Match.com profile went "live." Regrettably, Match.com has since wiped my profile bio and messages, so the best I can do is reconstruct the essence of my bio and recollect the core of the messages exchanged with Paul. Fortunately, I saved all my messages and emails from Paul, so his words will be presented verbatim!

Here is the gist of what my Carolpro bio read on Match.com:

I am a fun loving gal who enjoys meeting new people.

I take pride in my appearance; however, I don't consider myself a health nut by any stretch or spend hours at the gym working out.

It's important that my future partner get along with his ex and appreciate how I have a healthy relationship with my ex-husband. My children are my world, and yours should be too.

I like to dance, enjoy a cocktail or two, try my hand at golf, and experience the adventures of travel. Oh, and I LOVE a man in a suit—a business suit, that is.

I love my career as a Realtor® and am not looking for anyone to save me.

Carolpro,

42, Sterling Heights, MI, Seeking Male 42-57

Reflecting on the rollercoaster ride of online dating, oh boy, the array of matches that flooded my inbox was both thrilling and overwhelming. It was exhilarating to know that there were individuals interested in me. With a mix of anticipation and curiosity, I delved into the world of virtual connections, sending messages to potential matches and eagerly awaiting responses. Amidst the sea of possibilities, I even met up with one potential "fish" for a casual drink. This particular gentleman was a pro golf instructor—an impressive profession indeed—yet I could not help but feel a lackluster connection, an absence of that elusive "spark." He also carried emotional baggage from a past relationship, a deal breaker for me.

Little did I know that on January eighth, after seven days of my foray into online dating, my life would undergo a transformation that would forever leave its mark. Destiny was about to make its grand entrance:

Travelwithme365 noticed you in his Daily 5, and he's interested

Those were the words on the computer screen looking back at me.

Travelwithme365, Mount Pleasant, MI

You Both Share an Interest in Golf

You Both Enjoy Nightclubs and Dancing

You Both Enjoy a Drink or Two.

Oh, the allure of an enigmatic screen name! I couldn't help but be captivated as it sparked a whirlwind of questions in my mind: *Who the hell travels 365 days a year? Or could it possibly mean embarking on a lifelong journey together?* Regardless, his profile picture was even more intriguing. He was in some kind of aircraft—possibly a helicopter—and wearing an aviation headset as he gave a thumbs-up to the camera. At that moment, I thought, *Wow, this man emits confidence, and that casual hand gesture and infectious smile… It's like he's subconsciously luring me in.*

Fueling my curiosity, I decisively clicked on the "I'm interested" button and read Travelwithme365's bio:

> *Life's an adventure, enjoy the journey and travel in style.*
> *If you like attention, dressing up, fine dining, visibility,*
> *and romance… keep reading. Travel, days on the boat, and*
> *cooking are some of the other activities I enjoy. Life is full of*
> *exciting activities, and I'm fortunate enough to have time for*
> *plenty of fun. Happiness is what life is all about, so let's be*
> *happy together. Be it good or bad, I'm a confident person, and*
> *I like to be…*
>
> *Travelwithme365*
>
> *56, Mount Pleasant, MI Seeking Female 30-40*

Ah, the inevitable pause that comes when faced with the number of someone's age. As my eyes scanned his profile, a slight hesitation settled upon me when I discovered he was fifty-six. You see, I was only forty-two, and I had set a dating age limit of fifteen years older for the men I was willing to explore romantic connections with. In a stroke of fate, Travelwithme365 had just made the cut, so I sent him a message.

January 8, 2010
Message from Carolpro via Match.com

> *Hello. I'm Carol—great bio and profile picture. You have a*
> *great smile!*

Here are some important things to know about me right off the bat… I love my life, have three amazing children, my career fulfills me, I'm close with my family, I believe in maintaining a healthy relationship with my former spouse, and I've only had a couple of relationships since my divorce in 2007. I hope to hear from you.

Carolpro

P.S. I also love dressing up to the nines and showing off my high heels—to my mom's dismay. She always told me that I was ruining my feet, and, of course, she was right. Did that stop me, though? Hell no!

As the hours ticked by, anticipation and a hint of doubt began to creep into my mind. No response from Travelwithme365. The familiar thoughts danced around my head: *Okay, so maybe he's not interested after all? If so, well, it's okay, Carol. Whatever will be, will be, right? After all, optimism and resilience are essential in this unpredictable journey.*

However, fate had a different plan in store for me. A message appeared from Travelwithme365 the following day. My heart skipped a beat as I read the words on the screen.

January 9, 2010

Message from Travelwithme365 via Match.com

My sweethearts are 23, 21, and 18. Three of the best daughters any dad could ask for. I could go on and on but maybe another day. I love the fact that your life is great. You must be comfortable in your own skin. I also share that luxury!

Between my daughters, friends, and career, I've been very lucky and fulfilled. I've been divorced 9 years and have spent the last two or three taking a break from serious relationships. My kids are all well on their way to successful lives, so it's now time for Dad. Sorry, I'm not closer to Sterling Heights but don't think that's a real barrier to getting to know you. I'm sure your mom is cool, but don't give up the fight… I love a woman in heels!

Travelwithme365

My reply was simple and to the point. ;-)

January 9, 2010

Message from Carolpro via Match.com

Does Travelwithme365 have a name?

January 10, 2010

Message from Travelwithme365 via Match.com

Hi Carol,

Just wanted to make sure I wasn't talking with a sexual predator before I give out my name :) which is Paul. I've worked my whole life, starting at age 13 (ah, the joy of being a Detroit Free Press paperboy in MI in the winter!). I worked full-time during college and launched my career as an accountant. From there, I went on to become a certified public accountant, accredited in business valuation, and certified in financial forensics. Now I occupy most of my time working with attorneys and judges, valuing companies, and providing litigation support. I love what I do, so it never seems like work. Since I've been at it so long, I've earned some perks most accountants don't enjoy. I have a great staff of 19 in two offices who are loyal and cover my ass while I'm away. I often thought I'd retire by now but what for?

Anyway... my daughters have helped me maintain a young attitude. They gave me a skydive for my 52nd. We tube and water-ski Tawas Bay in the summer and snow ski in the winter. Some people just don't get that it's not about the finish line; it's about the journey.

My profile may look like I'm a dirty old man looking for some tail, but the real truth of the matter is I'm looking for attitude and have found that many women my age have lost the fire in the belly. Write back when you can and tell me more. Then maybe we can plan a rendezvous but don't get any ideas. I won't take candy from strangers!

Yay. Mr. Mount Pleasant had a name! Although, I never imagined it would be Paul. It seemed strange and yet oddly fitting. He knew my name, too, and the prospect of him soon learning all about me was exciting, with a hint of vulnerability. While I tended to be an open book, Paul appeared to be more like an onion, each interaction peeling away another layer, gradually revealing who he was at his core. It was a dance of discovery, a delicate balance of revealing and concealing. What I remember most during this time was Paul sharing more information than I requested. It was unexpected, and yet it pleasantly surprised me. It spoke volumes about his openness and willingness to let me into his world, nurturing our growing sense of connection.

Compared to Paul, my other matches before him were far from as interesting or compatible. One guy told me his spare time was spent drinking beer and playing with his cat. While nothing was wrong with those pastimes, they didn't align with my interests and desires. And then there were those men who demanded my attention with, "Why haven't you responded to me," or "We'd be great together," or "Give me a chance." It was like navigating a battlefield to reach my ultimate destination: Finding someone who ticked all the boxes on my wish list.

With Paul, however, I felt like I was getting closer to "that someone." Despite wanting to reply to his message right away, I held off for a day. After all, he had done the same, and I didn't want him to think he was the only game in town. It was like mirroring, a tactic often employed in sales, where you reflect the actions of potential clients, gradually building rapport and comfort. In the realm of dating, we are all salespeople, presenting our best selves and hoping to capture the hearts of those who truly appreciate what we offer.

January 11, 2010
Message from Carolpro via Match.com

Hello Paul,

Nice to know you have a name! Thank you for sharing so much about yourself with me. You are so fortunate in life with your business and lovely daughters. I can tell just by your messages that you are a genuinely happy person. I won't lie—there's definitely some fire in my belly. We sound very much alike in that regard. Since my divorce in 2007 I've dated a bit. My last boyfriend was a public speaker, charming and a great communicator. My babies are still young, 16, 14, and

8 and are the most important people in my world. Whoever I "date" has to know and understand that.

January 13, 2010

Message from travelwithme365 via Match.com

Hi Carol,

So nice to hear back from you. I'm often amazed at how fortunate my life has been... yes, I am happy. Happy people are more optimistic, kinder, more compassionate, generous, and my ED doctor tells me... ... ... haha, got you there!

Sounds like I have some pretty big shoes to fill from your last love! I like a challenge. I normally review and answer my emails quick. I'm on a grand jury, and today was jury day in Bay City. No phones allowed. They keep you locked up and give you coffee and water (thank God for the coffee). So I would have responded much sooner if not for my day of solitary confinement.

I assume you'd rather have me come to your neck of the woods on our first "date." How about lunch Saturday at your favorite sports bar? Call me if you'd like. 989-289-...

Looking forward to meeting you,

Paul

Of course, I called him but had to leave a message. My interest was definitely peaked at this point, especially after reading how he liked "a challenge." As for the distance between us? Well, I hadn't given it much thought. Typically, anyone residing more than fifty miles away would be categorized as "GU" or geographically undesirable. But hey, I wasn't looking for anything serious—or so I thought!

To my delight, Paul returned my call within the hour, and I remember thinking about how youthful his voice was and how he didn't sound like a Paul. And, at that moment, my heart fluttered like a teenage schoolgirl's when daydreaming about her crush. Crazy, I know.

As it turned out, our schedules conspired against us. That upcoming weekend, I had a real estate conference on Friday and Saturday, so we decided to meet up the following week.

In the days leading up to our much-anticipated meeting, we emailed, texted, and spoke to each other on the phone. The momentum was undeniably building, propelling us closer to when our "digital avatars" would become real-life faces!

Email TO Paul:

January 20, 1:00 p.m.

Subject: Photo for today...

> *Hi Handsome,*
>
> *Thought I'd send another visual for you... Sorry about all the files on the floor... Usually, I'm quite organized. But lately... well, that's another story... Xoxo*

And no, the photo was not X-rated. I was so enamored with this man I had not even met. It was nearly impossible to keep my mind off him.

Email FROM Paul:

January 20, 2010, 8:38 p.m.

Subject: Re: Photo for today...

I'm interested in you...
Your appearance
Your style
Your face, oh that beautiful, gorgeous face
That smile, so intoxicating
Your hair... perfect, so wild
The body I want to ravish, all I would ever need
Or could handle
Your presence is powerful
You... are the perfect package

I want to get to know you...
Your attitude so positive
Your youth... way younger than your years
Your priorities... nothing more be said
Your past, more stories to tell
Playful, oh yes
Promiscuous, I would bet not
Heart, so, so, huge
Connecting, you, me, phenomenal...

I have to have her in my life...
Stole my heart... absolutely
Excites me (I wouldn't be writing this corny phrase if she
didn't)
Compassionate... about life period
Caring, her heart must burst occasionally

Grounded... the excitement of finding out
Confident... over what's important
To Be Continued

I received a beautiful surprise on Thursday, January twenty-first (the day before our first meeting). A courier arrived with a bouquet of pink roses at my doorstep, accompanied by a note from Paul that said, "***Have a Great Weekend***." I will admit that Paul won himself extra points that day. No man had ever showered me with such a thoughtful gesture arriving before a date. It made me even more excited to see him and brought home the truth to the old saying, "Actions speak louder than words"—and his words were already making me gush over him. He was treating me like I was a princess on both counts.

Email TO Paul:

January 21, 2010, 12:46 p.m.

Subject: Wonderful... exceptional you...

I didn't think I could get more excited... but I was wrong... Thank you, Thank you...

Hope you can see from my photo how eager I am to be drawn into your arms...

Xoxo

I also included a picture of me with the pink roses.

Email FROM Paul

January 21, 2010, 2:09 p.m.

Subject: RE: Wonderful… exceptional you…

*You are a PRINCESS!!!!!!!!! We may just spend the whole
weekend in bed. Where to next… Belize, St. Maarten, St.
Bart's, or Key West?*

The momentum continued to build up to our "first date," and
I found myself heeding the sage advice my dear mom had imparted:
Always arrive bearing a small gift for the host or hostess. With this
golden rule guiding my actions, I embarked on a quest to find the
perfect gift for Paul. As fate would have it, Paul's surname, Murray,
danced in my mind, triggering memories of our previous conversations about our respective heritages. A bottle of whiskey seemed ideal,
an homage to his surname and our shared appreciation for life's finer
pleasures. And so, I ventured out in search of that liquid gold, my
favorite elixir of choice—Crown Royal. Of course, my ever-amusing
girlfriend, Cara, couldn't resist chiming in with her own unique sug-
gestions: A bottle of olive oil paired with the game Twister, a blend of
practicality and playfulness. While the idea made me smile, I decided
to stick with the whiskey—this time. :-)

Take Away:

**Step out of your comfort zone.
You might surprise yourself.**

Chapter Two

D-Day

Friday, January 22, 2010

Okay, what was I thinking? Why did I offer to drive to Mt Pleasant and meet him at his home, approximately 115 miles from mine? Well, I guess that was the Realtor® in me. Naturally, before I did, I Googled him—as most ladies do before a date. From my "important research," I learned that Paul had multiple businesses, served on numerous boards in his community, and had investment groups. All evidence pointed to him being very established with a beautiful home and children, which made me freak out even more, as what could such a man want from me, a simple gal from Sterling Heights? Just in case, though, I had to tell someone where I was going, so I told a handful of friends from my office. I would text them on Friday and again on Saturday. After all, I did not want to end up in some guy's freezer in the middle of nowhere, especially since Paul told me he could stand naked in his yard without anyone seeing him—a bonus for the hot tub use.

Hmm, how do I describe the moment I pulled up outside his house... First off, I wondered where the hell to park. He had an expansive circle driveway, with additional parking off to one side, so I was somewhat spoilt for choice. After choosing to pull up halfway, I noticed the huge front door—and I mean huge. Then there was the intriguing architecture, flat roof, floor-to-ceiling windows, and the lack of gutters. This small mansion was unassuming from the street but boasted nice curb appeal. Only then did I remember Paul telling me how he had an Alden B. Dow mid-century modern home and that the Michigan architect had studied under the famous Frank Lloyd Wright.

My heart was pounding as I got out of my car and approached the door. However, I'd come this far, so I figured, what the heck? I got this. Then the door swung open, and there he was...

Now, this is the part that becomes interesting and totally contra-dictory to everything I knew—I was speechless. Paul welcomed me in, and I awkwardly handed him the bottle of whiskey. He leaned over and gave me a quick peck on the lips, which immediately revealed how confident he was. He took charge and clearly had the advantage, as I was still in shock. You might be wondering here why I still hadn't said anything to him, but it felt like I had been a little robin, happily flying through the air, getting ever closer to a special destination, and then *bang!* I hit a window. I was stunned because what I could see through this window was a man who quite possibly could change my world, and I wasn't sure I wanted to hand over my heart. Don't get me wrong; I wasn't some heartless girl who would date and then ditch to move on to the next exciting thing. It was just that I had danced this tango before. I had loved and been loved. I had given my life and soul to someone, only for it not to end up happily ever after. If I was going to commit to a man again, I needed to know that he would be my ride or die, my forever.

Okay, so back to Paul and the front door scene… In between the peck and the formalities, I noticed beyond him, in the background, an entire wall of windows that looked out on a gorgeous yard and river. I noted the brick interior and parquet flooring. The décor was classy yet had that welcoming feeling. Yes, I couldn't help it—for a few moments, the Realtor® in me took over again. My brain was also on overload from this striking man whom I had only experienced from online and phone conversations remotely, without even knowing if we would be attracted to each other. But the second he opened that door, I felt the sexual chemistry, and so intensely that the only thing I could manage to say was, "Can I use your bathroom?"—I know, so not a Romeo and Juliet moment.

Back again to the door scene… As we walked up a few steps into the dining room—with the built-in wet bar—he pointed out where his primary bath was in his bedroom and the other ones down the hallway. Interestingly, there did not seem to be a door on that bathroom, so I went and shut his bedroom door and went into the bathroom that I actually didn't have to "use."

I looked in the mirror and said, "You got this," pointing at myself and then the mirror.

Then, internally, I was like, *What in the what, Carol? What has gotten into you? You never, ever needed to do that in any relationship. Game on, girl!*

After a few deep breaths to compose myself, I left the bedroom and found Paul sitting at his dining room table with two glasses of red wine.

"Is everything okay?" he asked.

I gave him a warm smile. "Of course" .

I found out later that Paul had thought I was bailing on him and was waiting for me to come out and say there was an emergency with my kids. This is obviously not how love stories are written—or is it? After all, everyone's "How I met you" stories are unique.

Once I had a glass of Caymus Cabernet Sauvignon—so smooth and much needed—in my hand, Paul gave me the "tour." And boy, do I love house tours, whether visiting family or friends for the first time or even for a listing appointment as a Realtor®. During the tour, I found out that he did have a door to his bathroom, a pocket door.

How could I have missed that?

I was thinking that maybe he's an exhibitionist. He did have some questionable artwork hanging in his room. Alden B. Dow homes are appealing on so many levels, so the layout utterly fascinated me. I was also on the lookout for "the freezer," haha.

As we continued to walk, talk, and sip the way-too-easy-to-drink vino, Paul showed me his theater room in the basement—*No freezer here. I'm almost home free!*—followed by his "car room," located up another flight of stairs and off the garage. The room had shelves of die-cast cars—hundreds of them—trophies that Paul won for his 1957 Corvette, and other car memorabilia. Then I saw it... a large box freezer, capable of fitting two or three human beings, probably chopped up! Seriously, my heart dropped. I had no warning signs that I'd end up in there. I was being irrational.

This is just a coincidence. And, of course, he has a freezer. He's a guy, and he loves meat.

To banish my paranoia, I asked for another glass of wine, and we retired to the expansive living room with the piano-keyboard wood-work surrounding the ceiling. There was a complete brick-to-ceiling fireplace and a built-in ivory-colored sofa that reminded me of melted unsalted butter. Directly next to the window was a low, glass cocktail table and four rolling upholstered chairs that matched the sofa. This was where I fell in love—or started to fall—holding on tightly to whatever will I had left.

The rest of the evening was quite enjoyable. Paul had scheduled a masseuse to come over to give us massages; however, unfortunately, she had to cancel—something about a wheel falling off her car. I was actually quite fine with missing out on the massage, though, as I still wanted this guy to myself so I could keep getting to know him better—including what he saw in me. In addition, I wanted to ensure that I was not just some toy for the weekend for a playboy. In truth, he had so much going for him, and he picked me out of an overabundance of beautiful women on Match.com. So, I let it all soak in and went with the moment. As long as I made it back home to my children, all would be okay.

Now, earlier, I mentioned a hot tub… He said I could go in with my bra and panties or a full "birthday suit." I remember thinking, *Oh boy, this is the part where he sees my tad bit overweight and curvy naked body in broad daylight.*

But what the heck, I had nothing to lose. Besides, Paul told me prior to coming up to see him that I could always stay in one of his daughter's bedrooms if there wasn't a connection between us. However, that wasn't going to be necessary…

Saturday, January 23, 2010

The following morning, Paul prepared a fabulous breakfast of scrambled eggs with cheese, toast, bacon, and a side of cantaloupe. I knew that between this and the previous evening's meal—bone-in ribeyes, asparagus, and baked potatoes with all the fixings—he enjoyed cooking and was damn well good at it. As a bonus, I learned that the "elusive freezer" did, in fact, have animal meat in it, not human!

The plan for the day was to head over to Soaring Eagle Casino for dinner and a show, the act being the comedian Carlos Mencia. We would end our evening by staying overnight at the resort. As the old saying goes, this "put the final nail in the coffin"—I'm becoming my mother every day.

Dinner at the steakhouse was terrific. I even let Paul order for me—little did I know this was the beginning of handing my heart over and trusting in the unknown. Now, don't go thinking he chose what I would eat. That would be crazy; I chose it, and it was another steak cooked to perfection! But overall, that night, my suspicions were being confirmed: He was a gentleman.

While we waited to enter the comic show, we sat on a bench. I began to tell him how much I loved that he wore suits and how handsome he looked in them. His reply was to open his jacket and reveal the Paul Benjamin Murray custom label on the inside—shout out to Keith Pogarch Clothier, Inc. I will never forget that move. It wasn't a cocky "look what I have" move; it was him confirming that he had what I liked, as on my profile on Match.com, I had noted how I love a man in a suit, and the monogrammed shirt cuffs were a bonus!

Another box checked off.

The comic show ended up being really entertaining—and the gambling and dancing. Side note: Paul looks hot doing the Cupid Shuffle!

Another box checked off—not the gambling, the dancing.

I was falling deeper and deeper, and the evening ended as beautifully as Paul was in his suit…

Sunday, January 24, 2010

It was raining when we left the resort, but I remember not caring about the rain. Nothing could dampen my mood. Paul drove me around his town while pointing out various points of interest. I forgot to mention that my "chariot" to the casino was his hot little Mustang, a 2007 Carroll Shelby. This guy was seriously enamored enough with me to take his Shelby out in the dead of winter—or maybe it was just his normal m.o.? Either way, I was going with it.

Unfortunately, the day flew way too fast, and when late afternoon arrived, it was time for me to head back south, forever changed. I will say that our goodbye kiss was much more passionate than our hello one...

Email FROM Paul
January 24, 2010, 7:08 p.m.
Subject: Love You!

Hi Baby,

He's a guy I met online, and we decided to have wine
We then went on to dine and danced, which was just fine.
He's a guy I kinda like, and he's nothing at all like Mike
I think we may just date cuz I think he just may rate
As a guy, you may decide you'd like to have at Mom's side.

Sorry for the corny stuff, but I'd really like you to not feel you can't be honest with your kids when it comes to me, how we met, and where we may go. I know you will eventually, but I really don't want to try to keep any secrets or say something that may upset your children.

Love You.

Yes, he wrote the "L" word in his email. I wasn't surprised, though, as he'd said it the day before. However, again, I wondered, *Is this what he does to multiple women? Why does he want to pursue me, someone two and a half hours away from him?*

As a defense mechanism, I didn't reciprocate the "L" word or tell the children about my handsome, swooning CPA.

Email TO Paul

January 26, 2010, 11:30 a.m.

Subject: RE: Love You!

MMMM… I could kiss those lips and have those hands ravish me… You are really, really, really sexy… and I'm craving you…

Xoxo

Email FROM Paul

January 26, 2010, 11:53 a.m.

Subject: RE: Love You!

> *Baby… I am so excited… I just sent you some snail mail*
> *today. I would normally save it for a surprise, but I couldn't*
> *stand it any longer.*

In my head, I focused on the word "normally." Yet again, I wondered, *So is this what he does? He swoops in, tangles you up in his web, and spits you out when he's done with you? That's it! I'm surely in the web now, but how long will I stay here? And what has he sent me? A love note? A thanks for the great weekend, but I think we should go our own ways.*

The email was also sent on Tuesday. I didn't receive the snail mail until Friday.

Email TO Paul

January 28, 2010, 11:46 a.m.

Subject: Hmmmm…

> *Hey baby,*
>
> *My friends who love and care about me just told me they saw*
> *your profile active within 24 hours on that wonderful site I*
> *met you on…*
>
> *Am I all you really want??? Or are you looking for the big,*
> *better deal…*
>
> *Please don't play me…I have way too much self-esteem for*
> *that…*

Crazy as it is…I defended you…Maybe you were just check-ing to see if I was back on…

Yes, I know… When I sent that email, I was in panic mode, but only because I had fallen hard for this man in such a short time, and if it turned out that he was screwing me over, I would be devastated. So, my heart sank at the thought.

"See, maybe there's no fairytale after all," I told Elaine, my girl-friend at the office.

There was also one part of that email that was untrue. My friends had *not* told me they saw Paul's profile active on Match.com. *I* was the one who noticed that his profile was tagged active. I lied to him; however, I'm owning up to it now. And, of course, I was checking up on him. We had decided both to go off the site. I did; he didn't. There you have it.

Email FROM Paul

January 28, 2010, 12:41 p.m.

Subject: Re: Hmmmm…..

> *Baby… sweetheart… lover… I discontinued my member-ship!!! Play you????? You break my heart thinking that way. There is noooooo way I could even find a bigger, better deal. You are the real thing. I'm going to log on NOW to call and find out what the deal is!*

> *I Love You. I Love You. I Love You…please don't be concerned!*

A phone call from Paul followed the email. Apparently, there was an error in taking down his profile. But in the end, whatever happened, I trusted him and let my paranoia go—and my heart was happy again.

Oh, and I said the "L" word.

The next day, January twenty-nine, I received the snail mail. It was a note written on his monogrammed note cards:

1/26/10

Hi Baby,

Thank you for an unforgettable weekend and another to come. Can't wait to have you in my arms!

Love You,

Paul

In the upper portion, he wrote, "*If it's important to you, then it's important to me.*" A check was enclosed, too. To fill you in, on the weekend prior, we were talking about aging, and I told him that I thought it was time I crossed over into the world of fillers and toxic substances being shot in my forehead. Of course, Paul said I didn't need it, and needless to say, I was shocked that he wrote the check. Little did he know that it was the beginning of my transformation, physically and emotionally, and the start of another bill in his life... me!

IF IT'S important To You, THEN IT'S important to me

1/26/10

Hi Baby,

THANK You FOR AN UNforgetable WEEKEND AND ANOTHER TO COME. CAN'T WAIT TO HAVE You IN My ARMS!

LOVE You
Paul

Take Away:

Be cautious, keep an open mind, and go with your gut.

CHAPTER THREE

A Visit Downstate

Saturday, January 30, 2010

It was my daughter Madeline's seventeenth birthday, and our nuclear family—me, her dad, and brothers Joseph and Charles—had just met for lunch at her favorite Mediterranean restaurant. None of them knew about Paul, and I was not ready to tell them just yet. I had spent less than three physical days with this man, and, of course, who tells their former husband about their amazing new lover—especially when Paul was heading downstate that day to spend the rest of the weekend with me.

However, later that afternoon, my oh-so-handsome awaited surprise arrived. To top it off, he held a bouquet of two dozen stunning red roses and milk chocolate sea salt caramels. How delicious—the man and the caramels! In return, I gave him a kiss and a card:

Thank you, Baby, for coming into my life.
I so look forward to our future. I plan on loving you forever!!
You are my everything.

Love you, Love you, Love you

Carol xoxo

When the light faded to dusk, we headed down to Greektown in Detroit for dinner and danced and kissed the night away. We joined some of my friends at a local watering hole. Before the clock struck midnight, I had fallen even deeper in love with Paul—and he with me.

On Sunday, my parents were having a birthday party for my daughter. I went, and Paul stayed back at my house. It was a strange feeling knowing that a man I had just met was at my home, alone, while I was at my parent's place with all of my family—and no one knew anything about him. I felt like I was a secret agent hiding "the package."

After the party, I headed home to Paul like a female lion chasing its prey. We ended the day by visiting some of my other friends. It was like I was on tour with Paul and needed to get the "buy-in" from the people who knew me best. Luckily, they all bought in and agreed that Paul was better suited to me than the men from my previous relationships.

Another box ticked!

After a short trip but an incredible whirlwind of one, Paul headed back to Mt Pleasant on Monday morning. From that point on, the future was clear. The distance between us be damned. We were all in.

Email TO Paul

February 9, 2010, 3:36 p.m.

Subject: Time spread

> *CLOSING IN ON THE GAP OF TIME THAT OUR LIPS WON'T HAVE TO BE APART… LOVE YOU BABY!!!!!*

Email FROM Paul

February 9, 2010, 3:47 p.m.

Subject: Re: Time spread

> *WHY DO I LOVE YOU SO TOTALLY MUCH? WE'RE LIKE A COUPLE OF LOVESTRUCK KIDS!*

Yes, we were acting like a couple of lovestruck kids… and as a woman, I had never felt so goddamn happy about it.

Friday, February 12, 2010

It was Valentine's Day weekend, and Paul had come for another visit. We planned to go to the boat show downtown with Russ and Cara. Once again, Paul arrived with presents, but not the flowers and chocolate one usually receives on Valentine's Day—he'd sent those earlier. Instead, I unwrapped a beautiful wood-toned jewelry box with a gorgeous diamond pendant necklace and a cognac gemstone. In a nutshell, I was flabbergasted. Never had I been showered with jewelry like this, let alone in less than a month of knowing someone! In addition, he had given me not one but two pairs of very sexy high heels: A leopard print pair and a black pair with silver studs. They both had peek-a-boo-toes, so it was good that my pedicure was on point! I remember telling him how I hoped they would fit as most pumps slipped off my narrow feet—I hate that. He smiled and replied, "That's okay. They'll fit when you're lying down,"—and they did!

What I felt for Paul at this point was intense and the most real thing I'd experienced in a long time. I felt like Olivia Newtown John standing by that kiddie pool in *Grease*, singing about the man she loved. The man she was hopelessly devoted to…

The boat show was fun! Russ and Cara immediately approved of Paul. I felt so happy as we walked around, like I was walking on water.

Is this really happening to me? This hot, handsome prince—here with me?

The evening ended with us dining in Downtown Detroit and meeting up with some additional friends for cocktails and cheer. I felt like I was on parade with this man.

Wednesday, February 17, 2010

It was the early morning, and this time, it was my turn to travel up I-75 to Mt Pleasant. I was determined to spend two nights with my man (as he was going on a golf outing with his buddies for a long weekend) before returning to my ordinary home and work routine.

Email TO Paul:

February 17, 2010, 9:46 a.m

Subject: Your Pillowy Lips

> *Baby, Baby, Baby…*
> *Can't wait to jump into your arms…*
> *Love you, Love you, Love you…*
> *Want to make love to you…*

Hold you all night…

… Because it feels so right!

Email FROM Paul:

February 17, 2010, 9:54 a.m.

Subject: Re: Your Pillowy Lips

*You still love me!!!!!!!!!!!!!!!! I'm nuts over you, and I may just
hold my nuts over you.*

Take Away:

If you get heels as a present, use them :-).

CHAPTER FOUR

The Big Easy

Saturday, February 20 – Wednesday, February 24, 2010

I attended my annual work real estate convention in New Orleans this week. Paul encouraged me to drink, dance, and have fun with my colleagues and associates, knowing I would be 100 percent faithful to him. You see, I have always been a bit of a social butterfly. Life is here on this earth to be lived, and I believe in grasping every single moment. Paul even teased me one day and asked if I was looking for "a bigger, better offer out there in the dating world." I think he saw my zest for life only becoming stronger and thought that maybe he wasn't enough to satisfy me and all I desired. I laughed and thought, *I'm the one who should be worried, but at this point, I'm not.*

Email TO Paul:

February 19, 2010, 2:15 p.m.

Subject: MY BBO

Hey Lover…

You are the BIGGEST… BEST… OFFER… I will ever find… and I've stopped looking…

Love ya…

Email FROM Paul:

February 19, 2010, 2:38 p.m.

Subject: Re: MY BBO

Keep count, and I expect a full DETAILED report once you're back from N.O. I love you Princess.

This is a pivotal email as it marked when I became his "princess." No one had ever called or referred to me as Princess. I know it can be an endearing term that fathers call their daughters, and I also know that it can mean prima donna. But, to be fair, I questioned how many other girls he'd called Princess. So, as women often do when we're crazy in love with someone, I became somewhat obsessed with learning about Paul's past. I had been married for fifteen years and divorced for three years at this point. Paul had also been married for fifteen years but divorced for almost ten—and I was sure that a whole lot of "crazy" had occurred in those single years of his. I'm sure there was, and I'm happy to report that I no longer obsess about it because it is what it is.

By "keeping count" in the email, he was referring to how many men hit on me. But, of course, that didn't happen at the conference. I did *run* into a gentleman, Richard, though, on Bourbon Street, *physically,* that is. We struck up a conversation. He was in town for an insurance conference, and as we talked, he told me how I reminded him of his late wife, which was a bittersweet compliment. I told him about my boyfriend and how crazy in love I was. He said that he and his wife had felt the same way.

Later that evening, my colleagues and I danced it up on Bourbon Street and enjoyed our downtime. I ran into Richard again and his buddy. We chatted for a bit, and he danced with us. He had a camera—yes, cameras were still being used then—and was taking pictures of my friends and I dancing. Afterward, we exchanged business cards, and he offered for Paul and I to stop by his house if we ever made it to his part of California, Santa Maria. He said it was beautiful with perfect weather. He was a gentleman, and I sincerely believed he meant what he said as he never tried any funny stuff. Anyways, he went his way, and I went mine.

I ran into him one more time after that. He mentioned how he thought he'd see me running along the Mississippi River in the morning. This was truly hysterical as I'm not a runner—although the compliment was again appreciated.

Email FROM Paul

February 22, 2010, 10:42 a.m.

Subject: Planning your life

> *Hi Princess, I could just picture you this morning, all snuggled in your bed, hair like a wild little lion. Please save some time to share your life with me:*

•*Friday, March 5 to Tuesday, March 9, come to Mt. Pleasant anytime Friday, but I'll have to work most of the day. Friday night we'll go out dancing and partying. I'll see about having another couple or two join us. Saturday, we'll head for Tawas and return to Mt. Pleasant Sunday or early Monday (I'll probably bring the dogs with us). I'll have to work most of Monday and Tuesday, you are free to hang in MP or head back home as you wish.*

•*Thursday, March 11 I'll be heading to my Princess Carol's award presentation and will return to Mt. Pleasant Friday morning.*

•*Let me know what other times we can spend together in March. I'll have to spend time in the office but Sundays are always open and Saturday is flexible and if you come to Mt. Pleasant, you could spend as much time as you like here. I'll come home each day for lunch!*

•*Let me know what you have available for me during the first half of April. Thursday, April 15, is our big party. We grill steak and lobster in the parking lot and celebrate the end of tax season. I would love to have you stop by and take me home (significant others are normally not to invited to this bash but I'm sure I can find you a pass). Friday, 4/16 is a holiday for us, so we can stay in bed all day or find something weather appropriate to do.*

•*April 22nd to 30th, we'll vacation together!!!!!!!!!!! Details to follow.*

•*I've already RSVP'd us for the Barberi wedding on May 22nd.....I hope you still love me by then!!!!!!!!!*

I love you PRINCESS and want you forever and a day!

When I received this email, I was still at the real estate convention in New Orleans and thought, *Wow, this guy does dig me. He's already planning into May.* Elaine and I were rooming together at the hotel, so she had to deal with me being all sappy and head over heels. She was a good sport and sounding board, though. Plus, she was over the moon for me and happy that I had moved on from the other men I'd dated.

Email TO Paul

February 22, 2010, 11:01 a.m.

Subject: Re: Planning your life

Oh, I love you so much… you can plan the rest of my life…
Have to jump in the shower… wish you were here…
You are too cool… and I am your girl…
Love you

Email TO Paul

February 23, 2010, 9:32 a.m.

Subject: One more day baby!!!!

Hi Love,

I need you, I want you…

I am crazy in love with you…

You are my world…

Baby oh baby... thank you for treating me so well... I am sooooo grateful that you love me... I miss your tender kisses....

Email FROM Paul

February 23, 2010, 9:35 a.m.

Subject: Re: One more day baby!!!

You are so BEAUTIFUL! I love you forever and a day.

I finally made it back to Michigan but suffered a dreadful snowstorm en route. Paul had even headed down from Mt Pleasant and shoveled my driveway—in his dress shoes. He either really loved me or loved shoveling snow! Either way, I was excited to see him and couldn't wait to live out our "planning my life" email with him.

After a week of being home, though, I opened my inbox to find a surprising email, which was not from Paul.

Email FROM Richard

March 1, 2010, 1:00 p.m.

Subject: Pictures of New Orleans

Hi,

I wish we were all back on Bourbon Street tonight. It's rainy here and boring. I tried to email some New Orleans pictures to you, but I recently downloaded a new picture program, and something isn't working right on my computer. Most likely, it's me.

So, I mailed the pictures to you yesterday, and I wanted to let you know they should be at your office early next week.

I sent a note along with the pictures, and I said you were the best-looking 42-year-old woman I had ever met, but that isn't exactly true. My wife would have given you a little competition in that department. But there is more than beauty in a pretty face. There is class and substance. My wife had it all, and everyone admired her, and my guess is you're very much like her. I think that's why I felt very comfortable with you. I attached a photo of my wife when she was about 48 just to prove I'm not lying. No, that's not me standing next to her, it's an actor at Universal Studios.

I told my cousin about you. He's a retired Secret Service Agent. When he saw your last name, he said I hope she is not related to the Provenzano that was a mafia boss, or I might get "WACKED" just for talking to you. I told him you were worth it. Enjoy the pictures, and if you ever come to California, give me a call. I'd be glad to show you some great places on the Central Coast. If you didn't have a boyfriend, I'd send you an airplane ticket to come while the weather is so bad in Michigan. I promise you'd have fun here.

Email TO Richard

March 1, 2010, 1:50 p.m.

Subject: Re: Pictures of New Orleans

Hi,

Thank you for sending me the photos. I look forward to receiving them. Yes, we all did have a great time on Bourbon Street. I certainly did take in the flavor of New Orleans. I am grateful for my career and the opportunities it provides me.

Your wife was very beautiful. She had great legs. I can tell from the way you speak of her she was your world. There are many people who never get to feel that feeling. I spoke to you in New Orleans of my boyfriend. He is my world. I never thought it was possible to feel such love, desire and the feeling of never wanting to be without that person... He encouraged me to go to New Orleans... drink... dance... and have fun... knowing I would be faithful and come home to him... As you could probably tell I'm a bit of a social butterfly... Life is to live, and I believe in taking in the moment....

As for the Mafia Provenzano connection... if there was, I'd probably be dead by now....

It was a pleasure meeting you, and thank you for sharing a cocktail and dancing.

I hear California is beautiful... I've never made it to that side of the country. Thank you for the offer, but as you can see, I have to decline... Thank you for being such a gentleman.

Gratefully,
Carol

I was surprised to see the email from him. It was nice knowing he thought highly of me. A little affirmation every now and then doesn't hurt. He genuinely seemed like a good guy. After I hit send, I forwarded the email to Paul. I wasn't concerned, as Paul knew about my interaction with Richard in New Orleans. He even joked about telling him to "keep it in his pants" and "She's my girl." I learned fairly quickly that Paul's pang of jealousy actually wasn't a pang at all. He was more than confident; he was self-assured and undaunted by any possible suitors. And with such trust comes true love.

Take Away:

Go on vacation when you are falling in love, but without the one that you're falling in love with. Trust me, you will be on cloud nine, smile at everyone that crosses your path, and tell them how much in love you are.

CHAPTER FIVE

The Interrogation and a First

March 2010

Paul and I were heading out on our first trip together to Fort Meyers, Florida, to visit a couple he had been friends with for years, Bruce and Sue. They lived on a boat and had invited us to stay with them. I was looking forward to it; it felt like I was in a real and natural relationship and having the time of my life as it played out.

Paul arrived the evening before Trip #1, and I finally introduced him to my children. I was somewhat nervous about all my loves coming together for the first time; however, it went relatively well in the end. My daughter, Madeline, had come prepared with "the notebook," which had a full page of questions she wanted to ask. Paul was a little taken aback—although he happily answered all the questions like he was testifying in court. Both my boys, Joseph and Charles, thoroughly enjoyed meeting Paul. Joseph even took him downstairs to listen to some vinyl, and Charles played the drums for him. It was magical and loud. The boys gave their unspoken approval—not that Madeline didn't; she was just being more cautious. After all, her mom was getting on a plane the following day with this "new guy" who had come into their lives. I understood how she felt; knowing how much she cared was a nice feeling.

The following day, we stopped at my parent's house on the way to the airport. They were also very interested in meeting the "mystery man" who had made quite an impression on their daughter. My older sister, Cindy, was there, too. Many might think that parading a new lover before the family is unwise when the relationship is still fresh. However, my family was my rock, and I was fortunate to have been blessed with a solid one. Like the meeting with my children, this one went incredibly well. My mom, ever the hostess, made Paul feel comfortable, my sister was conversational, and Dad talked about his classic cars with him.

Friends, check. Kids, check. Parents, check. Sister, check. Is this real? Can everything I'm feeling actually be true? And is this man genuinely feeling the same way as I am?

We got a drink at the airport bar while waiting for our flight to Florida. This has become our tradition: I would order a Mimosa and Paul a Spicy Bloody Mary. To date, we have done this fifty-five times. Fifty-five trips multiplied by 2—because you have to fly home, too, right?

This first flight with Paul was a memorable one… Let's just say I became a card-carrying member of the "mile high club…"

As for Florida, we had an absolute blast. His friends were fantastic hosts, and I kept being swept away as the sugar-like sand kissing the emerald-green water of a stunning shore receeds.

Take Away:

When in doubt, take a deep breath and take the leap.
Things might turn out perfectly!

CHAPTER SIX

That's a Wrap, and That Wasn't Very Nice

It was early April, and I met two of Paul's three daughters, Diana, the middle, and Erica, the youngest. We met at one of the local restaurants, a brewpub, whose owners also were clients of Paul's CPA firm. They were delightful and seemed genuinely pleased that their father was happy. Time would tell for them, though, if I was in it for the long haul and true love. Having heard stories about his past relationships, I wondered again why he chose me out of all his other matches to pursue.

This was my first "tax season" with Paul—busy days for him, especially March and April. I would travel up to see him. He and the other CPAs worked six or seven days a week until mid-April. I tried to stay in the background as much as possible. The staff at Paul's office were so lovely to me. Some even thanked me for dating him and stated how different he was now. He was happy, smiling, and generally in a good mood at work. It brought home the fact that love can put a spring in your step—and at any age.

Excerpt from a card for our three-month anniversary—from when we started communicating on Match.com—that I snail-mailed from back home in Sterling Heights. You know you do that silly stuff when you're head over heels for someone.

"Thank you for loving me. I hope we have many, many more consecutive three-month anniversaries. I Love You, Sweetheart! Can't wait to see and touch you. Xoxo"

The last day of tax season came, and I returned to Mt Pleasant for the "after party" in the parking lot. It seemed tame from what I heard about the past parties. Paul was happy tax season was wrapped up, and soon, we would be back at his house, celebrating in the hot tub and wrapped up in each other.

The following morning, we were traveling to his vacation place in Tawas on the bay when his phone rang. It didn't sync with the car, and I heard him talking casually with the person on the other line. As the conversation came to a close, he chuckled and hung up.

I looked at him and asked if everything was okay.

Yep, the skeletons from the past always seem to come into the present at the worst times.

The great thing I loved—and still love—about Paul was his honesty. He went on to explain how the call was from his ex-girlfriend, who was wondering how the end of tax season went for him. She'd also asked if he was heading up to Tawas.

Ah, yes. This is what he did with her, too.

My mind naturally wondered about how long they had been together and why she was calling him.

Hasn't she moved on and married someone else? If so, why did he take her call in the first place? Are they good friends? Am I right to question things? Is it okay to judge whatever relationship they have?

Then came the worst thought: *What happens when I'm not in Mt. Pleasant?*

To make matters worse, he told me she had seen a picture of me on Facebook and asked him if he was still dating "that cross-eyed chick"? In response, he chuckled and ended the call. Now, every girl wants to feel special and know their man has their back. However, it didn't happen in this instance, and I was not too thrilled about it.

Paul's defense was, "It's just easier to hang up than get into a conversation."

But he had a long history with her, long enough, apparently, that it was still partially present. As you read this, you might wonder, *Carol, what's wrong with you? You seem jealous. So what? She's a past girlfriend. Get over it. Technically, Paul didn't do anything wrong. When his ex said something nasty about you, he ended the call. That means he refused to keep engaging with someone who was immature and insulting his new Lover.* Okay, yes, perhaps there was a tiny thread of jealousy on my behalf there. However, mostly, I felt annoyed. A good metaphor for the situation is when you get a piece of fuzz or hair on your eyelash, and it's not bothering you until you blink. So, you try not to blink, but you have to because you cannot stop. I eventually stopped. When I met this woman in person at a restaurant in Mt Pleasant five years later, I wondered why I put my energy into those past thoughts and realized that Paul was truly in it—committed to me—for the long run. He introduced me as his future wife, which didn't go down well with her. Let's say there is always a reason we stop dating someone and move on. I also decided that having empathy for her was the best emotion to feel. And just like that, I never gave it another thought.

Take Away:

When people say unkind things about you, it is really about them. Worry is a useless emotion.

CHAPTER SEVEN

R609, a Balcony, and a Safe Word

April 2010

The "planning my life email" clearly stated that Paul and I would be on vacation from April twenty-second to April thirty. Paul even came up with a crafty rhyme for me to guess what we were doing—oh, I wish I could find it. At any rate, I shared the rhyme with my mom and sister Cindy, who guessed it: Paul was taking me on a cruise. A trip in March with him and now Trip #2 in April... This unassuming girl from Sterling Heights was utterly ecstatic!

We flew to Fort Lauderdale and boarded The Emerald Princess. I had taken a cruise with my former husband back in 1991 and hadn't been on one since—and I'm pretty sure, back then, I didn't walk around in heels all the time. From the welcome party to the moment we disembarked, we partied. Remember, I was forty-two, and Paul was fifty-six, so we could still "hang" as they say—or at least he could! I was still learning my limits. This was the occasion when we coined our "safe word"—and I don't mean for BDSM. It is easy to get tipsy quickly when you have dropped close to twenty pounds because all you've thought about is this incredible man 24/7. There is not enough body fat to sustain the alcohol, and I barely ate to boot. Thus, that proved itself one day, after returning from a catamaran cruise where the rum punch flowed with Captain Marky Mark's encouragement… Back on the boat, we had a cocktail before heading back to get ready for dinner. By this time of the day, I was mixing my light and dark liquors—a dangerous move for anyone. Paul and I returned to the cabin, had crazy sex, and then planned to go to dinner. However, the last few minutes of the evening went like this:

"Time to go to dinner. I'll wear what I have on," I told Paul.

He raised his eyebrows and eyed the very minimal amount of material I was wearing—in truth, the outfit was certainly not appropriate for the dining room of a cruise ship.

"Are you sure that outfit is the right choice, Princess?" he asked.

I grinned. "Sure. Let's go."

Our butler, Salvadore, stood outside the cabin in the hallway.

As I opened the door, Paul said, "Let's ask Salvador if he thinks it's a good idea."

Salvador smiled at me. "I would recommend some pants, ma'am."

With a playful sigh, I conceded, returned inside the cabin, and sat on the bed.

"How about we stay here for a few more minutes? I need to do something on my laptop quickly, and then we'll go to dinner," Paul said.

He knew me better than I knew myself because I passed out less than a minute later. For the record, I wasn't "pantless." There was some—but not much—material. Now, we always use the word "Salvadore" when one of us gets a little too rambunctious. The experience taught me a lesson in liquor management—or so I thought. I would continue to learn this lesson a few more times. Paul was a seasoned drinker; he could handle it. He was also a Baby Boomer, so he came from a generation that enjoyed alcohol consumption.

For the rest of the cruise, as we were in the Eastern Caribbean, we visited a private island, St. Martin, St. Thomas, and Turks & Caicos. I felt like an actual princess—I was wined and dined and introduced to new experiences.

How could something so wonderful happen to me? I kept thinking.

I always tried to do the right thing, see the good in people, and care for my family, and I am generally a "good" person. But, as Julie Andrew sings in *The Sound of Music*, "I must have done something good"—to deserve this remarkable man and life.

Returning to "my life" after being with Paul for eleven nights was incredibly difficult. The longer we were together, the harder it was for me to break away. The tears flowed as Paul pulled out of my driveway. This would be a constant now in our relationship. I had to leave him; I cried. He had to leave me; I cried. It was strange; I couldn't help it. This had never happened to me before. It would take a few minutes, and then I would accept that I had to leave, knowing we'd see each other again in a few days. This pattern played out for almost ten years. It never got any easier for me.

Diana, Paul's middle daughter, graduated from Michigan State University on May eighth. This was the first time I met Paul's former spouse, Sue. It wasn't like they had just divorced, so I was not concerned. I met her, and, of course, it's always a bit awkward to begin with—although now I've spent many family events with her, and she is a lovely woman. I actually believe we are alike in several ways, so when someone else mirrors you, you instantly like them. Plus, she's the mother of three incredible daughters, and Paul spent many years of his life with her. People change, circumstances change, and it's never the end, just a different beginning.

May 17, 2010, my 43rd birthday

Dear Princess,

We are so lucky to have found each other.
We are so blessed to be such a perfect match.
I am the luckiest guy in the world to have you for my own!
I Love You Princess

Paul

Take Away:

Live your life authentically because you only get one. It is also okay to cry.

CHAPTER EIGHT

Under the Knife; Goodbye Front Butt

June 2010

Yes, that is correct. I had a "front butt." I had all three of my babies via C-section—being cut vertically instead of the tiny horizontal incision doctors make right above the pubic bone. I was opened up like a book, and the spine on that book had seen better days—with the pages all wrinkled and creased.

"If it's important to you, then it's important to me." Remember those words Paul said to me earlier? Well, it was important for me to undergo plastic surgery, and not because I was vain—well, maybe a little bit. I just wanted to be the best version of myself, including for him. After all, we would both reap the benefits. I did tease him first, though, saying that recovery would mean a period of abstinence. However, I was still learning how unique this man was and how he always kept things interesting. He pulled out a pad and began to write…

Article 1

Volume 1

Sexual Favor Exchange

****

I, Carol Provenzano,

Acknowledge My Delinquency

In Providing Sexual Favors

To Paul B. Murray. In Exchange

For Valuable Consideration, I Agree

To Provide Sexual Favors Of Any

Nature Requested By Paul B. Murray

For A Period Not To End Before

June 7, 2020

Dated June 5, 2010

Carol Elizabeth Provenzano

Some women may have taken a contract like that, especially from their new boyfriend, the wrong way. But not me. I mean, did you think I was not going to sign it? Of course I was—and I did. It was a fair exchange, and I very much looked forward to seeing out…

Note to Paul

June 7, 2010

Surprise- A Love Note!
Thank You, Thank You, Thank you
For giving me such an awesome gift today.
I Love You Forever and a Day!

Xoxo

I spent a week recovering in Mt Pleasant after my tummy tuck. While Paul worked during the day, Diana and Erica helped me when needed. I will not lie; the pain for the first seven days was only bearable with medication, and the drugs made me constipated and nauseous. The girls were invaluable, though. Being sliced open and put back together from hip to hip was no walk in the park. Was it worth the pain? Most definitely!

Note to Paul

June 13, 2010

Baby! Baby! Baby!

Thank you, love for all the tenderness and care you gave me this week. You were the perfect caretaker! Your lovely daughters were incredible too! I can't tell you how much this surgery meant for me as a gift to you and from you, but I think you already know that. I'm so excited about the many great memories to come that we'll share. Hopefully, not many more enemas, though:(I love you darling soooo much. You are wonderful, super-duper cute, and soooo sexy. I can't wait to make love to you again! Good luck this week. You'll be on top of your game. I know it!

Thank you again, Lover-

I appreciate everything you do for me!

Xoxoxoxoxox

Take Away:

If you are willing to take the pain, you both share in the gain—at least when it comes to plastic surgery and fulfilling a sexual favor contract.

CHAPTER NINE

I Trust You With my Life

July 2010

This month was filled with weekends in Tawas, outings with friends, and family events. Paul and I were getting so ingrained in each other's lives that we almost refused to come up for air.

Our friends, Russ and Cara, live off a canal and have a boat. So, since this new man in my life was a boater, it was only appropriate for us to do the "boating" thing down here as well. My experience with boating is basically nil—although putting on a two-piece bathing suit now that I had my tummy tuck was something I definitely could do! Russ and Cara were always the ultimate hosts. In fact, Cara was there for me as I rolled backward down a hill one evening—don't ask what I was doing. She hoisted me up and led me back up to the top. Yes, where was this new man, the one I was trusting with my life? Let's just say he and Russ were obviously in their own worlds—or should I say their own patches of grass enjoying the night sky.

Note TO Paul:

July 12, 2022

Hi Sweetheart-

"Betcha thought I forgot your love note:) I can't thank you enough for another beautiful weekend in Tawas. Thank you for being so generous with the boys and I. They love sharing time up here with you-as, do I! You have given me so many wonderful memories thus far, and I can't wait to experience more of life with you! You are so deep in my heart - and I love you so much. You are my Captain, and I trust you with my life and my heart. You are my Rock Star, and I am yours Forever and a Day!

Xoxo
Carol.

I was always so sad leaving him. But I understood it had to be that way, as we both had our own lives we had to live and obligations. Sometimes, back home, I would think of him and have to send a quick email. I needed that connection.

Email TO Paul

July 27, 2010, 5:46 p.m.

Subject: Lover… Lover… Lover…

You are so hot… I can't stand it… You looked soooo good on Sunday…. oh and Monday morning…(and everything in between)

*Just wanted to tell you I love you more than my peanut butter
and chocolate chip morsel spoon snacks… and everything
else… xoxoxoxo*

Response FROM Paul:
July 27, 2010, 9:35 p.m.

Thank you for loving a pudgy little guy like me!

Then on another day, I sent this one.

Sweetheart,

*I am so amazed at how much you love me and take care of me.
I always dreamed of my Prince coming but never believed it
could be so wonderful. I love being with you whatever we do
and falling asleep, and waking up with you. God sent you to
me, and I pray we'll always love each other more than the day
before.*

Xoxo

Sometimes, I would make the emails visually appealing or throw
in a rhyme. I did not want Paul to get sick of my sappy letters and
emails. Little did I know then that we would carry on this way for
ten years!

Thank You Lover-
For… Being so kind to Charles
… Keeping the house warm
… Snuggling

… Taking us on a canoe ride

… Feeding us

… Racing cars with Charles

… Sharing your hot tub with us.

And for Loving Me!

Xoxo

I Love You

Xoxo

Take Away:

The meaning of gratitude is the quality of being thankful, the readiness to show appreciation, and return kindness. The act and feeling of gratitude is free. Show gratitude daily, and your life will improve immensely.

CHAPTER TEN

Gray Skies

August 2010

Paul had invested in a movie, and a special screening was planned at the Broadway Theatre in Mt Pleasant on his birthday weekend. He had invited several people to the event, along with some friends of mine and my children. In addition, Madeline brought a friend, Tina, and my nephew, Michael, joined my son Joseph. Why is all of this important? Paul's house was full of overnight guests, including my family and friends. We started with the pre-party at his place—with no shortage of alcohol—and then a large party bus took us to the theatre. The movie's star, from California, also came in for the screening. Everything was going smoothly, and everyone seemed to be having a great time. After the movie, we all jumped onto the party bus and headed to a local restaurant. We had delicious hors d'oeuvres and some beverages and generally just socialized more.

Upon reflection, insecurity often finds the most inappropriate times to rear its ugly head...

Paul never spoke much about the movie and the filming of it up to this point in our relationship as it was made "pre-Carol." It was filmed in a community in Michigan not far from his house, so he could attend the filming when he wanted to. I guess you could call it checking on your investment. In truth, I had no right to be upset about what—if anything—had happened between Paul and anyone during the filming, let alone a woman in the movie or someone he met off-set. You know what they say, "Take a shot of courage." Well, I found myself ordering shots for my friends and I at the bar in the restaurant. Paul was not with us; he was still working the crowd—as one does when you're the host. What happened next, to this day, I am still ashamed of. As previously mentioned, alcohol and I didn't always mix very well, and I definitely didn't need anymore at the restaurant. At one point in the evening, Paul wandered up to my group, and we all did another shot. Then, I made the most inappropriate toast of my life: I toasted to Paul sleeping with one of the girls in the movie. FYI, this didn't come out of just anywhere; however, what did it matter what he did in his past with women? He was with me now. The truth of the matter was that I grew up the "good girl." I was not experienced, and maybe—yes, probably—I thought at that moment how I wasn't going to keep Paul's attention, and I was desperately looking for validation. I was judging myself against all the other women Paul had been with, and comparison *is* the thief of joy.

The fallout was that Paul decided he was done talking with me for the evening—and everyone else, for that matter. I tried to talk to him, but to no avail, so we all retired to the bus and returned to the house. As soon as we walked through the door, Paul went to bed and shut the door. I again tried to talk with him; however, he needed some space and shooed me away. At that point, I knew one thing for sure: I was likely going back home with my kids in the morning, which was also Paul's birthday.

Feeling awful over my behavior, I went to say goodnight to my kids. They were sad about what had happened, which made me feel even more ashamed. They didn't need to see me over-imbibing, and what sort of role model was I for them? It was a huge mess! My youngest son was sitting in Paul's car room and said he didn't want to go home. My daughter, on the other hand, was looking for some nail polish remover to take off Paul's initials, PBM, that I had on my nails. Yes, I was that crazy for him! After the kids went to bed, I slept in a guest room.

The next day, I woke up early and went and sat by the river, thinking about the previous night's shit show. I was hoping, at some point, that Paul would come looking for me. My friends were waking up, too, and came out to the patio for a coffee. Paul soon joined us. It was awkward and sad, and I was confused because he acted as if nothing had happened.

We decided to get bagels for the crew, and I was silent pretty much the entire time. Finally, when we were almost home, I mentioned to him how I was going to pack the kids up and head home as I was sorry about the stupid toast, and I figured the damage and words said were irreparable. However, he didn't expect that, and I didn't expect him to say what he did next:

"Are you going to let a little bump in the road ruin our relationship?"

You see, I'm a runner and not the one who runs to see the beauty of nature, health, or to win a race; I run because I don't want to get hurt. I run because it's easier to start over than go through the pain of figuring it out. I've always run; it's my fatal flaw. But Paul stopped me and made me think, *Is he still in it for the long run? Do we apologize to each other and continue our journey?* A feeling of relief came over me. I was still heartbroken about what happened and knew we had to have a longer conversation later when we were alone. However, I also knew that alcohol played a role in the evening's activities, so I needed to learn how to manage my intake. Paul and I also had to improve using the word "Salvadore" to help nip such instances in the bud.

After my friends headed home later that afternoon, it was time for the kids to try out the rope swing on Paul's property. Yes, it was time to take the leap and jump into the adjoining Chippewa River, as I had done earlier in the season. Side note: I vowed never to do it again, as the first time, I didn't let go in time and swung right back into the embankment. I did go a second time to prove to myself that I could do it. Regarding the kids, I would say they half loved it, and half were terrified.

In the early evening, we all went to the steak house at the casino for Paul's birthday dinner, and his daughter Erica came along. It was the perfect end to a slightly bumpy couple of days.

Love Note TO Paul
August 9, 2010

Lover,

Thank you for the great weekend. Thank you for being so generous with my family and friends, and most importantly, thank you for talking to me and allowing me to feel comfortable talking to you. I love you so much and value our relationship. I want "us" to be the best "us" possible. I hope you enjoyed your birthday and our anniversary. I'm glad we were able to spend it together. I miss you already as I write this, although I am excited to come home to you again in a few days.

Love you Baby xoxo

Take Away:

Drunk words are sober thoughts. So, stop running, love yourself, and one of my favorites: The rear-view mirror is smaller than the windshield for a reason.

CHAPTER ELEVEN

The Beginning of Fall

Love Letter to Paul:

September 6, 2010

It's always so hard leaving you. I thought it would get easier but it doesn't. My head knows I have to go, but my heart wants to stay.

You have become so ingrained in my life, so much so that I can't even imagine a future without you. Thank you for being so kind and generous and liking my babies.

You know how much I hate this transition day, but I'll go home knowing we'll be together again soon and prepare for another adventure along our journey together.

I Love You more than I could ever express and will love you more with each passing day-

Thank you for Loving Me Captain!

Xoxo

Paul became my "Captain." To this day, that is what I call him. It is a combination of his history with the water and boating and him being the Captain of my Life. It fits him well, and it makes me happy.

I prepared for Trip #3 (September 11–14). This time, we were headed to New York to visit Paul's middle daughter, Diana. We had a fabulous time. I was getting used to our routine of heading to the airport, then to the lounge bar, and talking with other patrons. This was exciting. I'm a talker as it is, and having an audience to tell how much I love this man sitting next to me felt incredible! I wanted to share how I met Paul and how life was perfect with the world. Life was **perfect** for me at this time. I remember thinking, *I'm in a fabulous relationship, my kids are happy, my parents are alive and doing well, and I have a fantastic career, which allows me to travel and still work. How lucky am I right now?* And I remember trying to hold on to that feeling, knowing life constantly changes. They say the bad never lasts, but neither does the good. Life is an ebb and flow. All I knew was that life was good, and when the changes came, I would deal with them. Why ruin today's happiness with worries about tomorrow, right?

Our New York trip was lively and entertaining. It was great to see Diana and hear about her new job and life in Manhattan. We did some touristy things, like going to the financial district, which was amazing. So much happens in those buildings, so much commerce. Seeing the iconic Charging Bull sculpture or "The Bull of Wall Street" was impressive, to say the least. We also dined at some great restaurants and enjoyed craft cocktails and many laughs.

Love Note to My Captain

September 26, 2010

I absolutely can't stand leaving you. But—this time, we'll be back together sooner. I love and adore you - you are my everything. Thank you for the Rock Star sex and making me feel so special. I love you bunches and bunches, and I Love You Forever and a Day!

Xoxo

Take Away:

There is no sense in wasting today's time on tomorrow's inevitability.

CHAPTER TWELVE

Fire Up Chips!

October 2010

Football season had hit, and it was time to head to the box suite for the games. This is my kind of football—where we can sit inside, have a glass of wine, and not have to be bundled up in fall's chill. In addition, it was a great time to socialize and meet more of Paul's friends. We would hop from suite to suite. It was so much fun! Of course, we would watch the game, too. I was fortunate that Captain had several tickets to bring up the kids, friends, and other family members through the years. We made great memories, and I look back fondly on how we shared things with my family.

Love Note to My Captain
Oct 3, 2010

Sweetheart,

Thank you for being my rock, support system, and best friend. Each day I'm more amazed at your ability to love me and your tenacity to get through "my" rough times. I love you so deeply and hope you are 100% aware of that. I know you are always with me, even though we may not be physically together. I appreciate your honesty, intelligent decision-making, and your ever-present generosity and selfless ways with me. Thank you! Thank You! Thank You! I am so glad God brought us together. I Love you Baby! Xoxo

Card to Paul:
October 16, 2010

Sweetest Day-

Thank you for Rocking My World.

P. -Positively

A. -Absolutely

U. -Undeniably

L. -Love of My Life.

Trip #4 took us to Nashville for a Tanning Convention—at least, that is what it was supposed to be. We went with our friends, Rob and Tina. Going anywhere with them is an epic experience. When I first met Tina, the second weekend into my torrid romance with

Captain, I was not sure what to expect—as Tina is the sister of one of Paul's former girlfriends. However, Tina was warm and friendly and never made it feel awkward. Some of my fondest memories of Mt Pleasant include her and Rob.

I had never been to Nashville, so I took in all the sights, sounds, and experiences I could. I danced on the bar at Coyote Ugly, and Paul partook in the body shots. At this time, Paul was dealing with an ingrown toenail and could not wear his seriously sexy cowboy boots. Instead, he walked the streets of downtown Nashville in his Michigan State flip-flops. Go Green! I bring this up because half a dozen times, one of us stepped on his bad toe. Thank goodness for the numbing effect of alcohol, right? We stopped at another bar, and Rob decided to participate in karaoke. Song picked, beer in hand, and now the wait to be called up. As a general assumption, even though I do not do karaoke—I would clear the room—one usually picks songs they are somewhat familiar with. None of us are quite sure why Rob decided to change his song when he went up on stage, and I'm sure he regretted it when the boo's started coming from the crowd and possibly us, too. He attempted a redo with a new song but was quickly escorted off the stage, the mic literally being pulled from his hand. We all laughed uncontrollably—and still do to this day when we recall that trip. So many crazy moments with Rob and Tina. My travels with Captain have all been wonderful; however, this one holds an exceptional place in my heart.

Love Note to My Captain

October 25, 2010

A 10+ Vacation we just had - and the funny thing, it didn't include bathing suits or water, and it was still a blast! I love being your travel companion, lover, and partner. Thank you again for loving me and taking care of me. Leaving your physical presence is difficult, but I carry you in my heart as I know you do. I look forward to many more fabulous times and the times that I'm just snuggled up on your lap.

I Love you my Captain! Xoxoxoxox

Carol

Take Away:

Wear a pretty bra if you plan on visiting Coyote Ugly. You may just dance on the bar and leave it there with all the others to be hung up…

CHAPTER THIRTEEN

The Washington Monument

November 2010

It was Trip #5, and Captain had scheduled us to go to Washington DC for a business valuation conference he was attending at the Washington Hilton Hotel, where President Reagan was shot in 1981. The hotel was beautiful, and the grounds were lovely—Captain always loves a travel companion, and I am so glad it is me. We took a few extra days and spent some time in the city. I had been there once when my mom took us on a one-day charter trip—a junket, so to speak. I was eleven, but I remember visiting the National Archives and a couple of the Smithsonian Institution buildings. This trip introduced me to so much more, and my appreciation was greater being older. I fell in love with D.C. I loved its architecture, history, and vastness—even walking around the Washington Monument way too many times to catch the Hop On Hop Off Bus.

It was also on this trip that I met Sara, Paul's oldest daughter. At first, she seemed a little suspicious of me, probably because of the PDA between her dad and I. I vividly remember her asking me what

I wanted with her dad. I replied that I loved him and was not looking for anything else. I added that I would happily sign a prenup if we married one day. Looking back, it's crazy that I was even talking about marriage, but she did ask! The prenup comment was genuine. I had told Paul your girls come before me; they are your kids. I believed it then, and I believe it now. As a mother or father, your babies will always take precedence before your spouse, especially when they're young—at least in second marriages, third, or whatever number you are on. Of course, others may think differently, and that is their prerogative. I'm sure Sara was just concerned about whether I was with her dad for the wrong reasons. Luckily for everyone, that could not have been farther from the truth.

Love Note to My Captain
November 14, 2010

> *Sweetheart,*
>
> *What a wonderful time we had together. I love you so much and enjoy every minute we spend together. You are my everything, my future, and I am sooo in love with you. Thank you for taking me to Washington, D.C.*
>
> *Xoxo*
> *Carol*

What I did not say in the love note was *thank you for trying to stop me when I wanted one of your cigarettes.* Unfortunately, though, I persisted and smoked one. Thus, I thanked Paul for taking care of me that evening and sleeping next to me on the bathroom floor. The next day, I persisted again. I became a weekend smoker who shared her Captain's cigarettes. I was not supposed to let this happen; I knew better. Oh, but what fun it was...

Love Note to My Captain
November 22, 2010

> *Sweetheart,*
>
> *For some reason, this time, leaving you is especially difficult. I had such a wonderful weekend with you. As Christmas approaches, I am incredibly grateful and excited to share it with the world's most handsome, loving, and generous man. Sweetheart, you mean everything to me. Thank you for loving me, and thanks for the great Sex! :) xoxoxo*

I believe I see a theme here... Love and Sex.

Love Note to My Captain
November 28, 2010

> *Baby,*
>
> *Here I am, getting ready to leave you again, well, leave Mt. Pleasant, you know what I mean. I hate this part. I love every minute we spend together. Thank you for a beautiful weekend. As long as we're together, I don't care what we do! Thank you for enhancing my life and being my partner. You are everything to me, and I love you to the moon and back! Xoxoxo*

Take Away:

Dial back on the public display of affection when first meeting the children.

CHAPTER FOURTEEN

A Death in the Family

December 9, 2010

Today was a dark one for Paul. He called early in the morning to tell me his mom had passed away. She had been in an assisted living home in Bay City. I was fortunate to have met her; she was such a lovely, happy woman. Paul resembled her, and you could see the excitement on her face whenever we would visit. The funeral was two days later. Paul's girls came into town, along with his brothers and sister-in-law. This was also when I met the rest of the family. I was sad for my Captain and supported him throughout the loss. I had yet to lose a parent, so it gave me a bittersweet taste of the enormity behind losing someone you have known since birth, the grief and celebration of a life that becomes intricately entwined.

Love Note to My Captain

December 14, 2010

Sweetheart,

Thank you so much for letting me share this last weekend with you and this time in your life. I'm happy I had the opportunity to meet your mom before she passed. I could see how much she adored you. I learn something new about you each time we're together, and these past few days prove what a wonderful man you are! I am so fortunate to be in a relationship with you and excited about all we have to share in our "journey." I Love You So Much, Baby!! Xoxoxo

Christmas quickly approached, and I was excited to see how the annual Christmas Eve Open House Party would go at Paul's. I had heard about the past parties and knew Paul enjoyed hosting them. He loved having his girls under one roof, celebrating with him and all the friends and family that would stop in for a quick drink and a bite to eat. Paul was—and still is—very organized. He has a file folder for everything—I believe that is the CPA in him, one of the many things I adore. Of course, he has a file for me, too—at least he did when we started dating! At any rate, he would pull out the file, go over the menu, the guest list, and anything else pertinent to the event. This is the Christmas folder, and it has become quite thick. Keeping track of receipts is what good accountants do; great accountants record them, and even better accountants put them in the correct column. I loved this about Paul, and I loved his signature.

The party was a hit, as expected.

The open house was a success and Paul gave me a Christmas present after all the guests had left that evening. It was a beautiful bracelet. He wrote in the card:

Dear Princess,

Thank you for being my Princess Forever and a Day. You are My One and Only. You are so thoughtful and loving, and I adore the way you take such good care of me. You are my Treasure. I Love You. :-)

Your Captain.

I was grateful, and it came at the right time because I felt melancholy over how it would be the first time I would not be with my kids when they woke up on Christmas Day. Holidays can be depressing when the other parent has the children. Fast forward ten years, though, and we sometimes spend holidays together—my former husband, the children, Paul, and I. I will always be thankful for both of these men. I think they like each other. Currently, they are on a text message chain with other guys texting guy stuff, like sports, politics, and probably scantily clad women, so I guess it's all good.

We headed downstate later on Christmas Day to celebrate with my family. My parents enjoyed being around Paul because he was fun—heck, everyone loved being around him. He always made holidays and times with my family better by being around. Of course, it did not hurt that he was so handsome...

Love Note to My Captain

December 28, 2010

Lover,

Thank you for spending the holidays with me. It was a wonderful Christmas. Thank you for my beautiful bracelet. I love it!! As we "journey" into 2011, I know my love for you will continue to grow, and we'll share many more great moments together! You are my forever and a day, and I'm so grateful for match.com :-)

Love Ya, Baby!

Takeaway:

It is an old sentiment, but cherish the ones you love while you have the chance because you will have to say goodbye one day.

CHAPTER FIFTEEN

A New Year; One Year Down

January 8, 2011

Today was our one-year anniversary, a celebration of the day Paul "noticed me and was interested" on Match.com. To commemorate this special day, he had orchestrated a weekend of enchantment—an indulgent stay at the Soaring Eagle Casino & Resort. After we checked in and went to our room, a sight took my breath away: I found a dozen red roses waiting for me. Our evening unfolded like a dream, with a sumptuous dinner followed by dancing. In the tender embrace of Paul's arms, I realized that he had effortlessly made our first anniversary utterly perfect. Like a princess enveloped in a cocoon of love, I marveled at the depth of his devotion and sincerity. I could not wait for our next adventure.

Note to My Captain

January 10, 2011

Amazing! That's how I would describe this past weekend. You made me feel so special and beautiful, and we had so much fun! This past year has been a whirlwind and a year full of firsts for me. Thank you for exposing me to all the beautiful things in life with you. I love you so, so much and can't wait to see what this year brings!

Love You Baby

Note to My Captain

January 16, 2011

Thank you, Sweetheart, for sharing your time and daughter with us this weekend. It was fun! I love you unbelievably— You are so loving, kind, and damn hot. I can't wait to be with you again- 3 sleeps! 2011 has been wonderful so far, and I can't wait for the rest of it. Have a wonderful week, and know that I'm here with you in my heart.

Love you Bunches!

Xoxo

Note from My Captain

January 16, 2011

Dear Princess,

Forever and A Day, that's what we say. My love for you grows, as everybody knows, day after day. My poetry is gay,

*but will you love me anyway? Just want to tell you how much
I love my little Princess (105 or 112 lbs). I love and appreciate all the things you do for me and us. You wait on me, and
I don't want you to think that I ever take it for granted. I'm
such a lucky guy.*

*I love how all my friends like you for who you are and not just
how you look! I love my little arm candy, but you know that's
not all you mean to me.*

Love you,
Captain

I always begged Paul to write me love letters. Now and then,
I would get one, and it was terrific. Each one became a cherished
artifact that left me feeling euphoric as it would cement Paul's long-
term commitment to *us* in my mind. We would always say that love
was not a destination to be reached but a breathtaking voyage to be
savored.

Love Note to My Captain
January 24, 2011

Sweetheart,

*Although it didn't seem long enough, I'm grateful for our
time together. I love coming up here (Tawas) and just being
with you. I love that I can let myself go and just be me. Thank
you for accepting and loving me and not minding all the
tears I shed when I leave you or even think about leaving.:(*

My Captain came into "Port" and "Docked" in my life, and I gladly grabbed the "Lines" and "Knotted" them tightly- :-)

Seriously Lover, thank you again and again for sharing your life with me. As I said before and will continue to say, I am the luckiest girl in the world! xoxo

The Super Bowl weekend was right around the corner, and Paul was heading out with his golfing buddies for their annual retreat.

Love Letter to My Captain
January 31, 2011

My Captain, My Prince, My Heart-

Every time we're together, I fall more in love with you. With each shared moment, I feel I grow closer to you and realize how lucky I am to have you as my own. Your kindness, generosity, and sheer funniness make my life so enjoyable. I don't know what I'd do without you. You have become a huge part of my heart, and I love you deeply. Thank you for another great weekend- and for always keeping it fresh.☐ Sex was excellent as usual, and oh, so much fun!! Baby, I will miss you so much this coming week and weekend. I want you to have fun with your boys. You deserve it! I'll miss you but will be happy you're having a good time and making memories. I love you, Sweetheart, and I will be counting down the days until we are together again! Love you with all my heart, Forever and a Day!

P&C

Tax season was ramping up again. My weekends were spent with my Captain, working extra hours and spending time together at his beautiful home. Winter was gorgeous in Mid-Michigan. The trees and beauty of the river in Paul's backyard were breathtaking. The snow and icicles that formed on the trees looked like still-life paintings. Not to mention the floor-to-ceiling windows in the living room and how the sunroom let the rays beam in, keeping us warm and cozy.

Love Note to My Captain
February 20, 2011

Sweetheart,

Today is one of those days that I still can't believe I'm yours. It's not that I don't feel worthy enough, but I guess I can't believe someone as wonderful as you could love me! Thank you for making me feel so special, beautiful, and loved. If there's one word in my vocabulary that I never want to use again regarding my love life is "next." I pray you'll always be happy with me and that we continue to grow together and strengthen our bond. I'm so excited when we're together; leaving becomes harder and harder. But knowing we'll be together again in a few days makes it palatable.

Thank you for being so great to Charles and all of my babies- and thank you so much for giving my daughter the wonderful trip/opportunity this week in D.C. You are my heart, soul, and Prince who's rescued me in so many ways. I love you, my handsome Captain, and I will always be your First Mate as long as you don't throw me overboard. XOXOXOXOXOX

My Captain and I continued interweaving our lives, and I could not believe the sheer generosity and selflessness he showed toward me and my children. He was like a miraculous gift bestowed upon us from the heavens. With each passing day, I found myself embracing the reality that he was truly mine and the notion of a long-lasting future together.

Takeaway:

Outstanding sex isn't the only quality to look for in a partner, but damn… having it...Priceless!

Chapter Sixteen

Wrapping up Tax Season

April 2011

April always brought the looming crunch time—and clients who waited until the last minute to set up an appointment with Paul. I always dreaded the days when he would tell me about a past girlfriend who was also coming in to drop off her tax info. Thankfully, that only lasted a couple of years into our relationship. Was I worried? No. I was more aggravated. However, who was I to tell my Captain whom he could have as a client? I looked at it as, "Well, if it's good for the firm, it's good for him." And when it came right down to it, I trusted him because with trust comes real love.

Love Note to My Captain
April 4, 2011

Sweetheart,

The tears are flowing as I write this. It's hard to leave you and return to my other life. I am so grateful and blessed to be given this fabulous opportunity to love you and for you to love me back. Sometimes I think when I write these notes, they become redundant, or at least I worry that you think I just may be writing the same thing repeatedly, but I am grateful and feel that I've found my Prince and am living my own fairy tale. When I'm with you, I feel so protected, like nothing could ever happen to me, and I know you're there even when you're not "physically" present. I'll begin this week by counting down the days till the end of the week and when I can be back in your arms. I know your next few weeks will be hectic and stressful, I'll try to stay in your background and not burden you with the little things going on in my life, and I'll anxiously await our time together in California. I Love You Baby! Thank you for everything this weekend!

Xoxo

Card to My Captain
April 8, 2011

Baby,

Thank you for the beautiful "15" months. You have taken me down a fabulous road, and I have loved it! Our journey has been exciting, arousing, and event filled. I would challenge anyone to have a more fabulous boyfriend who's hot, sexy, and everything all in one package!

I Love You!

xoxo

Happy Anniversary!

Love Letter to My Captain
April 11, 2011

Why is it that every time I sit down to write your love note, the tears begin flowing? It's because it leaves a hole in my heart whenever I have to leave you. I know you're always with me, but I love just being with you- or at least in the same town with you.:) Fifteen months, no fifteen incredible months- and a fabulous weekend to boot! Thank you for treating me like a Princess. I'm living the fairy tale! I loved every minute of this weekend and am so excited about California.

And you know I can't begin to thank you for the opportunity you've given Charles. I'm so grateful. Captain Paul, you have the most enormous heart and .. 😋

You are my forever and a day- and I LOVE YOU SO MUCH!!

Good luck getting through the week, and know I'm loving you always!

Xoxoxoxo

Finally, the 2011 tax season ended, and I visited Paul for his work's annual parking lot celebration.

Love Letter to My Captain

April 16, 2011

My Captain, My Prince, My Heart-

Every time we're together, I fall more in love with you. With each shared moment, I feel I grow closer to you and realize how lucky I am to have you as my own. Your kindness, generosity, and sheer funniness make my life so enjoyable. I don't know what I'd do without you. You have become such a huge part of my heart, and I love you so profoundly. Thank you for another great weekend- and for always keeping it fresh. 😲 Sex was excellent as usual, and oh, so much fun!! Baby, I will miss you so much this coming week and weekend.

Captain flew out on April 17 to Palm Springs, California. He had booked a rental home for two weeks and wanted to visit the California faction of the family. The kids and their significant others would come out, too, at various times during the stay. I joined them the day after Easter, for Trip #6 (April 25 – May 6). I needed to spend the holiday with my kids and family. I remember boarding the plane and being so excited. I also remember running into my love's arms at the airport. We had a fabulous time: Sun, fun, and no shortage of frozen cocktails!

Take Away:

Make sure your significant other has time with their children without you being present. It makes a stronger relationship.

CHAPTER SEVENTEEN

Sleepover with the Ex

July 2011

My baby was now ten years old and cute as a button. Of course, a mother would say that, but my boy Charles had curly brown hair, blue eyes, and an adorable personality to match! So, we did what everyone told us to do, "Carol, this kid needs to be in commercials." Charles participated in a local commercial event and was chosen to go to the nationals in Florida. However, this was not a cheap endeavor, I and my former husband could not afford the enrollment fee, so my Captain offered to front the money. He believed in Charles, and even if it did not work out, he would have a write-off. Thus, we formed an LLC for Charles, and a contract was drawn up. I could not help but wonder if this was the start of something big for Charles. Would he end up famous? In my heart, I didn't know if that is what I wanted for him—especially when you hear of stories of child stars, and all you want to do is protect your children. Of course, the thought of it was still intriguing, though...

Love Note to My Captain
July 3, 2011

Oh, Sweetheart,

Six sleeps and a different state without you. I am going to miss you so much! I hope you realize that. Thank you for another fantastic weekend! I know I've said that many times, but they keep getting better and better! My love grows stronger and stronger with each day you're in my life.

I hope my love notes don't seem redundant to you. As I said before, I wish I could come up with additional words to express how much I love you-

I HATE BEING WITHOUT YOU!!!!

I know it's impossible to be with you always, but my heart feels differently. Again, I can't thank you enough for giving Charles this opportunity. You have invested so much in him, myself, and my children that I could never repay you. I appreciate all the love, kindness, good times, and financial aspect you've brought into our lives.

We have many more good times ahead of us and much to look forward to. It's those times that get me through the times when we're apart.

I know I'm a sap, but with you, I've never experienced such love and feeling of being so satisfied and fulfilled in a mate/ partner/almost husband !

I know it wasn't just chance that I met you on match. Thank you for seeking me out and giving me all your love.

You'll travel with me this next week in my heart, all the time, and I'll count down the sleeps till we are together again. I love you forever and a day, and then some. ♥ *xoxo*

Letter FROM My Captain
July 4, 2011

Dear Princess,

Forever and a day, now, in the beginning, and in our future together. You treat me like such a "Captain," and I appreciate that. I wish I could take all your cares away and cuddle you every night. You are my one and only. I look forward to when we can always be together, and you'll never have to say goodbye.

I hope you know I trust you and certainly don't have a worry while you're in Florida. You mean everything to me, and you know you don't have to worry about me. I love you, Princess, and can't wait until Saturday when you return, and I can make love to you.

I hope Charlie does well and the trip goes smoothly. Just remember, if you hit a few bumps along the way, your "Captain" will be there for you.

Love you Princess.

Love
Paul

So, Charles, his dad, and I headed to Orlando. Boy, it was hot! Charles did well and had fun. He had to participate in skits and walk the runways. At the end of the program, we were given an envelope with the names of talent agencies interested in talking to us more about Charles's prospective career. We had a handful of names, so we spoke with the agents and left Charles's information. It looked like we were not packing up and moving to California just yet. I was happy we went, though, and Charles got to walk the red carpet. Was it the end of my son's career that never started? Actually, no. There was a local talent agency back in southeastern Michigan that we became affiliated with instead. Charles auditioned for a few commercials and did get some local air time! The experience was also a great example of my and my ex's success at co-parenting and being friends. The three of us shared a hotel room with two double beds. My Captain had no issue with it at all. He wanted the best for Charles, too, because, at the end of the day, it is about what's best for the children.

My profile on Match.com had mentioned that I was not looking for someone who trashes their ex. I understand that separating, whether married or not, can cause many emotions, and specifically, a long, drawn-out divorce tied up in the court system for months or years can create some nasty feelings. However, I wasn't interested in dating anyone who would bring that negative energy into a new relationship. In addition, they would have to be content with my former husband being in my life, and Paul was.

On July 4, Captain gave me a card to open on our monthly anniversary when I would be in Florida. Yes, we were still celebrating monthly anniversaries. Why not? It had a general anniversary message to which he added:

I Love You Princess forever and a day. Thank you for being all mine.

Can't wait to hear the stories about Florida and then our adult entertainment.

Paul

Also, that month was my daughter Madeline's high school graduation party, which was being held at her dad's house. Paul came into town for the weekend. We were a year and a half into our relationship by this time, and Paul had fitted in seamlessly.

Letter to My Captain
July 10, 2011

Too Short!!! But I am so grateful to have had 2 sleeps with you! Thank you, Sweetheart, for coming this way this weekend and for being there for me at Maddy's grad party. You were the hottest guy there, and I still can't believe you're mine! :-)

Thank you again for giving Charlie this wonderful opportunity. I'm excited to see where this all goes for him! I know we have so much to look forward to but I still get so sad when we have to part. I love you more than you'll ever realize and can't wait to be Mrs. Murray one day!!

Love you Bunches and Forever and a Day! Xoxo

Take Away:

If you have a great relationship with your ex, be grateful and tell them how much you appreciate them. If you do not have a great relationship, still be thankful because gratitude breeds gratitude.

CHAPTER EIGHTEEN

A Quiet Birthday

August 2011

Captain's birthday was a much quieter one than last year. No party buses, free-flowing alcohol, or apologies needed!

Letter to My Captain

August 8, 2011

Thank you for spending the weekend down here. It means so much to me. I'm sorry it wasn't as action-packed as it could have been. I love spending time with you, whatever we do, and I know you feel the same. I love you so much, and I'm so glad we've made it to your next Birthday from where we came last summer. You are my Captain and have stolen my heart; I trust it in your hands.

Thank you for looking so good in a suit, really good!

Baby, I love you forever and a day. I'll miss you this week counting down the sleeps!

Xoxoxo

When my parents were alive, they would have parties for almost any occasion. Captain was fortunate to experience several of these parties; some were even thrown for him—as was this year's one at my parents' home. I loved including him in our family birthday celebrations and any celebration for that matter! After being stuffed with dinner and cake, we returned to my Sterling Heights home, and the next day, Captain headed home. I would meet up with him the following Thursday in Tawas.

Letter to My Captain
August 15, 2011

Another great weekend in Tawas with the love of my life!!

Thank you so much for letting me bring Charlie up and for making it so much fun for him.

Again, I'll say the hardest part of this is leaving you and having to say goodbye. I'll miss snuggling with you, and I'll count down the nights.

I'll probably miss your you know what...more though- hehe-.

I love you, Captain, and thank match every day.

Xoxo PnC ♥

August finished up with the annual Dream Cruise party held at my sister's house in Royal Oak. The location was perfect, and she always opens her home for anyone to stop by. The Dream Cruise and the week that leads up to it mark the end of summer for me. It is like a rite of passage. After we clean up from Dream Cruise, it's time to start thinking about fall. In Michigan, though, we can guarantee a few more 90-degree days. Luckily, we had one for the company canoe trip in Mt. Pleasant with Paul's firm. I brought up Madeline and Charles, and they enjoyed the sights down the Chippewa River, followed by a party for the staff in Paul's backyard. Fun times!

Take Away:

Sometimes, it is ok to have a quiet birthday. After all, no drama and no tears, right?

CHAPTER NINETEEN

Finding Paradise, a Cognac Gem, and Accepting Truths

September and October 2011

Several times in our relationship, I would make the trip up to Mt Pleasant for one day or even drive up in the morning and back downstate in the evening. September was one of those months…

Letter to My Captain
September 22, 2011

> *My Captain, My Rock, My Life-*
>
> *I HATE LEAVING!!*
>
> *Do you get that??*
>
> *As the season changes, I look forward to all the fun fall brings and our journey progressing. I have so much fun with you; you have captured my heart. I can't even imagine my life, my existence, without you. Thank you for including*

me yesterday at your luncheon. It makes me feel special that you want me in your life. I didn't mind all the driving on Tuesday. I would drive for hours to be with you. Thank you for your generosity and for making me feel beautiful and sexy, and your forever and a day.

God has given me such a special gift, and I still can't believe you are mine. I love you, Captain, and can't wait to share our Sterling Heights bed together!

Have a great weekend with your shareholders, and know I'll be downstate missing the shit out of you!

**The following weekend, Paul invited my parents and sister up for the weekend to watch the Central Michigan University football game. I was pleased knowing my mom and dad could now see the home and community I had grown to love. They were not new to Mt Pleasant, though. My dad would golf with my former husband's dad and a large contingent of his uncles. The wives would also come on this trip and do what wives do when their husbands' golf, lunch and shopping.

Back to the weekend... Paul was the ultimate host and made my parents and sister feel comfortable. My dad loved the football game and being in the suite. He and my sister could experience the game from the field, too. By this time, my mom was on oxygen; however, she was able to attend the game and stayed in the suite. She had a great time!

Love Letter to My Captain

October 2, 2011

Oh, Sweetheart,

Thank you so so so much for sharing your home with my parents and sister this weekend. It was vital to show them where I am for half of my life. You were the ultimate host. Thank you for sharing your football tickets with them, also. I feel our relationship is cemented deeper every time we're together. Every time I look at you I continue to melt inside and wonder what it is you see in me. How did I get so lucky that you chose me to spend your life with? I promise to continue loving you as I do, if not more, if possible, and make you proud to be with me.

I want to stand next to my Captain forever and a day and share all that I can with you. As I said, I love you, and I like you, and I get excited when I think about being with you and how much fun we will have. I love you, my Prince, and will be anxiously awaiting your arrival at our home in Sterling Heights!

xoxoxoxox ♥

Another family function would be happening for Joseph and my mom the following weekend. We had a special menu planned, and the party was going to be a big one!

Love Letter to My Captain
October 10, 2011

Captain,

Thank you Thank you sooo much for the great weekend!!! I know you were sick, and I'm sorry I made you sick, but it was still awesome! You were so kind to do all you did around here and cleaning all that garlic. It meant so much to me. Thank you for socializing with my family. I know, at times, it can be work- :-)

You are so wonderful, and I love you so much. You have made me the happiest girl in the world!! You know how hard it is for me to say goodbye. Every day I spend with you makes it more challenging to be without you. When you leave me to go home or when I leave you to come back to Sterling Heights, a big part of my heart is empty. The only benefit is, is the fact that I get to get all excited over again and look forward to seeing and being back in your arms. We have such a beautiful life- and you are my Rock, My Captain, My Prince, and the true love of my life. Thank you for making me your Princess! I love you Forever and A Day!!!

Xoxoxoxoxo

Today, the guests arrived at the house around 3:00 p.m. for a seven-hour party. The main dish was a garlic extravaganza and a family favorite from my mom's side. It is officially called Bagna Cauda—we pronounce it as Bonya Calda. You start with oil and add five or six garlic bulbs into a frying pan. Once they are browned, add anchovies and butter—lots of it—and stir for a long time. Each family member usually takes a turn stirring it. Then, you toast to the simmering pan of deliciousness, have a shot of whiskey, and voilà! The dish is ready. To serve, everyone makes a circle around the frying pan—you must do this outside, or in a basement or garage, as the smell is pretty strong—takes a piece of celery, cabbage, or lettuce, and dips it in the frypan. You then use a thick slice of crispy bread to catch the drippings on the way to your mouth. Paul was a huge helpful addition to this party as he sliced up all the garlic. The dish was a hit with him, too—or at least he acted like he loved it. It was a fantastic party, and everyone enjoyed themselves. Life could not have been better on that beautiful fall day.

Love Note to My Captain
October 24, 2011

Another beautiful time spent with My Captain- I love you so much, and I like you- 😃 *I really enjoyed sharing this past weekend with you and experiencing the Athenium (hotel in Detroit). I feel like such a Princess, I laugh when I'm with you, and I cry when I leave you, but the times with you far outweigh the times I'm alone. Loving you has made me so happy. My Captain is so cool, so hot, so much fun, and so easy for me to be with. I feel we are perfect for each other, and I couldn't imagine life without you. Thank you for being so kind and generous to my babies and me. You are my heart, and I love you.*

Xoxoxox❤

FYI, we had spent the weekend in Detroit, attending a Lions game with some of Paul's friends from Canadian Lakes, Michigan. The Lions won that game. So, it was a good day!

The following weekend, a family friend of ours was getting married. Unfortunately, Paul was in the middle of passing a kidney stone, so I headed up to Mt Pleasant on the Thursday before the weekend. We planned to drive downstate on Saturday for the wedding and then back up on Sunday. However, Paul spent most of Friday in bed, in pain. The stone did not seem to be moving. To help, I googled home remedies for passing a kidney stone, as we really wanted to make it to the wedding. You can only imagine what I made him drink—it included castor oil and hot spicy seasonings. Yuck! He was a trouper, though, and suffered through my special remedy.

Love Note to My Captain
October 31, 2011

My sunshine-even in the rain,

Stones or no stones, I love being with you. I'm never bored.

Thank you so very much for coming to the wedding with me. I feel so special when we're together, and because you always look like a million bucks, I feel like a million bucks too!! 😜 I'm sorry you weren't feeling well the last few days, and I apologize for making you drink that god-awful concoction.! I think it made a difference, though.

As I head back to Sterling Heights, you'll be with me in my heart and the touch of your lips forever ingrained in my memory. I've found the love of my life, and it is so satisfying, emotionally and physically! I'm super excited about our upcoming trip. I love experiencing things with you- and I will finally head back to Vegas with my True Love! So sexy, hot, seductive, and extremely intelligent, Captain. I'll see you in three sleeps and will love you more when I return. Xoxoxo

Take Away:

Taking care of your significant other when they are ill can be no easy feat, but the extra bond you form in the process makes it all worth it.

CHAPTER TWENTY

Viva Las Vegas

November, 2011

Paul's annual November valuation conference was held in Las Vegas this year, so I got to hit up Sin City with my man! I had been there once before, in 2007, for work. My buddy, Robert from my office, and I watched the fountains go off at the Bellagio, and I told myself that the next time I would come back, I would be in Love—I guess I was putting that energy out there. It took four years to return, but it was worth the wait.

While my Captain attended the conference, I managed to fill in my time exploring the city. After he was finished every day, we went out for fabulous dinners, shows, and he played a little three-card poker. We stayed at the Aria; however, my Captain showed me around the strip and Downtown Vegas. I finally had made it to see the Bellagio fountains again—with my Captain—but we were having such fun that night that we almost missed it as it was well into the evening, and I had downed a few Crown and diet sodas by then. It was truly one of those moments a girl dreams about, yet the dream is way better than the reality. Still, I had made it happen and was utterly content.

By now, you might think I was an expert at packing, having gone on so many trips throughout my life. But I am a girl, and one who likes to travel with her stuff, and nowhere in Captain's bio on Match. com did he say travelwithme365 and pack light! Captain always teased me about the number of high heels I would bring on trips, but a girls gotta have her shoes, right? Show me a girl with one pair of shoes, probably flats, heading to Vegas or anywhere, and I guarantee she is sensible, level-headed, practical, and does not check in her luggage as it is all in her carry-on. Well, that's not me. I have a suitcase and a carry-on bag stuffed to the brim. After all, besides shoes, I needed my toiletries, two outfits for each day, lingerie—which, of course, doesn't take up much space since there wasn't much material—and purses/totes.

Not long after Vegas, Trip #8 took us to Key West. We left the day after Thanksgiving, and it was my first time traveling to the Keys. My Captain pulled out all the stops and made it a memorable trip. We stayed at a boutique hotel on Duval Street, where each room had its own private patio. They also had a complimentary Happy Hour! The staff was delightful, and Paul treated me like a Princess more than ever! We took a seaplane to the Dry Tortugas, snorkeled, and toured Fort Taylor. We had delicious dinners and took in shows.

One evening on Duval Street, we wandered into a gallery and instantly connected with the proprietor. One of their artists whose work was displayed also caught my Captain's eye. In conjunction with his Love of Bill Mack's art and the complimentary beverages we were served, we left with Paul purchasing a beautiful relief piece of art. Her name is *Elusive*. This began the collection of the Bill Mack pieces, along with future trips to follow the artist. It felt like I was living a dream. I loved the laid-back feel of Key West. I can honestly say now it's one of my favorite places to travel.

It was tough to return from Key West to the cold and impending craziness of the approaching holiday. I cannot fully verbalize it, but I felt different returning from this trip. I felt more connected. Maybe large purchases do that? It's not that I had any "skin in the game" because I didn't; I just felt like Paul valued my opinion, and he made it seem like it was *our* purchase.

Take Away:

When in Love, travel—and then travel some more!

CHAPTER TWENTY-ONE

Jingle Bells

December 2011

The holiday season was ramping up, and I was excited to spend another Christmas with my Captain.

Love Note to My Captain
December 13, 2011

Captain,

What a wonderful weekend! Thank you for always making the time we spend together special. How did I get so lucky? I'm still trying to figure it out! Well…the bottom line is I'm so appreciative of what we have together and unbelievably grateful we were one of the "1 out of 5" that met online and made it. You're perfect for me - your kindness and generosity may beat out your hotness!! No, you're HOT!

What I'm saying is you're as beautiful on the inside as your physical beauty. But, most importantly, I LOVE being with you and HATE leaving. As I said before, the only good thing about that is getting excited all over again for our next reunion.

As Christmas approaches, I'll continue to thank God for all the blessings in my life and be grateful we're spending our 2nd Christmas together!

Thanks for the Hot Sex this weekend!

Forever and a Day

Xoxo

For the next couple of weekends, I was busy preparing for Christmas, but we managed to take in a Red Wings game. The Red Wings seem to play often— at least, that was how it felt :-). Captain was in a group where they would have the ticket draft, and the guys would pick the games they wanted to see. We had four tickets and went to plenty of games through the years. We got to know the ushers, and I enjoyed chatting with them. Of course, Paul took these games much more seriously than I did. I have to say, though, we did have some great experiences at The Joe—except maybe the time Paul slipped down the unending concrete steps one icy winter evening. Yep, karma can be a bitch.

I was in Mt Pleasant a couple of days before our Christmas Eve party. One of the days, Paul's jeweler—yes, he has one—stopped by to drop off a package. We both answered the door, and the jeweler seemed surprised to see me. He handed Paul the bag and did not say much else. We small-talked, and he left.

Paul and I headed downstairs to the theatre room a couple of hours later. This was not uncommon for us to do this as it was also "the smoking room" in the winter. Paul had an excellent ventilation system, and it was much better than freezing outside. Even better, though, would have been quitting. Anyway, my Captain said he had something to give me before the party. He handed me a beautiful gift bag, and in it was a small, wooden, ring-sized box. Naturally, the first thing that popped into my mind was, *Is he about to ask me to marry him already?* Surely not, as he knew Charles was still young. *Could it be a long engagement, then?* Maybe it would be a scenario like when you ask someone, they say, "We haven't picked a date yet," and two years later or more, they still have not picked a date. The previous summer, when a salesman was trying to get Paul to purchase a classic Bentley, he said it would be difficult to get it serviced in Mt. Pleasant. The salesman asked about us getting married or engaged, probably thinking along the lines of having it serviced downstate at the Bentley dealership, hoping to make a sale. Paul responded, "We won't be engaged long." I remember that moment exactly. Doesn't every woman, who is head over heels for a guy, have that supersonic radar scanning for those commitment words? I was dazed at first. Did he actually just say that in front of other people?

Anyway, I opened the wooden box, and looking back at me was a gorgeous sparkling ring. The center stone was a cognac diamond, and surrounding it were diamonds set in a two-toned gold infinity pattern. The ring was stunning. I peered up at my Captain and was speechless, so thankfully, he took the lead and said, "This isn't an engagement ring. That would be bigger"—not that the ring was tiny by any means. He then went on to say, "This is a promise ring." It's funny because I wasn't disappointed. I would always go back and forth in my mind about living in Mt Pleasant full time. I loved it there. It was my playground. It was like I was on a continuous vacation every weekend I was there. My heart wanted that; however, being so far away from my kids would be impossible. Not to mention leaving the career I had worked so hard to sustain. My parents were also getting older, and I wanted to be around to help and spend as much time with them as possible. I knew all too well that this "time" with them would end one day. So luckily, my Captain wasn't thinking of getting engaged just yet.

Love Note to My Captain
December 26, 2011

Lover,

Today I Love you More Than EVER! I'm amazed to think that's even possible, but it is. Again, this holiday season was excellent! I felt so much more a part of it than before. Not that you didn't make me feel like it then, but just being more connected to you, your daughters, and your friends and extended family meant so much. My ring is BEAUTIFUL!!! I love it so!!! I know that you were always committed, but just having the symbol on my finger means more than I can say or explain. I still can't believe that you chose me!!! You are such a beautiful man, with so much going for you; I just can't believe it sometimes that God brought you to me. As we journey into our third year together, I can only imagine how much more I'll love you.

Thank you for being so generous to my children and for appreciating them. Thank you for understanding my position with Charlie and how torn I am between being with the little Brussel Sprout and my Captain. Thanks for not "cutting me loose":-) Since I can't be here full-time right now! But I promise one day I will! Thank you for always satisfying me sexually; I love being intimate with you. You're so hot! My Captain, My Lover, My Life- I love you Forever and a Day and Then some. Thank you for loving me! Xoxo ♥

So, we closed out 2011 with a commitment to each other to continue our journey. I loved my promise ring. Now, you might think that Paul was pacifying me for the time being and that the ring was on my finger to symbolize I was his and thwart any possible suitors that may cross my path when I was back downstate alone. However, it was a lovely piece of jewelry, and I wore it with pride. Plus, how many people can say they have a cognac diamond? :-)

Chapter Twenty-Two

Back in the Groove

Love Letter to My Captain
January 1, 2012

Baby,

I sit here feeling so loved by you today. I can't tell you how surprised I was with my beautiful Christmas present! The ring means so much to me, and I love it. It's gorgeous and boasts how much taste and class my Captain has! You may think it's silly, but I feel closer to you. I know you were committed before, but just having this ring on my finger means more than I can explain. I don't know what I did to deserve you, and I continue to pray that we will be blessed with a long, loving life together.

This holiday season has been so much fun! I enjoyed the Christmas Eve party and being with your daughters. They love their Papa so much!

I wish I could be here with you 24/7. I think you know how torn I am, but even in the sadness I feel when I leave you, I say a little prayer and thank God you are in my life. I realize that having my Captain in my life and his heart and Love, even if physically we can't be together, is all that matters! Baby, you know how much I love you and like you, and I want to add again how sexually satisfied I am. Being intimate with you makes me feel so connected and so good! I love when you reach out, grab my face and kiss me- out of nowhere. Thank you again for being so hot and handsome and finding me on Match. We're perfect together!

I Love You Sexy Captain!

Xoxo

At this time, I headed back south and returned to my "other" life.

Card From My Captain
January 8, 2012

It was an anniversary card:

You're In My Heart
We'll Never Part
Forever And A Day
I'm Here To Stay

Love,
Paul

I used to leave tiny love notes throughout Captain's home, making sure to put them in places that I knew he would find after I was back downstate:

- The pocket in his robe
- His drawers in the bedroom
- The silverware drawer in the kitchen
- The coffee pod holder
- Other random places

One such note read:

I Promise to Love You Forever and A Day.
I Promise to Never Leave Your Beautiful Sculptured Ass.
I Promise to Be Your Princess If You'll Be My Captain For
The Rest Of Our Days!!

Xoxo
Carol

I brought Charles and our little dog, Skittles, to Mt Pleasant the following weekend. Charles always loved being there with me, especially when it came to the hot tub. To him, it was a mini swimming pool.

Love Note to My Captain
January 16, 2012

Captain,

Today, I can only say, Thank God You're Alive!!!!!

Seriously, I love you so much that the thought of anything happening to you tears me apart! Love, you mean the world to me, and I wish I could be there by your side as your partner 100% of the time, but until I can you have to promise me you'll be careful and not put yourself in jeopardy. You need to be the Captain of my boat, not of that stupid moat! 🤪 *Thank you for your generosity and for putting up with Skittles. He's cute, but a lot of work!*

Thank you for picking me to be your girl!

Your Princess

In Paul's backyard, interwoven in the patio, were four large trees. Surrounding the trees were poured circular walls that formed individual moats. These were approximately seven feet deep, with landscape beds around them. Paul loved to feed his birds, especially in the winter. You could sit in the sunroom and look out the floor-to-ceiling windows to catch the action. In addition to the deer, wild turkeys, run-of-the-mill squirrels, and chipmunks, we also would come across turtles that would wander up from the river. One not-so-little guy fell in the moat one summer day. Good thing Captain noticed him—he was probably filling his bird feeders at that time. Good deed done for the day with a turtle rescue! Balls, dog toys, leaves, and sticks are fine falling into the abyss of the moat, not a turtle, and definitely not my Captain!

Charles, Paul, and I were later in the hot tub enjoying the warmth of the water, gazing at the stars through the steam, and having a great time. Paul decided to get out—usually, he is the first one out. I loved being in the hot tub. It was charming on a cold, snowy winter evening. The next thing we saw was Paul filling the bird feeders with nothing but his bathing suit.

"Captain, it's freezing out here. Plus, I don't want you to slip on the patio and hurt yourself," I said.

Like a typical man, he said he was fine. Paul is the kind of guy that cannot be told what to do. So, when you think something unfortunate, adverse, or harmful will happen, good luck convincing him otherwise. Therefore, I looked at Charles and shrugged.

"Oh well," I said.

The next thing we heard was a loud noise and a shriek. We looked over to where Paul had been but saw nothing. Then, a second later, a head popped up.

"I'm okay," Paul said.

Without hesitating, I climbed out of the hot tub and ran to help him. It was a comical scene, yet he could have really hurt himself. Luckily, the buildup of leaves from the previous season had cushioned his landing, and he was only left with a few scratches. I remember thinking at the time, as I stood there and shook my head at him, that I was meant to be the girlfriend and not act like a mother reprimanding her child. After all, Paul was a grown man with sound judgment. But, statistically, it had to happen at some time—falling into one of the moats, that is. I was constantly worried that it would one day happen to me.

A handful of times, we drove up to Tawas in the winter. We would spend the weekends taking in the beauty of the state's eastern side bordering Lake Huron. It is a different feel in the winter; no bustling crowds downtown, lighter traffic, and several restaurants close until the vacationers return. The marina next door is free of vessels, and the once-filled slips sit empty. The boaters with their dogs and cocktails alongside their boats on the dock have now retreated to warmer destinations. The bay is snow-covered, frozen underneath. It is quiet and calm.

Love Note to My Captain
January 22, 2012

Baby,

I'm so grateful to have had four sleeps with you. I'll head back downstate and anxiously await coming back into your arms again- and those kissable lips! I regret the little "incident" we had. I'm not a very good actress and didn't want to bury any-thing. It's just hard for me sometimes. I love you deeply and don't want to feel that I'm just another girl along the way. I know they were only words, but that's all I had to go on.

This is why I needed to talk to you about it. I know I'm spe-cial, and you have been my best gift, and sometimes I wonder if I'm that deserving. That said-thank, you for clearing the air and confirming I'm not just another girl passing through your life.

I Love You
Carol

Okay. At this point, I was becoming vulnerable again. Please do not view me as some pathetic girl who has no self-confidence and whines about the past women their men have dated. It is indeed not like that. Being fourteen years younger meant my Captain had more time and experience than me. I will never catch up—nor do I want to. When I first met Paul, I was fascinated by everything leading up to us: His childhood, work, marriage, children, and the post-divorce period. As I have mentioned, I love conversation. If you are not talking to me, I am asking questions. I find relationships fascinating. I'm always asking couples how they met and their "story." During the first couple of years, some of these past relationships would be brought back into Paul's realm by a phone call, email, text, visit to his office, or running into one another at a social event. It seems I could not escape it. They were nowhere and everywhere at the same time. It became an annoyance. My Captain did not discourage them, either—at least, that is how I felt. I actually think that my former Lothario, or ladies' man, enjoyed it.

As our relationship grew and the years passed, we created our own stories. I would remind myself, at times, about my previous mantra, "Comparison is the thief of joy." I learned that it didn't matter who else had previously shared experiences with him; I couldn't change anything, nor should I want to. Experiences with others make us realize what we want, need, and can do without. The irony is that as we get older, our preferences may change.

So with that all said, the incident that made me vulnerable at this point in the relationship was a note a former girlfriend wrote for Paul. It was not a long love letter, just a note found in the kitchen drawer expressing one's "love" and referring to the great times they've had in "our place"—their place, not Paul's place, or how he now referred to it as "our," as in his and my place. There we go again. I can't seem to escape it. Truth be told, I was sad he had kept the note—although, in retrospect, I would not have been able to write this book if he hadn't kept my love letters.

I believe I'm not the only girl that would be upset by an ex's love note. But by this time, I had given not only my heart to him but my present and future and my time physically away from where I made a living—selling real estate while being out of town on three of the four weekends a month. It was challenging. Plus, everyone who knew me knew my Captain. So even though I had a ring on my finger, financial support, and much more, and I thought I felt secure with our relationship, my thoughts didn't always mimic my words. As my friend Tom used to say, "You can't control your feelings, but you can control how you respond." I'm not a very good actress, nor do I feel that relationships are equal in the love each person has for the other.

Take Away:

Do not inquire about past loves, likes, or conquests. Instead, choose present happiness over silly bouts of jealousy that have nothing to do with your relationship.

CHAPTER TWENTY-THREE

Back to the Sunshine State

February 2012

Trip #9 took us back to Long Boat Key. The little note I kept in my wallet, where I would scribble the trip number and place we were heading, was getting some use. Captain got a kick out of my record keeping, and if by chance I would forget to record the trip—while we had our pre-flight Mimosa and Bloody Marys—he'd remind me. I had never traveled so much in my life, so looking forward to the trips, taking the trips, and then wondering where we were going next always seemed to be on my mind. I was—and will continue to be—grateful for all the travel and new adventures I experienced with my Captain. While this was a business trip for him, we did enjoy staying with Bruce and Sue—this time on land. It is always nice to escape the Michigan winters, even for only a few days. The sun on your face, the greenery, and the fact that you can see your arms in public make these little getaways renew hope that spring in the Midwest will soon arrive.

Love Letter to My Captain

February 7, 2012

Wow! Our 9th trip finished! Who knew I was going to be so lucky and not only find the Love of my life but go on numerous vacations! Thank you, Baby, for taking me along with you. I had an excellent time. You know how much I love being with you, no matter where we are. Our hosts were lovely, and I tried to behave my best. You know I can't keep my hands off you sometimes, actually all the time, for that matter. As you begin your busy season, I'll try not to be so needy when it comes to wanting to be with my Captain. I love you so much.

I couldn't think of a better Captain or better mate for me. You have brought me so much happiness, and I'm so grateful for everything you do, and knowing how much you love me back makes me feel so special. Thank you for being my Rock Star! Thank you for the morning cuddles. 😳

As you can probably tell, I am still incredibly enthralled with my lover. Some might say it was because we did not see each other daily—but I beg to differ. Captain just had this "thing" that I could not put my finger on—an X factor. I was drawn to him in a way that I had never experienced with other men, almost like an electric current.

Love Note to My Captain

February 12, 2012

Oh, Baby-

You're so good to me and to Charles also! Xoxo

It is unimaginable that I was so lucky to find you and that you picked me! My world has grown so much as my heart has. I've never given myself to anyone as unconditionally as I have to you. As I said before, it's scary, I always had a wall up, and I let that wall crumble when I met you. I believe it when you tell me I'm the only one, but sometimes my heart worries that someone will come thru and steal you away from me. But, believe me, you have never done anything to make me feel that way. You are so wonderful, and I can't believe God chose me for you! From the trips to the snuggles, from the bling to the cup of coffee, I appreciate and love them all. You are my Forever Captain, and My Prince, and a handsome one at that-The Only One- Love You, Baby, and I'll be counting down the sleeps! Xoxoxo ♥

The following weekend, I headed north only to come back down for a Red Wings game with our friends, Rob and Tina, from Mt Pleasant. I am weird like that. I will go out of my way just so "we" can all be together because why not? Isn't life more fun that way? Unnecessary miles, wear and tear, extra gas, and time spent on the road? It was just the way I wanted to do it. Wolves travel in packs, elephants in a herd, and dolphins in pods. I would compare us to the dolphin pod, which is more social. Studies show dolphins are highly intelligent and some of the smartest animals in the world. I would not push it as far as to say that I'm a brainiac—although I try to absorb as much knowledge as possible.

We traveled with our pod to Downtown Detroit and checked in at The Atheneum Hotel. They have a neat bar and shuttle their patrons to and from the game. The Wings game at Joe Louis Arena—now moved and renamed Little Ceasars Arena—was fun, and the afterparty even better. My Captain can be a "bad" boy sometimes, though. He has that *thing* most men have as a reflex—the wandering eye. Yes, I know, it is a primitive reflex, but geez, guys, try to keep that concealed from your loved ones, savvy?

Love Note to My Captain
February 20, 2012

> *Captain, 25 months and counting! Crazy. No, not really… the only crazy, unbelievable part is that you love me and have made me such a big part of your life! I had such a lovely weekend with my Captain. We had relaxation, excitement, family time, and great plentiful Sex! Who could ask for more?*

> *Again, I want to apologize for being so sensitive at times. I know in my heart you love me - but deep down, I'm still just a girl who wants to be that special, only one, and feels vulnerable when other women catch your gaze. But, Captain, I know how high sexual you are - and that's one of the qualities I adore about you, so maybe I'll work on toughening up my shell, and you can keep reaffirming your undying Love and devotion (hehe) to me, and all will be better! Or, if it's easier, make sure I don't notice when some smokin' hot sexy chick catches your attention.*

Ok. Ok… I'll stop… I'm not trying to change you or what you do. I need to accept this and not feel embarrassed or "less than" when it happens. Men are from Mars, and women are from Venus… or, in my case, Sterling Heights. I'll end my love note by saying, "You're my Captain, the love of my life, and one day I'll be your wife…" I ought to do this shit professionally… lol.

Love you Baby!
Your Princess

Xoxo

Three sleeps!

Some women would straight out not tolerate this behavior, some would, and some would while trying to change their partner to better the relationship. I am in the third camp—although I realize no one really can change someone. Remember when I said I was a runner? Or, as Captain had told me in the past, I tend to be an ostrich, sticking my head in the sand. Was this bad habit of his worth throwing in the towel? Of course not. Plus, do you also remember the part where I said I was so drawn to him? I had discussed this at length with Tom, my dear friend who encouraged me to keep dating Paul early on in the relationship. He was a man, and I wanted to get his opinion.

He asked me, "Do you really want someone who follows you around like a puppy dog?"

"Wouldn't that get boring, Carol?"

You see, Tom knew me. He knew how easy it would be for me to say "next" with my relationships. He gently reminded me that it did not mean Paul loved me any less or wanted someone else; it meant that he appreciated the beauty of women—okay, loved looking at a hot chick. Tom noted that most men do gaze—they just do a better job of covering it up. This journey with my Captain was by no means pot-hole less. We would have a bump, and then the repair crew would come out to repair it—figuratively speaking.

February 2012 also brought me peace. Peace in that Paul purchased a life insurance policy for me, so my children would be taken care of if I met my maker before I was old and gray. I am old(er) and gray(er)—hair dye can do wonders, though. Thank you to my hairdresser, Jessica, and the Headliners salon in Mt Pleasant for all the magic you have worked on me throughout my years there…and to my sister-in-law, Monika, for the current upkeep!

In a nutshell, during this period of our relationship, Paul and I were traveling so much that I was always on the expressway. But, as one could say, I was living my life to the fullest, doing things I would never have done before meeting my Captain. I just had to keep reminding myself that it is rare to strike gold, let alone find a diamond in the rough, so questioning the little things that are, in truth, completely trivial was a road I had to drive far away from.

Love Note to My Captain
February 26, 2012

> *Thank you for another great weekend in our journey! I tuck away all of our memories in a special place in my mind and heart and revisit them often. This weekend was monumental for me because you're genuinely looking after my well-being by caring for me if something happens. I pray we have many years together, but knowing that I'm the one and you're sure about that means the world to me and takes a great deal of*

stress off me. So, I'll head back to Sterling Heights, missing my man but returning knowing I have obligations to fulfill and kids to kiss and snuggle. I'm excited about Thursday evening! We should have fun with whoever goes with us. Also, thank you for letting me get my hair done, the hot rollers, the steam cleaner, and a few miscellaneous Meijer items. Oh, the gas and the oil change too! Wow, I'm expensive. Good thing I'm your Princess!

Love you, My Prince xoxo

4 Sleeps!

Take Away:

There are few flawless diamonds, and flaws make character.

CHAPTER TWENTY-FOUR

Barry Manilow and the Hard Rock T-shirt

March 2012

It was always on my bucket list to see Barry Manilow. I thought I would have to return to Vegas to see him, but he had a show date in Detroit. Captain knew how much it meant to me to see Barry in concert. Remember the saying, "If it's important to you, then it's important to me"? (see January 26, 2010).

Love Note to My Captain
March 10, 2012

Hey Lover,

This will be a short note because we'll be together again shortly - one sleep! I'm sorry I must leave, but I know you'd understand. Tomorrow afternoon can't come soon enough! I am so in Love with my Captain - people probably think I'm goofy... but what the hell do I care!! Thanks for the great dinner last night and the extra pound of meat... hehe. I'm super excited to see Barry tomorrow evening - we'll have fun!

Okay, short, sweet, and to the point, like a guy... 😋... not my Captain, though - you're the complete package! Can I say one more time you looked so hot yesterday—mmmm—I am so lucky!

You and Me... Forever we shall be! Xoxo

It was probably not on Paul's top 20 list of things to do on a Sunday night in Detroit, but he's my Captain, so we went.

Love Note to My Captain
March 11, 2012

Captain,

Thank you so so much for taking me to see Barry Manilow! It meant a great deal to me. I know you suffered through it, but I hope you enjoyed a little bit of it. I know wearing the Hard Rock T-Shirt helped you. :) And thank you for taking me to Boogie Fever after. I love dancing with you! We need to do more of it! Well, here we go again. I hope you have a good week, and I'll count downtime sleeps one by one. I love you, sweetheart, and I adore our journey and can't wait for all that's ahead of us!

Missing you already——
Xoxoxox

Your Princess

Let me stop at this point and tell you again how good my Captain was to me. I was living in a four-bedroom Cape Cod home where I was stretching to make the mortgage payments and continue to do everything else needed when you are an independent contractor who lives on commission income. I made it five years post-divorce in the home with my Captain's financial help. I loved my home. Many great memories were made there: Parties, renovations, more parties, more renovations, and that was where we brought Charles home to welcome him into our family. My parents lived only a few miles away, which made the location even more attractive.

What I tell people, who ask me about the real estate market while wondering if it is a good time to buy or sell, is usually this: People are always going to need to move. There will be births, deaths, divorces, and downsizing. I fell into two of those categories. When I met Paul, he had several real estate holdings, including rentals. At about this point in our relationship, he probably realized we were dropping money into a dark hole in my current home. It was time to pass it on to another family who would appreciate it and cut his financial losses. In addition, my kids were already going to a parochial school that was further north, so moving to a location near their school would be beneficial.

One afternoon when Paul was downstate, I made some appointments to view some condos currently for sale closer to my kids' current schools. It was a tough pill to swallow. Most were older, not renovated, had no basement, or maybe just had a carport. We had looked at about five of them when we ended at Normandy Forest in Clinton Township on Ridgeway Court. I think Paul and I knew right away that this was the one—or at least the only one we saw that day that would come close to Captain pulling out his checkbook and writing an earnest money deposit.

It was in a lovely development with only one way in and one way out, which made it safe. As you turned into the complex, you could see a gazebo surrounded by landscaped beds that abutted the edge of the retention pond. These differed from your run-of-the-mill condos stacked two high, two together, four or eight, or any number other than one. Instead, these were standalone condos with basements and two-car garages. So, after five years of selling in this area, why had I yet to hear of this complex?

This particular condo was a two-bedroom, two-bath. As you walked in, the kitchen was on the right, with a small serving hatch opening into what would become our dining room, and the rest of the open space was our great room with a cozy stoned gas fireplace ceiling high. The two bedrooms were off this room, separated by a hallway. The primary bedroom had an extra-large closet space. Imagine a walk-in closet without the fourth side while opening up to the bathroom with a Jacuzzi tub. I have sold many homes with these tubs, and what most people say about them is true: You use them initially, and then they sit, getting used only a few times afterward. However, knowing the option exists to soak that bad back, have a glass of wine after a tough day, or immerse yourself with your significant, it is worth having a Jacuzzi! Some unsolicited advice: If you are burning candles and have long hair, ensure the two do not come into contact, or your significant will yell, "Your hair's on fire!"

The condo unit was also at the end of the court, with a treed lot line and shrubbery between the complex and the subdivision next to it. It had a deck that was accessible through the French doors of the bedroom in addition to the great room. We did get use out of that feature, especially during our nicotine days. The condo was in decent shape, and it was cute. A three-bedroom could have been a better move—looking back on it—though Charles was the one who spent the majority of the time sleeping there. Oh, it had a substantial expansive open basement, a godsend during my daughter and her husband's move back from New York after graduation. At times, this was a detriment—as my kids would sneak boxes over from their dad's house to store some of "their" things when I was out of town. And my former husband sent the kids over when he ran out of room at his house... lol. Anyway, the point is that the basement was huge, and I took advantage of every square foot of it.

The next day we made an offer on the condo and were later told another one had come in. The agent asked for our highest and best offer. Captain said he didn't want to bid against himself, especially as we were a tad already over the asking price. So, I left it up to him, knowing he would do what was best.

Email from Captain
April 3, 2012, 11:00 a.m.
Subject: Condo

We may already have the most attractive offer submitted. 143 Princess

Email to Captain
April 3, 2012, 11:19 a.m.
Subject: Re: Condo

Not sure...

I don't want us to get caught up in something that isn't the best financial situation... It's pretty clear to see that getting a great deal now... for something in decent condition... probably won't fly... That being said.. .I do like it... but it wouldn't be

the end of the world if it passed us by. You're the Captain and
MY ONLY... the decision is yours... 143

And with that, we were informed the next day that the seller accepted our offer.

Love Letter to My Captain
April 4, 2012

Oh, Sunshine,

What a journey we're sharing! I still can't believe to this day how good you are to me. It's truly shocking! You have enveloped me in your life and made me feel so special. I never doubted that you love me, but as I said, I still can't believe how giving you are to me. These last few days have brought that to light. I can't thank you enough for investing in the condo, our new home and making my life so much easier and less stressful. I felt like my home was falling apart around me, and I didn't know how to handle it. I'd lie awake at night and wonder how or what I'd do and the next move, if any, to make. But, as I said before, this is one step closer to me being with you every day. Think you can handle that one day? :-) Now, when I'm in Clinton Township, a part of you will be with me. I know now that I can call my super hot landlord "almost husband," and you'll take care of whatever needs to be handled that I can't handle alone.

My heart holds so much Love for you, and I'm so grateful we found each other. As I said, good things happen to good people, and we're both blessed. One in five relationships begin online- but I wonder how many miracles there genuinely are because we are one! I think I'll call you Captain Miracle now! 😋 *I love you forever and a day. I'll count down the sleeps. Love you so much! Xoxo*

Am I actually going to move? Am I really leaving the stability of my home and going to hand over my security to Paul? There were no guarantees. Life has no guarantees anyway, so I figured, "What is the worst that can happen? I move again?" Plus, we had almost a month before we would close on the condo. Paul was giving me a tremendous gift; the gift of security. My Captain had always made good decisions, and how could this one be any different?

The month passed, and while it did, I started packing.

Love Note to My Captain
April 30, 2012

Our love story just keeps getting better and better!... And each step of the way, I love you deeper and deeper.

Take away:

In the end, Lewis Carroll knew best: We only regret the chances we didn't take.

Chapter Twenty-five

A Moving Truck and a Transition

Love Note to My Captain

May 6, 2012

Captain,

As I look forward to this next week, I have many emotions and thoughts going through my mind.

First off and most importantly, I'm grateful, so grateful that my Captain has chosen to spend his life with me and help me out in so many ways too. Invest in a home that will be "our" home and thus make my life substantially easier.

My next emotion is excitement. We have many exciting things to look forward to, starting with the condo and a wonderful summer ahead. I'm looking forward to christening the new place with you!

Finally, I can't help but be a little scared. It's a big deal to move and so much to do, but knowing you'll be there for me takes some of the edge off. I want to make this fun for us and not work- and I hope I don't get too emotional!

Rolled up in all these emotions is Charlie. I hope this won't be too difficult for him. I don't think it will, but I know we have to make it exciting for him and let him know it's a good thing, and hopefully, we don't run into any spiders too soon; that may be the deal breaker for him. Lol

Captain, I love you more than my heart can hold, and I continue loving you more each day. I'm so sad when I leave you, but know I must leave to be able to come back. You are truly the Love of my life, and I've never been happier; emotionally, physically, and sexually. God did send you down from above for me, or at least downstate! :-) I'll say it again; we are the one in five, and such a love story we share! Captain, next time we see each other, we'll have our new place together- four sleeps -

I Love You, My Prince - You are My Forever and a Day!

PBM, you are Mine!

Closing was scheduled for Friday, May 11. Charles's eleventh birthday was the day prior, so I decided we should have one last party at the old house before the moving truck arrived on Saturday. So, we celebrated while moving around piles of boxes and took in the final hours of the "Kozak Drive" home. It was bittersweet. I was excited about the future and yet would be closing the door on the home where I raised my babies.

The move took all day on Saturday, with the truck taking two loads from Sterling Heights to Clinton Township. However, again,

Captain was a good sport—although he chided me a bit about all the stuff I had...

Love Note to My Captain
May 13, 2012

Baby, I love you so much!!!! Thank you for being so wonder-ful. You are the Love of my life, and I am so blessed. I love our new home! I'm looking forward to many happy memories here. You are my forever and a Day and my One and Only -

I Love You, Captain!

Your Princess

Thank you so much for our home!

xoxoxo

May 17, 2012

I celebrated my forty-fifth birthday in Mt Pleasant. Captain gave me a beautiful card he had customized by cutting out pictures of a table with a couple of chairs. He had written *High Top & Stools* underneath. There also was a picture of a TV with the words, *A Flat Screen*. The kitchen of the new place had a little corner area where we could put a bistro table, which ended up being one of my favorite places to sit and talk with Captain. The television that I currently had needed an upgrade, so that was also a welcome gift idea.

The day after, we went shopping in Mt Pleasant at a family-owned furniture store with interesting pieces. We saw the table and knew it was perfect immediately! So, we packed it up, and I headed home to our home—or, as I called it, our home downstate. It did not matter that I wasn't on the deed; I still considered it ours, and Captain never said otherwise.

Love Note to My Captain
May 20, 2012

Cocktails for 2! I'm looking forward to sharing that with you at our new table! My Captain is so amazingly generous and kind. Even though I know this, I still get surprised at your generosity towards me. I know I'm your Princess, but I still can't believe it sometimes!

It was a super special weekend. I love sharing time with you, from evenings with other couples to our own private time just sitting by the river or snuggling in bed-our bed - right Captain??? Lol. The journey has been so incredibly wonderful. You have swept me off my feet. As I've said before, I love you like I've loved no other, and honestly, honey, the "things" have nothing to do with how deep my Love is for you. Granted, they make my life better and add an extra dimension, but what's inside you and the Love you choose to share with me matters the most!

I can't wait for you to come home to Clinton Township within the next couple of weeks or whenever you can. We need to make Love in our new bedroom to seal the deal!

I love you, my handsome Prince, Forever and a day and then some- You are My Rock Star! Love you so Much! Your Princess xoxoxoxoxo

The next three weekends were spent either in Tawas or Mt Pleasant. Captain could not come back downstate until June 13, a Wednesday. Even then, it was only about thirty minutes before he had to head back up to his place.

Love Note to My Captain

June 13, 2012

Thank you! Thank you! Thank you - soooo Much! My Prince came to my rescue. 😊 *I love you till the ends of the earth and back again and forever and a day. You are my one and only and such a handsome Prince. Am I really yours? Love you, Baby, and Thank You Again! Oh, Captain!*

Your Princess

There is a gift in every situation, event, or time in our lives. We just may not know it. The flood occurred by a malfunction of a dishwasher connector. I would have been able to handle a water-logged kitchen, dining room, and living room. However, I thought I had protected myself during the move by storing all the photo album boxes far away from the sump pump. There was no battery or water backup system when we purchased the condo. Having the sump pump fail when I was out of town would be my luck. So, guess where I stored all of my precious photos— directly underneath the kitchen! I was a mess. Captain could tell from my phone call to him that day. He lined up Servpro, and they were there within the hour. It was a total blur. Boxes were coming up from the basement, and photo albums were being disassembled with pictures being laid out onto the driveway in an attempt to salvage them. We quickly discovered that more room was needed for all my photos. Hence, the decision was made to return the photo albums to the warehouse, as laying out 30,000 plus photos warrants some serious space. I was so happy to see Paul and could not believe he drove two and a half hours to comfort me. He couldn't stay long because he had another appointment that day, but just having him for a few minutes meant so much to me. We ended up having to replace the kitchen flooring and cabinets. The gift in this situation led us to receive a brand-new kitchen, complete with beautiful wood flooring.

Two days after the flood, Captain and I left on Trip #10. This trip was a byproduct of our visit to Key West and our contacts at the Gallery. We were invited to Bill Mack's studio in Minnesota, appropriately named Camelot.

It was a fascinating weekend spent with others who owned Bill Mack's pieces. Learning more about his artistry and the processes was only some of what we were treated to. We were shuttled to our hotel, ate fabulous meals, walked the red carpet, and were presented with a live show on the grounds. It felt like we were nobility! As a bonus, Bill had animals roaming around the yard, including a white pony and peacocks. It was magical. The trip was successful—both for Captain and Bill Mack. An original Ronald Regan on the former Hollywood Sign was commissioned, and Bill Mack did a phenomenal job!

Love Note to My Captain
September 10, 2012

> *Lover,*
>
> *32 months! I'm in awe at how fast the time has gone by! And yes, I love you more today than 32 months ago. Back then, I was wowed and swept off my feet by this handsome Prince who already loved me. Who knew??? 😊*

Sweetheart, thank you for the fun weekend. I'm always so amazed how things flow with us. It's so easy to be with you. I'm so comfortable. I think you feel the same! 😜
Thank you for letting my daughter and her friend attend the game and stay at "The Mansion." (as Charlie refers to it)

You are always too kind and generous and open up your home without conditions. Giving her the cash and some food to take home was much welcomed by her and appreciated by me.

I'm excited to see the progress this week on our Ridgeway Home. I hope Dan will have the moldings and door up by this week and our bedroom painted. Do you know why? Because I love having Sex with you! You are such a turn-on. You make me feel so sexy and give me such pleasure. I never imagined it could be so good, well - I knew you'd be good. I didn't think I would be so satisfied and turned on by my Hot, Hot Captain! I Love You, Baby, So Much!

Xoxo, I Miss You Already!

Love Note to My Captain
September 20, 2012

Needless to say, I'm bummed we are not together right now, but of course, we all have commitments we have to keep and business that needs to be done. I realize without that, we wouldn't be able to do all the wonderful things we do, and I appreciate you so much. You are so smart-brilliant- and have such a great mind for business. I wish I had 1/4 th of your intelligence, but I'll get by on what I have. I do have a big heart that loves you so much!

Thank you for letting me get my hair done and for all the financial support. I know we're a team. You always seem to do the "carrying," though. I pray that you'll never think of me as a financial drain but as your Princess. We have a great couple of months ahead of us, from our kitchen to our travels, and you know how much I love to travel with my Captain! Thank you for always talking with me when I need advice and genuinely caring about what's going on in my life. I love sharing everything with you. I hide nothing.

Well, my handsome Prince, I hope you hit them long and straight and have a productive shareholder retreat. I'll be back at our Ridgeway home getting ready for our new kitchen and missing you! Thank you for the great Sex last night, and when I start missing you (every few minutes), I'll recollect our intimacy together.

I Love You, Captain, Forever and a Day!

Your Princess. Miss You Already! Xoxo

It is fall, which means Captain's shareholder retreat, the changing leaves, and all things pumpkin spice and Football! Captain and I attended the Lions game and stayed overnight again at the Atheneum in Detroit. We did add one more stop in the evening. So, read on, and remember: I am being authentic.

Love Letter to My Captain

October 1, 2012

My Handsome Captain -

Another first in our relationship! It was fun going to the strip club with you. What an interesting experience. I could have done without you telling one of the dancers you loved her ass, but that's only because mine is flat and giggly... It was entertaining, and I actually enjoyed the flirtation by you and to you. You, my Love, were going back to sleep (and then some) with me! I'm glad we went. It was a great time. It's always fun to get away with you. You are a perfect traveling companion.

I also want to thank you for coming in for Joseph's birthday party. It meant a lot to me. I know you were tired and exhausted and could have easily just returned to Mt. Pleasant for the night, but you made the trek to Clinton Township and made me happy, as well as the other family members that really like you!!!

I'm getting more and more excited about our kitchen now. It really is going to be nice, and I love our granite piece we picked out together. Thank you for making me feel so special and always saying wonderful things about me to others commenting on us. I genuinely believe that I am the fortunate one in this relationship. You have given so much of your heart and included me in many aspects of your life, not to mention that you're always there for me. I'm not too fond of all the miles between us, but I realize this is how it has to be now. Every time you leave, though (or when I leave you), I always feel that a piece of me is missing, and I pray that we will both live long lives to carry out our journey and love story. You are my Fabulous Captain, my one and only, my forever and a day Handsome Prince, and I mean handsome- How did I get so lucky? I love you, sweetheart. You are the best and the best Lover ever!

Love You Always!

Your Princess

Take Away:

Don't let being uncomfortable stop you from trying new experiences.

Chapter Twenty-six

From Concrete to Asphalt, Walking Paths to Burnouts

October 2012

We went back to Manhattan for Trip #11. It was for another conference, and we stayed at the iconic Roosevelt Hotel—which sadly closed permanently after 100 years on December 18, 2020, due to the pandemic. The hotel was gorgeous, with its exquisite chandeliers, architectural columns, history, and general grandeur. I loved staying there. While Captain was at his conference, I would head out and check out the local area. It was always fun to explore. I would usually walk and later jump into an Uber—which is always interesting, especially in New York City. We, of course, spent time with Paul's daughter Diana, as she was still living in the city.

Love Letter to My Captain
October 25, 2012

Oh, My Captain,

It's incredibly difficult to see you leave today. Each moment I'm with you, I feel more attached than ever. You are so strongly woven into my heart, and words cannot even express the Love I feel for you. I know you already know this, but I must keep telling you because it's true.

I had such a wonderful time with you in New York. I hope you know how appreciative I am that you take me with you.

I love traveling with you. I want everyone to know that I'm the luckiest girl in the world. You are such fun to be around- "we fit." I can't imagine my life without you in it. Not only are you fun, but you are so much more. Your intelligence never ceases to amaze me. You always know the right thing to do. I'll say it again. I can't believe you choose "me"!!!

We make an incredible couple together. Thank you for the great Sex- you Rock It! Just looking at you is provocative. I pray that we'll always have this passion for one another and that our Love will grow deeper and deeper. I love my Captain, Forever and a Day, and many more after that. You are my heart.

Love you, my Handsome Prince-Your Princess xoxo

The holidays were right around the corner, and the year was coming to an end. Trip #12 came fresh off Trip #11 with Captain's annual business valuation conference in Orlando. We stayed at The Marriott, and after the conference, we hired a rental car and drove across the state to Longboat Key to see Paul's friends, Bruce and Sue, again for a quick visit. We stayed at the quaint Sea Club Beach Resort, this time with our room overlooking the Gulf Coast. As we walked on the beautiful, china-white sand, I remember thinking how grateful I was to be living this life and living it with my Captain.

After our trip, we went to the Nascar Race at Homestead-Miami Speedway. Paul's longtime friend, Joe, from Mt Pleasant had won four pit passes at one of their golf outings a few months prior, so he and his wife, Nancy, included us in their win. This was another first experience for me—although, for the most part, the women had clothes on, which surprised me! I learned quite a few things about Nascar. Their fans are intense, the noise is loud, and the drivers whiz by so fast that you can barely keep up with them. Overall, it was a time I'll never forget, and I was grateful for being invited by Paul's friends.

I was experiencing more and more with my Captain. He introduced me to things I had never done, and I kept thinking, *I know I'm your Princess, and I pray I stay that way. I pray that we remain healthy and nothing bad happens to us. I pray that one day we can wake up together and know that one of us doesn't have to leave. Thank you, God, for this gift. Thank you, God, for this life. Thank you, God, for My Captain.*

The day after we arrived back in Michigan was the closing day for my former marital home on Kozak in Sterling Heights. I would no longer have the security net of "running home"—not that I ever planned to. However, I would not be a homeowner anymore, which was a scary feeling. I had to trust the journey Captain and I were on and have faith, knowing everything happens for a reason.

Love Letter to My Captain
November 21, 2012

Oh, Sunshine,

Do we have to part????

I had such a wonderful vacation with you…It was so nice to sleep next to you every night and wake up with you in the morning.

Thank you for treating me like such a Princess… I do feel loved.

Today is a closing of a chapter for me… but our book has already begun, and I'm so appreciative for everything you've done for me and my children. Sometimes the road is not smooth with my babies, but you handle the bumps with me and make me feel better… just knowing I can talk to you means everything to me.

I know we'll make many memories at Ridgeway… we have already started… And our new kitchen is beautiful… I love it! It will be christened tomorrow for its first Thanksgiving. I only wish we were together, but I understand. This is what it is now. I'll miss being with you and your girls. I'm so happy you get to spend quality time with them. You'll have fun - but, don't go looking for a BBQ! That would suck! I know every-one will miss you, especially me.

I know I will see you in a day or two, but that doesn't take away my sadness about you leaving. You will be in my heart, and I know you're just a phone call away. Even as I type this, my heart is pounding since I know you're leaving in just a few minutes. I'm a big girl, and I know I can handle today. I have to, to get to tomorrow.

Needless to say, I want to thank you for the great Sex on our trip and thank you for investing time in me… smile… I never want it to end…

I love you, Captain… Forever and A Day, and you are in my heart…

I miss you already… enjoy your babies… and think about me… even if it's just a little… hehe.

XOXOXOXOXOXOXO

LOVE YOU MORE!!!

Your Princess!! Xoxo

Ironically, Thanksgiving was the day after the closing of the Kozak home. We celebrated with my family at Ridgeway, "our" new place. I can say that I was thankful for all the beautiful memories made at the Kozak home with my former husband, my three wonderful babies, and the many parties that took place. I was also thankful to have a supportive boyfriend who believed in us and our future—even though neither of us knew when our journey would culminate with I do's.

Card from My Captain
December 25, 2012

> *DEAR PRINCESS,*
>
> *I LOVE YOU MORE TODAY THAN YESTERDAY,*
> *LAST MONTH, LAST YEAR, AND THE DAY I FIRST*
> *MET YOU. I HOPE YOU WILL BE MINE FOREVER*
> *(AND A DAY☺) AND NEVER GROW DISTANT OR*
> *HARBOR NEGATIVE THOUGHTS. MY HEART IS*
> *YOURS FOREVER, AND I LOOK FORWARD TO*
> *SPENDING THE REST OF MY LIFE WITH MY*
> *PRINCESS!*
>
> *LOVE YOU, PRINCESS*
>
> *MERRY CHRISTMAS, HAPPY NEW YEAR*
>
> *YOURS FOREVER*

I had all the feels that Christmas. We celebrated with the annual Christmas Eve party in Mt. Pleasant and headed south on Christmas day to be with my family. I felt like the luckiest girl in the world.

2012 ended, and as 2013 breached the horizon, I wondered if—and hoped—we would always be madly in love with each other.

Take Away:

Be grateful for the broken road you have walked because,
one day, it will lead you to the happiness you deserve.

CHAPTER TWENTY-SEVEN

I Knew Better

Love Note to My Captain

January 2, 2013

Sunshine,

Your first love note of 2013! (And one of many, I might add)
Thank you for the spectacular holiday season together. I am
truly one lucky, lucky gal. Thank you for loving me- "all of
me" :-) and taking care of me. I love you so much and appre-
ciate all you do for me and my babies.

This journey sure has been incredible! As we venture into our
fourth year together, I know we'll have many more experiences
and shared times that bring us even closer. I love being on
your arm and "belonging to you"-A position I treasure and
cherish.

As we go our separate ways for two sleeps I'll miss you, but
the excitement of seeing you again-super soon- will keep me
pumped! I hate sleeping alone, but I'm good as long as I

know you'll be back, and we'll snuggle and partake in some extracurricular activities.

I love you, baby - have a great couple of days -

Yours Forever and a Day
Princess

xoxoxoxo

Love Note to My Captain
January 6, 2013

Captain,

Dislike, Dislike, Dislike!!!! When we part - ☐ Thank you so much for coming to our Ridgeway home this weekend and for coming a day early! I am the luckiest, most blessed girl ever that walked the planet! My Love for you grows stronger as our journey continues. I can't believe it will be three full years! Three years of Love, great Sex, wonderful travels, and so many happy times. Steve was right when he said we fit! ☐ I pray you'll continue loving me as we journey together. I know I'll love you more as time passes, even though that seems inconceivable because I already love you so much. Thank you for always being so good to me in so many ways. I love you forever and a day, and thank God for giving you to me! I'll miss you the next few days, but I'll be excited to see you, so hopefully, they'll go fast -

Love you Sunshine
Xoxo

Your Princess

When we took our trip to Camelot, Bill Mack had a personal driver, Steve, who shuttled us around in his limo. As we interacted with him over the weekend, he decided that Paul and I "fit." So, that is how "we fit" came to be. It was endearing, and Steve was fun to be around. Even today, I smile and think of Steve and his camaraderie when we use those words to describe us.

Love Note to My Captain
January 14, 2013

Captain,

Another Monday, and you've come home to just the pups! I hope you know you're always in my heart, whether I'm in the next room or a different city.

I am really, really sorry for our miscommunication last Thursday. I was feeling vulnerable. I know you're true and will always be there, but since I have nothing in the "hopper" with any closings. I just felt a little down on myself. Also, I'm trying to learn how to deal with our separations from each other better. I'm sure a factor of not being busy with work surely doesn't help matters. So please forgive me if I upset you or made you concerned; it wasn't my intention. I love you with all my heart and only want to share my life with you- and be a part of yours.

Thank you for being flexible this weekend, coming down with me for Charles' basketball game, and allowing us to paint the house. I love it so much already and am super excited to put our touches on it.

Sorry, I can't sleep next to you tonight, I'll miss your loving arms around me, and hopefully, you'll miss my ta-ta's

I love you, Captain. Thank you for making me yours!

Xoxoxo

Your three years and Running Princess….

Some say women are more emotional than men—although some studies say there is no proof in that statement. I can only speak for myself, and I would say I am sensitive. It is just who I am; I cannot help it. In many ways, being sensitive is a good thing. In my relationship with Paul, though, I tend to be overly sensitive and sometimes interpret things differently than him. I can't always pinpoint the reason for the miscommunication, either. For example, one weekend, I wrote the above love note, and upon reflection, I was really "poking the bear," so to speak, and looking for affirmation regarding our relationship. Yes, I know. My Captain has told me he loves me a million times and will always be there for me. However, you can't understand what someone feels in their heart until you have walked in their shoes. At this point, I had the best life and knew it, yet I could have appreciated it so much more if I had let go of those doubts. Today, I know better and can reflect on my less-wise self and chuckle. I learned that our whole lives are a journey, and it can take time to accept that good things can happen to us and that you don't always have to look around the corner for that semi-truck to derail you.

A Special Poem for My Captain

February 9, 2013.

(Included with the love note below)

For My Captain…

There once was a girl who tried
So hard for the pride of the Captain she loved…
So she strapped on the boots and gear and headed down the
hill in fear.
The ending wasn't as she had planned,
For all she was longing for was to prove to her man,
That his Princess could do what others could do.
But this, of course, was proven untrue.
After tears, ice, tests, and examinations
It was decided her knee was in trepidation.
But the Princess has learned that her Captain, for certain,
Loves her unconditionally and forever…
Even if she temporarily walks with a limp,
But do not fear; she'll be back in her gear!
Kicking up her heels, but never again to lace up the skis,
For she has learned to stick with other things that, please!

I Love You, Captain
Forever and A Day
You are my Rock

Xoxo
Your Princess

On February 2, Captain and I headed up to Cedar River to ski and stay with his friends, Doc and Cathy. Paul had purchased the cutest ski gear for me the previous weekend—because you have to look cute on the slopes, right? Even better would be knowing how to ski while looking cute! I had skied once in my life, back in high school. Hence, Captain and I agreed that I needed some training time with a ski instructor. In retrospect, I needed way more time with one... Let's say I should not have even tried downhill that day. The bunny hill was more my speed. The result? A torn medial collateral ligament (MCL) that would bother me for the next ten years until I had it surgically repaired in 2022. Needless to say, the weekend turned out drastically different than I had imagined. Who wants to be seen with the ski patrol on a sled being taken down the hill? The shame... What followed were X-rays, an MRI, visits to the orthopedic, and weeks of physical therapy. I remember talking with my mom after it happened. She casually mentioned that if I had asked her what she thought about me going skiing, she would have told me I was crazy for putting skis on. Then she added, "*But you never asked.*" I can still see her shaking her head. Hindsight is 20/20, isn't it?

Love Letter to My Captain
February 9, 2013

Hi Sunshine,

By the time you read this, you will have safely returned home. I don't even know where to start to begin to thank you for all the care you've given me this past week. I just want you to know I was having fun before my "incident" and thought it was so cool to share that with you. From what I can tell now, the only good that came out of this is that I could spend more time with you! 😃

Enough about my knee. I'm getting tired of this already. I want to get back to me so we can return to the prior me (pre Feb. 3rd). I will work hard to regain my mobility because I want to get back in my "heels"!

I hope this weekend was fun for you and the boys, and I hope the Wings win/won. I love you immensely and can't wait to see you in 4 sleeps. I hope you have a good, productive next few days that won't be too stressful.

My Love Forever and A Day!

Your Princess

On Trip #13, we headed to Dallas for the Keller Williams Convention. Now, Captain was joining me on my conferences. It was fun to see this reversal. I was the one going to classes, and he was left behind to explore the city. We were fortunate enough to meet up with my cousin, Lisa, who was living there, and we dined at a wonderful Mexican restaurant. We also met up with the new friends we made on our Minnesota trip, who gave us a grand tour of the area.

Love Letter to My Captain
February 20, 2013

Happy Thursday, Sweetheart!!

8 sleeps on, 1 sleep off, then back in the arms of my Captain! I can't even begin to thank you enough for taking me to Dallas and the Keller Williams Family Reunion. I know this is your busy time, and you're not nuts about "drinking the Kool-Aid":-). Incidentally, you do realize how much I love Keller Williams, and I'd drink that Kool-aid all day long! I did want you to experience it, though. It was important to me. So again, thank you for picking up the bar tab for my co-workers. The more time we spend together, I realize just how wonderful and generous you are, and I still can't believe you choose me to share your life with. I know you've heard these words from me before, and I want you to know that's how I genuinely feel. My heart still skips a beat when I look at you - and my knees buckle... hehe... Seriously, thank you for opening up my world to so many new experiences.

I love you so much, sunshine...

Thanks for letting me ride shotgun down this road we travel together.

Love Your Princess Forever and A Day!

During our summer at Camelot, we had met a lovely couple from Dallas named Larry and Cheryl. We'd mentioned how we were traveling to Texas early the following year for my work convention, and they insisted we come a few days early to spend time with them. We had a lovely visit, with our accommodations very comfortable. We met their friends and toured Dallas. They even scheduled a tour for us at the Cowboy stadium, now named AT & T. Amazingly, I managed to get around with my crutches. It was not the sexiest look—and I had to forego the heels for a bit longer. Thank God my Captain had fallen for me by then. The visit was fun, and the convention educational—combined with great camaraderie between work buddies. All in all, it was a successful trip to Texas.

It was March, and that meant Autorama time in Detroit. We would go with my dad, my sister, Charles, and, of course, my Captain. The group changed a bit through the years—although it was always a good time as I enjoyed seeing my dad happy around the classics (cars and his friends), my sister with her friends from the "car gang," and having Charles learn more about these cars. Needless to say, I also enjoyed being on Captain's arm. I would wear my heeled boots, cowboy boots, ankle boots, and other boots. I love my boots like I love turtlenecks.

Love Letter to My Captain
March 11, 2013

Hi My Sweet Lover -

Another Fabulous weekend and I've fallen more in Love with you.

Thank you for being flexible during tax season and coming downstate for Autorama and Mexican Village. It's always wonderful climbing in our bed at Ridgeway, knowing I'll wake up with my Lover. We really, really are blessed. And I'm one really, really lucky girl!! This week I'll focus on work and getting the basement back together. I want to keep my landlord happy! I hope your week isn't too stressful.

I love you to the ends of the earth and back again-and then some!

You are my heart, and there you'll stay.

Love You, Captain-

Xoxo
Princess

It was the third year of the "crunch time" tax season in my and Paul's relationship. He worked six days a week at the office and would bring files home to go through in the evenings and on weekends. Despite how busy he was, though, he always made time for my family and me if I asked—and even when I didn't. Captain was such a good guy, and everyone in my life at this point knew it, too.

Take Away:

Life does not stop when you get crutches; it can actually be more fun!

CHAPTER TWENTY-EIGHT

Snorkeling and the Safe

Love Letter from My Captain
April 5, 2013

Captain - As you wind down these last few days of tax season, know I'm your cheerleader, cheering you from the sidelines, silently saying a prayer that you'll get through this without too much stress. I wish there was something I could do to help, but know that I love you so much and would do anything for you.

Thank you for allowing Charles up here- my little active Brussel Sprout- he likes being with you. I hope we weren't too tiring for you.

I'll miss you tonight and the tenderness of your lips when I get my last kiss goodnight. The warmth of your skin next to mine is like the warmth of the sun shining through the windows when we lay together in the recliner at the end of the day in the Greenbanks sunroom.

My Captain - you put the spring in my step, the excitement in my heart, and the joy in my world, knowing you are always by my side, even if we're in different cities!

I Love You, and I'll Always Love You!

Your Princess!

Tax season ended, and Captain was ready to go on vacation. I was, too, despite how he had been doing all the heavy lifting. We were up to Trip #14 (April 20–27), which took us to Isla Mujeres, Mexico, the "Bay of Women." We flew into Cancun and caught a ferry to the island. Of course, the rum flowed before we landed on the island, and the entertainment was truly authentic, putting us in that island mood. However, within fifteen minutes of arriving, we were in a convenience store, and the power went off on the island. The locals said, "*No problem.*" Apparently, it happens all the time and always goes back on again. I remember thinking, *Well, this is exciting stuff!* Our hotel was surrounded by aqua-blue crystal clear water at the end of a long wooden planked bridge. There was a cute tiki bar just before the walkway to the hotel that was always busy, day and night, and it became our stop before heading back to the hotel every evening.

One day, we rented a golf cart and drove around the island, including a stop at a zip line over the Caribbean Sea at Garrafon Reef Park. The vibe of the island was laidback, and the locals were so friendly. We enjoyed cocktails and treated ourselves to massages on the beach.

On the second last day of our vacation, we snorkeled at our hotel. Before we left, we took a gamble and stored our essential belongings in the room's safe for the first time. Then, we rented snorkel gear from the hotel and spent a couple of hours viewing the colorful fish, like the Blue Tang Sturgeonfish, the Sergeant major, and the French grunt—to name a few—in the crystal clear waters. You might be able to guess what we found upon returning to the room... Although everything had been cleaned, when we opened the safe, some of our belongings were missing. Our passports, wallets, and credit cards were still there, but the cash and special money clip I gave Captain were gone. Immediately, we headed down to the reception desk, only to be met with a severe lack of empathy after Captain told the staff what had happened. They kept telling us that the safes only had one key—please, I'm no dummy—and it was the one we had. They didn't have a backup or master key. Finally, they said they would get back to us and let us know what housekeeping said. They were just appeasing us, though. They kept telling Captain to rent a golf cart and go to the police department, but then they said to be careful around police. Captain kept saying, "*Well, how do I get there without any money?*" The staff just shook their heads. Of course, they had several golf carts they could have let us use, but not for free. Thus, we were the tourists and had no other recourse. Luckily, we were at the tail end of our trip, and honestly, I was happy to be heading home after dealing with allegedly corrupt individuals. In all my experiences on vacations, something like this had never happened before.

Love Letter to My Captain
April 28, 2013

Oh Lover,

I can't believe it›s over!!! I had such a wonderful vacation with you. Thank you for being my Captain and knowing what's best for us. I have to say I was a little scared when we were speaking with the hotel staff. But you handled it well, and I felt protected by you. You are so handsome and beautiful to me. I'll never forget our beach walks and the sunsets. I love you so much and adore you! I have a great life! We have a great life! Thank you for searching and finding me.

I'm glad you didn't break up with me! Hehe, I was a bit shocked at the entire situation, although I'm happy to know we can always talk things out and, in the end, love each other even more. You are such a big part of me. I can't explain. I wish I could bring you your coffee every day. I love making you happy.

I hope you enjoyed your Sunday and that it was relaxing. I'll miss sleeping with you tonight but will count down the sleeps till I'm lying next to you again. I Love you, Captain, forever and a day!

Thank you for the adventure! Hugs, Kisses, and so much more!

Your Princess

Yes… the breakup word reared its ugly head, and it was not uttered by me. It happened one evening when the alcohol was flowing freely at the tiki bar. I was thinking, *Thank goodness. We only have to cross the bridge to get to our room*—but I was worried about Captain making it across. What I was not worrying about was him falling off his stool backward. It all happened so fast. He fell back, and two bartenders ran around to help him. Captain raised his hand and yelled, "Check!" Honestly, he can be so entertaining sometimes. He insisted we walk in the water to get back to the resort. Remember, even though I am Irish, I cannot handle large amounts of alcohol, partly because I did not weigh that much back then and partially because I barely ate. When we returned to the room, Captain was uttering something about how we should break up over my frustration in helping him stay on his feet and pulling him up a flight of concrete steps. At this point, I was 98.5 percent sure he didn't mean it, and we fell asleep. Sometime later, I woke up to find Paul gone. Feeling a bit panicked, I quickly ran out the front door, and it closed behind me, locking me out and Captain—who was on the porch. Now, I had to walk all the way back to the front of the resort in the middle of the night to find someone to let us back into our room. These resorts are unlike the large chain hotels or even the smaller ones in the States, where there is a staff member 24/7. I wasn't successful in finding someone at the resort, but eventually, we were sent assistance—see, there always is a master key! If you are wondering why I didn't send Captain to get help, he was still in no shape to venture out. Plus, he was in his PJs—or lack of them.

The next day, Paul and I talked. We agreed that no one ever truly knows if a couple will last. We can put all of our faith in someone, but the reality is that it takes two to stay together and only one to leave. My Captain didn't leave.

Take Away:

Never go out the front door without knowing you will be able to get back in.

CHAPTER TWENTY-NINE

The Best Birthday Present

Love Letter to My Captain
May 6, 2013

Captain,

You definitely win the prize for the best birthday present EVER!! I can't thank you enough for the new vehicle. I'm so excited to get it! I know you love and take care of me, but it still amazes me what you do for me, which is one of the many, many reasons I love you so. You melt my heart when I look at you, there's just something about you that my words can't explain. I'm so attracted to you, and again, tell you that I can't believe you picked me to be your Princess!

I had a wonderful weekend with you. It's so nice to be under the same roof. I know there was a ton of "family" time in there, and I thank you for being so flexible. Also, thanks for sharing details of your (our) future. I love you so much, and I'd be devastated if "we" became "you" without "me." You know I'm a chick, and chicks like to hear the words "us' and "we" :-)

Sunshine, only two sleeps, so excited about seeing you Wednesday and then a great weekend ahead. I Love you, Captain- you travel with me always in my heart! ❤

Your Forever and a Day, Your Princess xoxo

Here we go again, another May. It was always such a busy month, and I loved it! The excitement of the upcoming warm summer and all the blooming tulips and flowering trees always made me happy. Yes, my Captain did purchase a new car for me a few days before my birthday. The road trips back and forth for the last three years pushed an already old minivan into a much more driven minivan with the miles adding up, tires needing to be replaced, and, in general, already had one foot into the graveyard of used cars that dealerships sell for about two grand. The body was still pretty good, though, and as my mom would say, *"You'll be good till about sixty, and then everything will start to fall apart."* I am fifty-five now but feel sixty. I believe I'm heading in the wrong direction… haha.

I remember when Charles and I sat in the dealership the day we turned in the van, and Captain purchased a brand-new Ford Explorer for me. When he wrote the check, I started to cry. My precious Charles said, *"Mom, don't cry. This car is nicer than the van."* I was so grateful and could not believe this man was purchasing a car for me, in my name, and paying the insurance. Again, I'm just a girl from Sterling Heights, still wondering what I did to deserve someone like Paul.

Love Letter From My Captain

May 12, 2013

Happy Mother's Day!

*Although you're not my mom, you are my hot little Princess!
Enjoy the party today, and tell everyone I said hi.*

*I hope the blinds turn out how you wish… time to prepare
Dan's to-do list.*

*Only four sleeps, Princess… then I get to f—k to that hot little
body of yours. Can't wait!*

*Also, can't wait to be in Tawas with my Princess next week
and celebrate your "46" birthday.*

*I Love You, Princess, and will miss you, but I get to look for-
ward to our next days together.*

Love your Captain

We celebrated Charles's birthday and Mother's Day at Cindy's
with the annual brunch. These two occasions will always go hand in
hand with me. When I was pregnant with Charles, a few days before
Mother's Day, I had a scheduled C-section and was released four days
later—on Mother's Day. It was a perfect Mother's Day gift.

Love Note in a Card From My Captain

May 17, 2013

Always so Caring
Always so Sweet
Always so Sharing
Always so Upbeat
Always my Gal
Always my B…h
Always my Pal
Always my Rich…
Beautiful, Hot, Sincere, Sexy, Wonderful, Perfect, Skinny,
Shapely
More than any Man could ask for PRINCESS!

Dear Princess
I Love You
"ONLY" You Forever and a Day!
Happy 46th to My Hot, Sexy Princess

Love Your Captain

Love Note to My Captain

May 20, 2013

Hi Sunshine,

I sure wish you were coming home to me tonight, and I would
make your cocktail, and we'd have some time by the River, but
as you know, that didn't happen. Though… how lucky am
I to have so much time with you and share some wonderful
moments, activities, and adventures. Thank you for making

my birthday so special. Thank you for the heartwarming card. You know I love when you write special notes/poems to me.

I'm sorry I got a little tipsy on Friday. I guess I knew my captain was there for me. I love our mirror purchase and can't wait to find the perfect spot! That was so great you decided to purchase it for Ridgeway! You are so so good to me. Thanks for the kinky sex this weekend- and thanks for being patient... hehe... You are my Rock Star!! I love you more than Peanut Butter!!! Thank you for my beautiful flowers - I'll enjoy them this week and think of you often... like I don't already??? I'm silly, I'm sorry...

Thank you for your generosity in supporting me. I haven't given up on myself - don't worry - I'll bring you more checks. I'm working on it. Please don't let this ever stand in the way of our relationship, and please always talk to me if there's a problem. I worry you'll grow to dislike or have issues with me and my career. It's just challenging knowing I'm not there 24/7 to give my customers full service. It's a difficult balance, and knowing I can do both makes me grateful. Please, please, please tell me you'll always be honest with me and continue to understand or agree to figure out how I can make both ends work without having so much stress and worrying I'm displeasing you. I do love you so much and always want you to be happy with me. I'm excited to start working on our loving cup of flowers!

I Love You, Sunshine Forever and a Day! I can't wait to be back in your arms!

On my birthday that year, we attended the Humane Animal Treatment Society's (HATS) dinner and auction. It was such fun, and since Mt Pleasant is a smaller community, it was a great time to socialize and see so many people we knew all in one place simultaneously—hence why I had a cocktail or two while celebrating another year around the sun for me!

Love Letter to My Captain
May 27, 2013

Captain,

Here I go again, ready to say goodbye. I have so many blessings in my life, I shouldn't get so sad when I leave you, but I can't help it!

My Captain is such an integral part of my life. I love you dearly, and I could never put the words on paper that you would understand just how deep my love is for you. I'll say it again, you have opened up a whole new world for me and have given me so much- from your love and devotion to a place for your Princess to live and all things in between! You've opened your heart, your home, and your finances to me, and for that, I could never thank you enough!

This weekend was great, especially the sex!! I've never had such great sex in my life, nor have I been so satisfied!

I'll head home and try to sell a house for us and work on getting some additional business. I can't wait to see you again, Lover! I'll miss you a bunch!

That weekend opened up boating season—at least for Captain. His official start was usually Memorial Day. Tawas Marina was always a happening place during this time.

On June 5, my Dad turned eighty. The following Saturday, we had a big party for him at my sister's house in Royal Oak. We did a car theme, and each of the kids and grandkids had custom-made T-shirts that said "Mac's Garage" with a picture of a classic Ford and name titles printed underneath for all of us. Dad's said, "Founder & Patriarch," Mom's had a pin that was the same logo with the title, "Matriarch," and mine said "Wheel #4,"—as I am the fourth child. My other siblings had their numbers, too—"Wheel#1, #2, #3—and the grandkids were the "lug nuts," appropriately numbered in order of their age. Captain was "The Fifth Wheel." Oh, it was a memorable party!

Love Letter to My Captain,

June 9, 2013

> *Dear Lover,*
>
> *I can't thank you enough for everything you did for my Dad's party. You are so generous and giving. You have such a huge heart and something else… hehe…*
>
> *The party was a success, and you were a big part of that. Thank you for all the physical help you gave. It means so much to me.*
>
> *You've woven into every thread of my body, life, and heart. I am so grateful for you that God has given you to me. We have such fun together, and I love being in your presence. Thank*

you for trimming our shrubs, you worked so hard, and they look great!

Four sleeps and then "us" together again.

Love You Forever and a Day!

Xoxoxo

Your Princess

143

Take Away:

Milestones in life, whether yours or your family members, can be remembered even more fondly when shared with your significant other.

CHAPTER THIRTY

Good Times in Tawas With the Kids

July 2013

Paul's daughter Diana and her boyfriend Kevin flew from New York to visit us in Tawas. We took the boat out on the bay, and the kids tubed and water skied. A typical day for us in Tawas included starting the day with bacon—lots of it—followed by a leisurely morning until we packed the cooler for the boat. We spent the afternoons out on the water and/or in the marina sitting on the dock with our friends. Then, we'd usually go back and grill and finish the evening watching movies or playing euchre. I should not admit this, but we also smoked—a lot. During Diana and Kevin's visit, the fish flies were terrible, so our new smoking place was the garage, sitting on coolers and five-gallon upside-down buckets. I fondly remember this particular evening playing euchre, having cocktails, and running back and forth into the garage for our breaks. Captain had made his famous homemade spaghetti, which his girls loved. Pedro (the Jack Russel) was still alive at the time. He was snuggled up on Captain's lap during dinner. When Captain got up, he had red sauce all over the front of him. Diana looked at him and said, "*Dad, what the hell. Are you losing it?*" We all laughed so hard. Captain's reaction was priceless, too—he blamed it on poor little Pedro. However, low and behold, upon finding Pedro, we noticed his little paws had sauce on them along with the trail of little red paw prints. He must have regurgitated his spaghetti snack on Captain's lap! No one had heard anything except the surround sound of the movie track. We still laugh about this today.

There were so many good times in Tawas. Captain had purchased the Tawas place B.C.—Before Carol—ten years earlier. During this period, I was just another girl to his fellow boaters down there—as they'd seen so many on Paul's arm. Even though this was the third season I'd visited, they still teased me about how I may not last the distance with Paul and were always surprised to see me back the next year. Despite their little taunts, I took it all on the chin, telling them every time with a big ole smile on my face, "*There won't be anyone else, boys.*" They just simply had to get used to me. ;-)

Love Letter to My Captain
July 8, 2013

Hi Sweetheart,

3 1/2 years!!! Amazing! Not that I'm surprised we've lasted 3 1/2 years, but more of what an amazing time we've had. I know it's the journey and not the destination that matters, and what a journey it has been!

I'm so lucky that I found you. I can't imagine life without you, you are so embedded into my heart, and I'm so grateful for your love!

What a great extended weekend it was, lots of laughs and great memories. Thank you for making me feel special. 4 sleeps ahead without you is better than more, but I wish it were less. I'm excited about our upcoming trip. Thanks for letting me tag along!

I love you, Sunshine, and thank God for you. FYI, I'm looking at you as I write this, and you are so hot and f.....g handsome, and you love me! I can't believe it!

Love you, Captain

Forever and A Day!

xoxoxo

Your Princess

Trip #15 to Baltimore, Maryland, was for an American Institute of Certified Public Accountants (AICPA) conference. We stayed at the Baltimore Marriot Waterfront, and the harbor view from the room was incredible. Bonus: We were able to spend some time with Paul's daughter Sara. It was always nice when we could mix conferences with visiting family members. Sara took us to Fort McHenry, where the Battle of Baltimore took place in 1841. When the U.S. soldiers were victorious, they raised a giant American Flag, which inspired Francis Scott Key when he wrote *The Star Spangled Banner*. Fun fact: Allegedly, the melody is set to an old English drinking tune...

Overall, we enjoyed fabulous seafood, hilarious comedians, great shopping, and water taxing around the harbor. It was another successful vacation.

Love Letter to My Captain

July 18, 2013

Goodnight, my Love,

As I lay down to sleep this evening, I'll be wishing I was sleeping next to you. A six-night streak I'll be breaking, although I'll be back very soon! Thank you for the great trip to Baltimore. I enjoyed spending it with you and didn't mind the pampering you gave me. I love traveling with you, and the fact that you chose me to go with you is extra special.

I love you so much and trust you with my everything. It seems scary to some, but not to me.

I've given you my heart and trust you'll take care not to break it or break me in any way.

We have so many good times ahead, and our journey is so fulfilling! I'm already excited as I write this to see you tomorrow. Ok, enough of me babbling. My eyes are tearing up, and I'm at my desk. No one understands the depth of my love for you. I hope you sleep well. Love you bunches and with every cell in my body!

xoxo

Your Princess

xoxo

Love Letter to My Captain

July 24, 2013

Sweet Dreams, My Love!

My heart is unconditionally yours-

Hey Lover- I like seeing you during the week, isn't it wonder-ful? Of course, we both know what the perfect scenario would be. Until then, we keep on Keeping on. I loved being able to make dinner for you and you coming home to me. It's some-thing so unexplainable.

I can't thank you enough for your generosity with me and my babies, especially now with Maddy and the car situation. Your heart just keeps growing. I couldn't and wouldn't like to journey this road of life without you. I am the luckiest girl in the world. But, when I looked at you today as you left for work, you looked so handsome, and it made me realize again how in awe I am that you chose me. Not that I don't believe in myself, but there are so many other women out there that are more beautiful, more accomplished and have more than I can offer you. You have my heart, my love, my faithfulness, and my extended family:-), all of which are intangible, and I hope that will always be enough for you.

I'm so looking forward to the rest of the summer. Tawas will be fun, relaxing, and laughter-filled. Chicago will be awe-some, and you'll have all your babies together as we celebrate you- "Papa" and your upcoming bday. Then we'll head up north to experience "Pure Michigan," and you'll introduce me to additional new experiences. Now, not to forget the culmination of summer with the Dream Cruise and throwing in a baseball game at Comerica Park, a perfect ending to August.

Life is beautiful

Life is a vacation

And I appreciate it all-

Baby, Baby- I wish I could lay next to you and snuggle tonight, we'll be together soon.

Sleep tight, my love-

Close your Peepers and dream wonderful things-

Love You Forever and a Day-

Xoxo
Your Princess

My Captain was always there for me, and if my kids or I needed something and he had a connection, he would happily help us. So, let's just say that the Krapohl Ford dealership in Mt Pleasant received some extra business by Captain dating me.

Love Letter to My Captain
July 29, 2013

Miss My Captain Already!

I know I'm just weird -

Thank you for the wonderful weekend in Tawas with the kids and our friends. As usual - you were the ultimate host. Thank you for opening up your home to them and giving up your bed, well, "our" bed, and sleeping in a room with Maddy & Cody. :-) You always make everyone feel welcome, which is one of your many beautiful qualities. I can't even begin to thank you enough for what you've done for Maddy. Thank you for making her car possible. My Captain gets it done, another fantastic quality!

This weekend was tons of fun- especially starting on Thursday night! Sex with my lover is so awesome. I'm so into you! You are so handsome and make my heart skip a beat whenever I look at you. Yea, I know... STILL, I don't think that will ever change. Your heart must be so large in that beautiful chest of yours, and I'm surprised it doesn't break through.

Thank you for allowing me to take the kids to Chicago. It will be so nice to have my babies, all of them, with me and make some great memories. Thank you for making it possible, for your generosity, and for the fact that you support me in going with them. Five sleeps is going to seem like an eternity to me. I'll be missing you all week and wanting to be back in your arms. I Love You, Captain, so much!!

You mean everything to me!

Your Princess!

All 113.2 lbs of me. :-(

So, the last three years of dating Paul had been a whirlwind of amazing trips and experiences. However, after that tummy tuck back in 2010, I was always petrified of gaining the weight back, especially when we sometimes indulged in delicious food and drinks. Overall, I had to watch my calorie count a little, as many other women do. Some of my friends would say that I was obsessed with being skinny, and I agree that it was not the healthiest choice to sometimes live on scoops of peanut butter with semi-chocolate morsels—especially from a nutrition perspective—but what the heck? I was younger then, and it fit my lifestyle—at least when I was back downstate without my Captain, haha.

Take Away:

Gratitude and laughter combined are fuel for the soul.

CHAPTER THIRTY-ONE

Accepting What Is

August–September 2013

The trip to Chicago I was meant to take with my kids—and my girlfriend, Ann Marie, and her kids—had to be canceled at the last minute. I decided it would still be fun to take the kids somewhere and asked Captain if he would like to go to Double JJ Resort in Rothbury with us. We would stay in Michigan, and it'd still be a nice getaway. I had been to Double JJ before—this is probably the only place I had been that my Captain had never been to. Score for Carol! We stayed in a cute little cabin with an adorable front porch, perfect for taking pictures! The highlight of the trip was the horseback trail riding. Captain took it all in and was a good sport, especially considering that his buddy Carl had passed away two days prior. Carl was one of the foursome Captain would go on golf trips with every year. A good man taken too soon.

Love Letter to My Captain

August 4, 2013

Sunshine of My Life -

Thank you, thank you, for taking the kids and I to Double JJ. I wanted you to see it, and I'm glad we shared it with my babies!

I'm so sorry about your buddy. He was such a nice man, and I know you'll miss him. You were fortunate to have shared so many laughs and good times. There's so much sadness sometimes in life. Thank God we have our memories to look back upon.

I'm so excited about Chicago and about spending time with the girls. You are so special and deserve all the great things life has to share with you. Thank you for letting me walk that journey with you.

I love you more today than I did yesterday. I love it when we talk, and you share your feelings with me, and I can say whatever I feel without being judged by you. Two sleeps, and then it's my Captain Time Again.

I Love You Forever and a Day!

XoxoxoYour Princess

Trip #16 was Captain's 60th birthday celebration in Chicago. Before we left, though, I threw a party for my daughter Maddy and her boyfriend Cody as they were about to head back up to Aquinas in Grand Rapids for the school year. It was fun to celebrate them and send them off for another year of college. We had my family and Cody's parents join us, too. A party before a party. Isn't life grand?

Love Letter to My Captain
August 11, 2013

My Birthday Boy!!

What a great weekend in Chicago, it seemed like a whirl-wind! Time goes by so fast when I'm with my Captain. I hope you enjoyed your birthday celebration. Thank you for letting me share it with you and your daughters. I know you were surprised by Erica's decision, and I also know what you always say to me - "What are you going to do-they're your kids…"

Thank you for always going out of the way for me. Sorry about all the driving you have to do today. Hopefully, by the time you read this, you'll be snuggled up in bed with your cool covers, moving your legs… 😜
… and feeling content.

I wish I could be lying next to you.

As one fabulous weekend ends, we have more to look forward to. I'll get back into the office this week and work on making things happen. I am trying, Captain. I hope you know that. And the exciting news is, when I see you again, I'll have a check for you!

As I close this love note, you already know how much I love you and how much you mean to me, but I also want you to realize how happy I am and how much you've changed my life.

I'll continue to love you with all my heart as it will grow deeper in love with you. With every day that passes, I feel more blessed than the day before. I know God sent you to me, and I am forever grateful. I Love You, Captain - Forever and a Day!!! Xoxo

Chicago was an absolute blast from beginning to end. I am talking shopping, fabulous meals, limo rides, boat cruises, cocktails, pubs, and meeting Paul's daughter Erica's boyfriend, Isaiah. Erica and Isaiah were both in Chicago for work for the summer—although Isaiah is originally from there. They'd both be returning to MSU in a couple of weeks for school. However, the day before we were due to leave the hotel and catch our flight back home, Erica wanted to talk to her dad. She asked if he liked Isaiah, and Paul was agreeable. Erica then said they were moving in together back in East Lansing. I smile as I type this because Captain's first comment was, "Is he going to pay half the rent?" Isaiah fit into the family perfectly.

Love Letter to My Captain
August 26, 2013

Baby… Baby… Baby… :-(

Here I go again, but you know I always come back:-) What a lovely weekend, Sunshine. Thank you for introducing me to that side of the state and always wanting to share your life and past experiences. (*Feel free to leave the past sex conquests out, though* 😁). *I love hearing about all the wonderful things you've done, but sometimes I'm sad because I wish I could have shared them with you. At the end of the day, we are where we are, though, and I'm blessed with my beautiful children, knowing that God wouldn't have worked it out any other way. I thank him for bringing you to me… better late than never… right?*

I love being your Princess; truthfully, you were the most handsome man at the wedding. We make a great couple… we "fit." So I'll head home now and work my heinie off if only I could make it into a bubble butt for you. 😜 *I'll count down the sleeps till I feel your luscious, inviting skin against mine.*

I Love You, Captain - and take you home with me in my heart! ♥

Love,
Your Princess

Forever and a Day!

The Bay Harbor wedding we attended was lovely. The weather was beautiful, the venue was idyllic, and the bride and groom were simply stunning. Many of Captain's friends were there. One, who shall remain nameless, scoffed at me when I told him I would marry Paul one day. Once again, people were making assumptions due to knowing too much about Paul's past and stream of relationships. But, like the boaters, I would show this guy where he could stick his opinion…

Love Letter to My Captain

September 8, 2013

My h—d c——d Lover,

Handsome man, I'll miss you tonight and the next few, not just nights, though, but days also. 😳
Thank you for being so generous to not just me but to Maddy and Cody. Thank you for letting me take her shopping and filling her tank.

Talk about filling… you've filled my life with your love, your heart, your generosity, your awesome sex, and so much much more!! And, needless to say, something else..........

I hope you don't think about me "fishing" about getting married. I don't do it intentionally. I know how established you are and how you feel about marriage. My head tells me all of this, and I understand it, but my heart wants me to think I'm special enough to be your wife one day. That's all. You're smart, I'm smart, but I'm still a girl who wants to feel special.

The CMU game was fun. I love going to the games with you. I can't wait for the others. We have such a fun fall ahead of us. Happy 44th Anniversary - many more returns of this day - to us! Ok, Captain - I Love You Forever and a Day. You are my Rock Star, My Shining Star!

Xoxo
Your Princess

P.S. Can't wait to see you soon.

I loved the special times when Madeline would travel to Mt Pleasant from Grand Rapids. It was a nice getaway for her and Cody, and sometimes her friends. It meant a break from the craziness of school, plus I could see her, and Captain would feed them home-made family meals. At this point, Madeline was getting serious with Cody, so naturally, the idea of them getting married would come up in conversations I had with my Captain regarding marriage. It was also about this time when, now and then, Captain would throw a one-liner out there like, "Why should two people have to get married?" or "Isn't it about the journey and not the destination?"

Look, I loved this man, so much so that I even agreed with him when he said lines like that, but silently, in my heart, every single time, I felt like someone had blown the candle out on me.

I get it now, though. Back then, Captain was at the top of his game. We were enjoying a happy and organic relationship. He cared for me financially, and the system we created worked very well. I would put together my "accounting" and let him know what bills I had coming, what monies I needed for special occasions, my real estate-related expenses, groceries, and sundry items. Then he'd write me a check and always give me extra, saying, "You need some walking around money, too." And if an unexpected expense came up, and I was downstate, he'd tell me to put it on the credit card. I, in turn, would sign over my real estate commission checks to him, so it was a fair give and take between us—but just with him being the bigger give financially. The thing about being a Realtor® is that you can go a month without a closing, which would mean going without a check, but sometimes you could have three closings in a week. The point is that it was an unbalanced flow of income for me. I'm sure my lifestyle choices with being away so much didn't help. Every check I deposited from Paul, I kissed. I was filled with so much gratitude; it was my way of thanking Captain—weird but true. The tellers even got used to seeing the pink imprint of my lipstick on the paper! God only knows what they thought I was getting the money for… At any rate, our journey was moving along the road of life perfectly. Why would I want it to push it where it was not quite ready to be? And, to be honest, I was not in a real personal hurry to be a wife again. I wanted my youngest to graduate high school first. I also knew how much I loved my man, and I believed in fate, doing the right thing by my partner—not the easy thing—and putting love before fixed titles. Plus, when you receive flowers and the card says, "*Happy 45th! You've Made The Past 45 Months The Best Of My Life! Love, The Captain,*" how can you not have faith in the future?

Take Away:

The definition of belief perseverance is the tendency to cling to one's initial belief even after receiving new information that contradicts or disconfirms the basis of that belief. This is where faith steps in. So, have faith, and keep yourself grounded. Then, happiness will come.

CHAPTER THIRTY-TWO

Weddings Akin to a Baseball Lineup

November–December 2013

Trip #17 (November 9–13) took us back to Vegas for the AICPA Conference. This time, we stayed at Caesar's Palace. We took in some shows, ate great food, had plenty of cocktails, and did a ton l of walking. Yes—silly me was still walking around in my heels. But you know what they say: It's not how you feel. It's how you look, right?

Love Letter to My Captain,
November 14, 2013

To My Forever and a Day and the Best Lover Ever!

As your beautiful head hits the pillow, know that I love you immensely and wish I could be lying next to you. We had a fabulous time in Las Vegas, and I love spending every minute with you. You're so generous with your heart and your love and everything else. I am the luckiest girl in the world.

I can't help but tell you again how special I feel when we're out, and I'm on your arm. You are so handsome, and I pray I'm the one for you—Forever and a Day! I miss you so much when we have to part. You become one with me, and I feel I'm only a half when you're gone. :-(

I'm so happy I can bring you another check. It makes me fulfilled that I can contribute to us. I know it's not much, but it is something. Sunshine, I'll fall asleep wishing you were next to me.

I Love You and Appreciate You!! ♥

Xoxoxox

Your Princess

The holiday season was yet again around the corner. Captain and his girls were going to celebrate Thanksgiving in New York while I was hosting Thanksgiving at Ridgeway again. I was happy that Paul would spend much-needed time with his three daughters. I enjoyed the time with my family. I knew all too well that my folks were getting older, and the time I'd have with them was lessening as the years went by.

Love Letter to My Captain
December 2, 2013

Hi Baby,

I was so glad to have you back in my arms again yesterday. I know it sounds silly, but I had that excited nerves thing going on yesterday before I picked you up from the airport! I'm so attached. I hope that's a good thing. I missed you tremendously but I was so happy you spent time with your daughters. You guys did have a great time and made great memories. As we move into the holiday season, I want to tell you again how grateful I am for you. I couldn't imagine my life without you! As I've said before, I hope that doesn't scare you. It's probably not mentally healthy, and some would say to be so attached. I don't care - I am!

Thank you for helping me financially. I try not to spend money recklessly, oh, but I did buy those boots, sorry about that! I want to look good for you and always make you proud that I'm on your arm.

I'm excited to come to see you this weekend and decorate. I love you to the moon and back and miss having you next to me, around me, and you know the other one... 😜

Your Princess

Xoxoxo

Love Letter to My Captain
December 9, 2013

Thank you so much for the joint account. It feels so special to see both our names on the checks, like I'm a part of you! Two is Better Than One! I'm so grateful to have this account, but if I don't seem overly excited, it's because I think I look at it as if something tragic would happen to my Captain, which makes me sad. But, I am so so so grateful. Nothing can replace you, and I pray we are together for a long, long time, forever and a day...

Captain had opened a joint Charles Schwab account for us, as I always was concered something would happen to him. It made me feel secure and again taken care of. Right around the corner was Christmas, again always an exciting time. What made it even better this particular year was that on December 23, Madeline got engaged. Cody proposed by setting up a trail of roses in vases, signifying their journey together. We all celebrated, and the champagne flowed. It was the most wonderful way to end the year—or the beginning of a brand-new year with them as an engaged couple. I was ecstatic, and Madeline's father approved—and I would have, too, if asked, haha. Not long after, though, the reality hit: We now have a wedding to pay for!

Two days later, Captain threw the annual "Christmas Eve Open House." Since his daughters were in town, I thought getting all the kids together before New Year's would be a great idea. So, we planned an evening to see the Trans-Siberian Orchestra at The Palace and then a walk through downtown Rochester to see the lights and have dinner.

The Mt Pleasant crew met up with my crew at our Ridgeway house, and we had appetizers and some general Christmas cheer. Also, at that time, the game *Cards Against Humanity* was the rage, so why not play it? Maybe not exactly the right choice for the youngest—a twelve-year-old—but nonetheless fun. Overall, it was a success. Sara, Diana, Erica, Isaiah, Madeline, Cody, Joseph, and Charles attended.

The Christmas lights in downtown Rochester made the perfect backdrop for photos, and by now, I was known as Katie Kodak! Of course, the kids would roll their eyes, but I believe it is important to document with pictures. One never knows when you might need a pic of something or someone. Maybe it's because I'm so sentimental. Either way, the kids obliged me.

Take Away:

It is a domino effect—engagements and weddings, that is.

CHAPTER THIRTY-THREE

Statistically, It Was Bound to Happen

December 2013—February 2014

Trip #18 (December 29 – January 4) brought in the new year, which took us back to sunny Florida. My Captain and I were heading to Naples' calm waters and fine white "sugar" sand to meet our friends Russ and Cara for New Year" and then on to Longboat Key to see Bruce and Sue.

Love Letter to My Captain
January 14, 2014

> *Hi Lover,*
>
> *We had such a wonderful Christmas time with our families. It was great to have all the kids home and be able for them to get together. I love my beautiful necklace. Thank you again. You always put so much thought into my gifts.*
>
> *I'm sorry our vacation did not go as smoothly as we would have liked. At least you were able to spend some time by the*

water in Longboat Key. Maybe I should be off the vacation
planning board! 😂

Overall, I was fortunate to spend time with you, and I hope
it wasn't too much. Lol, I pray you stay warm and snuggly
tonight. I'm sorry I won't be there to lie next to you. I love you
with all my heart and miss you already!

Love,
Forever -N- a Day

Your Princess

Xoxoxo

So, Naples did not turn out exactly as planned. The first night was great; we went downtown, had dinner, and enjoyed the company. Russ and Cara were terrific hosts. However, the next day, Captain started feeling a little off and warm, so after a few hours of being out and about, we stopped at a local drugstore to buy a thermometer. It turned out that Paul indeed had a fever, so off to bed he went.

The next day, New Year's Eve, Captain lovingly shared his fever with me, and we were both down for the count. We stayed in our room and didn't come out to the condo's common area until we felt better—just in time for us to head over to Longboat Key. In all of our travels, that was the only time we ended up sick on vacation, excluding the brown bottle flu…

A few weekends later, on January 25, we celebrated Maddy's twenty-first birthday at the Ridgeway house. Captain had been exposed to many of our McEvoy parties. He knew they lasted a long time, and, of course, this was no exception.

Love Letter to My Captain
January 27, 2014

Hi Lover,

As you close your eyes and go to sleep, I want you to know how much I really, really love you. I mean really, really, really-

Thank you for coming to Ridgeway this weekend. Knowing you were at home when I was out working was wonderful. It's so nice just doing everyday things with you. But, I must admit, it's really nice and HOT when we're naked together! 😵

Thank you for all you've done for us - and for my babies -

Your generosity towards Maddy is unbelievable - so, so, kind - She was so happy. You know she won't blow the money. She'll spend it wisely with her Cody.

Thank you for the CLOSET - now I don't have to worry about turning the corner in the bedroom and holding my breath. My Captain's heart is so huge -

My Captain is also very, very handsome and hot -

My Captain is an awesome dancer -

My Captain is astute and intelligent -

My Captain is beyond words -

I love my Captain

Love Rocking this Life With You!

Your Forever and A Day

Xoxoxo

Princess…

    with the new closet

February hit, and the annual tax season began. Every tax season, I became more accustomed to the process—or should I say, the mood of my Captain and the culmination of a season of grind.

Love Letter to My Captain
February 3, 2014

Hi Sunshine!!

TOO SHORT!

Not your d—k, obviously, but the weekend. I shouldn't complain. At least I did get 2 sleeps with you. I wish I never had to leave. I love being here with you. I love being anywhere with you. :-)

Thanks for taking me out to the Optimist dinner. It was good to dance with you again! You look so hot on that dance floor!! Plus, it's a lot of fun! But the real fun started when we came home and played "dress up." It felt good in so many ways!

I'm a little concerned it's going to be a long week. I don't like not knowing how many sleeps before I see you again. But I know this is your busy time and that's what's important so I'll wait patiently!

Thank you for loving me. I carry you around with me in my heart. You don't have to worry about me or anyone randomly texting me. I'm all yours! Thank you for getting me new tires, and thank you for the check. I appreciate it.

I Love You, Captain, with every fiber inside me- Forever and a Day... and then some - Love Always.

Your Princess. xoxoxo

We usually had plans on the weekends, and the Optimist dinner was one that weekend. It's always amazed me how Mt Pleasant was such a small town, and Paul knew so many of its residents. By this time, I had been on the scene for a while, so the "nice to see you again" when referring to me was actually true. So many times, in the early days, I was mistaken for one of the other women. I eventually got used to it and knew it would resolve itself the longer I was around.

Love Letter to My Captain
February 10, 2014

Captain - My Love,

I am once again leaving you for the week:(As I write this, I realize how lucky I am and what gratitude you brought into my life. So many times, I still can't believe you chose me - I know I am kind and sweet... But you've got so much in your arsenal - looks, charisma, intelligence, success, sexual prowess, and you look so damn hot in a suit!! I mean all that, and you picked me, a struggling Realtor® with financial baggage. I hope you always love me. I fell in love with you so hard and quickly - as you turned my world upside down!! I can't even think of life without you, Captain. Our bodies will change, but my love for you will grow deeper - I pray you feel the same...

This weekend was wonderfully relaxing, and I enjoyed being by your side. Sex was off the hook, as usual!! I'll miss you this week. Try not to get too stressed; I know tax season can wear on you. I'll count down the sleeps, my love. Don't get too lonely in this bed, and stay in this bed, no wandering in the house!

I Love You Forever and A Day!

XOXO
Your Princess!

The following weekend was Valentine's Day. Maddy and Cody were planning on coming to Mt Pleasant. Captain was sharing budgeting ideas with them and spreadsheets for record keeping. In retrospect, I should have been the one he sent to budgeting school.

Card From My Captain
February 14, 2014

"You Are My Dream Come True Princess!

I Love How You Love Me and Love Loving You.

Forever & A Day."

Happy Valentine's Day To The Couple That "Fit"

Love, Your Captain

Love Letter to My Captain
February 17, 2014

My Sweet Captain -

Our 5th Valentine's Day shared together...

I am the luckiest girl in the world, as your card says... It's a Miracle!! I call it destiny. Although I didn't put together an ABC book of our love story, we could fill the pages of a novel with our journey. You are threaded so tightly into my world the thought of it ever coming unraveled is too much to bear.

Promise me we are Forever and a Day -

Thank you again for being so good to Maddy and Cody. I know that obviously, there is no obligation to my babies, but you have welcomed them into your life along with me - and that means so much. The flowers for her were so special, and you have such a loving heart.

The flowers for me were just beautiful, no spectacular is a better word, and the chocolates were delicious, they're still with me now... :-)

Seriously though, I wish I could give back to you even a smidgen of what you have given me, but I give you my tenderness, love, and all that I am, along with some bad decisions... like getting my car stuck in the snow....

As I finish writing my Captain this love note, I realize I'll miss sleeping in your bed, snuggling, and having breathtaking sex with my Hot Hot and Even Hotter Prince!

You are the Bomb Diggity!!

Enough said!

Your Princess.

Take Away:

The love notes from your significant other may be short and come only occasionally, but they matter.

CHAPTER THIRTY-FOUR

Tax Season, Autorama, and Easter

March 2014

Even though it was tax season, Captain made it a point to come downstate if it was important to me. Thank goodness for being able to work remotely! In March, we had my company's euchre tournament and Autorama. I especially loved going to Autorama and seeing all the hot rods and custom cars. The overhead and underneath lighting for the cars on the main floor highlighted the flawless, streak-free bodies and glistening white walls. It was a nice break in the dead of Michigan winters. I knew going made my dad happy, and having Paul there also made him happy. It was a win-win event all around!

Love Letter to My Captain
March 9, 2014

My Captain -

My heart is dropping sad tears. I needed more than two sleeps to get my Captain fix. Actually, I never get enough of my Captain! Maybe one day we won't have to count the sleeps?

I appreciate you coming down this weekend. I had fun at the Euchre Tournament, and you were a winner!! Actually, I am the winner, and you're my prize. For once in my life, I won the blue ribbon! You are so perfect, so handsome, so genuine, and so giving. Is it true you'll love me forever and a day? I pray that it is. I am so grateful. You treat me like a princess. I feel I'm living a fairytale, but it's actual life. Thank you for going along this journey with me. I wouldn't want anyone else by my side. Thank you for always supporting me in so many ways,

I Love You Forever and a Day and Then Some!!

Four Sleeps!!

The Euchre tournament was super fun. Luckily, Captain did not have me as a partner for the whole time; otherwise, he wouldn't have won second place! Everyone at my real estate office that knew Paul—and most did since I spoke about him all the time and had embedded him into all parts of my life—seemed to genuinely like him.

Love Letter to My Captain

March 18, 2014

My Wild Irish Rover,

Thank you for spending Saint Patrick's Day with your princess. Thank you for giving me your corned beef also!! :-) I know it was a quick overnight, but nonetheless, we did get to spend some time with each other. I'm getting out of your "hair" (not down there) 😵 so you can focus on your work. I would have loved to have stayed longer and probably could have snuck out another day, although I don't want to see you stressed. If it were after April 15th I'd stay in a New York minute-believe me! I don't relish the thought of not being by your side. I'll get through the rest of the week and rush to be by my Captain again.

I love you, Sunshine, Forever and A Day!

Thank you for being my Captain!

XOXOXO

As I mentioned before, the months of March and April were always busy for Robert F. Murray & Co. However, at this point in Paul's career, he had it down to a science.

Tax season ended, the parking lot after party happened, and I guess I talked too much.

Love Letter to My Captain

April 16, 2014

Oh Sunshine,

Sorry my naked body is not laying next to you to sleep. I hope you're feeling better when you read this love note. I'm sad when you don't feel well. Thank you for inviting me to your end-of-the-season tax party. Sorry I talk so much. I'm always just so happy to be around you. Thank you for everything you do for me. I am so grateful! I couldn't imagine you not being at the helm of my life. You're in my heart -wherever I may be - good luck the next couple of days on winding down. The weather will turn, and we have so much to look forward to.

I Love You Forever and a Day My Love

XOXO

Sleep Well and Sweet Dreams

Your Princess 🖤

The following weekend, we would celebrate Easter at Ridgeway with my family. We did plan an end-of-tax season trip planned—although it happened a month later, around my birthday. More on that later…

Love Letter To My Captain
April 20, 2014

Lover -

Wow - What a Weekend -

Thank you so much for coming downstate and spending the holiday with me and the family. It went by so darn fast, at least for me. You were so kind and great with the kids all weekend! Thank you_thank you_thank you_!

Also, sorry for getting a bit emotional this weekend. I love you so much that I get nervous if I am overwhelming you with family, children, and "my" stuff, especially since you have so much going on in your own life and you're in post-tax season recovery mode. Sometimes I worry we'll scare you away... lol.

I'll miss you this week, but I'll count down the days and run back up to see my Captain as soon as possible!

- Thank you for taking me into your life and loving me and all that comes with me.

- Thank you for being so kind and generous to not only me but my babies also.

- Thank you for embracing my family and appreciating my parents.

- Thank you for so much more than I could ever put on paper.

- Thank you for making Love to me. I needed that connection to you, plus it felt great!

I Love You, Captain -
Forever & A Day
Your Princess

Take Away:

You cannot change people, but you can change the way you react to them.

CHAPTER THIRTY-FIVE

My Favorite Month and the Return of the Brown Bottle Flu

May 2014

Captain came into town to celebrate Mother's Day and Charles's birthday. We gathered at my sister's house for our annual brunch. It was always so much fun and denoted the beginning of summer to me.

Love Letter to My Captain

May 11, 2014

Dear Captain,

Another weekend passed, and my Captain is snuggled safely in his bed - (alone, I hope) lol. I have to tell you how much it meant for you to come to Ridgeway and be here with me for Mother's Day. It seemed like a long weekend, but it went by quickly. One of the best parts was you making love to me!

Although a close second would be the pizza-ordering phone call, haha.

I'm so fortunate to have such a beautiful life with you and grateful for everything we share. Your generosity never ceases in your heart and is always open. Thank you so much for taking Charlie to get flowers. They're just beautiful, and you went out of your way for him means so much. Thank you for including him in your matching fund's gig and educating him in the market. Hopefully, you'll get a reprieve from him giving you back the same money we give him, and it getting "matched," lol.

Sunshine, I want to tell you how much I love you. I know I say it often, and I hope you still understand the magnitude of my words, even if I say it over and over again. I am so happy!

Well my love, it's the countdown to VEGAS baby! It seems like it would never get here since I've been so excited about it. You know how I love to travel with you. It looks like we only have three sleeps this week. Woo hoo!

I Love You Captain

Forever and Always - and much more than a day-

Can't wait to see my Lover again!

XOXO

Your Princess.

In our first year of dating Captain had offered all my children the opportunity to set up Charles Schwab accounts, and he would match the funds they invested. Madeline and Charles went in on it, and we set up investment accounts with their name and mine. However, Joseph chose not to do it, which was ok—he benefitted from Captain's generosity in many other ways. Being the youngest and having the most time with Paul, Charles naturally benefited the most. It still amazes me that Paul cared so much for them.

Love Note to My Captain
May 25, 2014

Baby, Baby…

So sad to be leaving you and your handsomeness. What a wonderful 19th trip we had!! I am the luckiest, I mean, the luckiest girl in the world! You have shown and given me so much that I could ever imagine. Your heart is so filled with love and kindness it never ceases to amaze me. I hate the thought that the trip and our time this weekend is over, but it allows me to start getting excited to see you again. I can't help but miss you immensely when we are apart, but I understand this is the way it needs to be for now. I want to thank you especially for my beautiful birthday flowers, the exhilarating rafting/helicopter ride through the Grand Canyon, not to mention the shows and the fabulous dinners. I want to apologize for the afternoon at "Liquid" It was fun, but I'm filled with a tad of regret that it ended the way it did. Thank you for taking care of me. I can always count on my Captain to be there for me. I never want to embarrass you. I hope I didn't.

Thank you for letting me take this journey down the road of life with you. It sure is exciting! I look forward to this next weekend; while I miss you at Ridgeway, have a fabulous week and play some great golf! You are my world and in every cell of my body.

I Love You Captain, and I proudly wear your "PBM" x 2.

Xoxo

For Trip #19 (May 16–22), we celebrated my birthday in Vegas, and by celebrate, I mean *celebrate...*

We stayed at the ARIA Resort & Casino on Las Vegas Boulevard and indulged at Liquid, the adult-only and luxurious upscale pool and lounge. You can "purchase" the use of the daybeds and/or cabanas and get credit back for food and beverages. Let's just say I went in looking much different than I came out… Again, I am not a seasoned drinker, and I should have known better—especially since it was scorching hot and I was more than likely getting dehydrated in addition to drunk. I recall not feeling well, and as we walked out, I needed assistance from My Captain, so we changed direction and found a nice shady area for me to "rest"—apparently, what I found comfortable was a nice piece of cement for a pillow. It is all a blur, but I remember Captain sitting next to me, and each time a passing civilian stopped to ask if I was all right, he replied, "*Oh, yes. She's just got a serious case of the brown bottle flu.*" Not one of my finer moments, I know. To top it off, I had to be taken back to our room in a wheelchair.

After sleeping it off for what seemed like hours, I woke up only to find Captain missing in the suite. Thankfully, he'd left a little love note on the mirror that read:

Princess I Love You! Went to the Casino, back at 7:30.

I remember feeling so regretful for what happened and still so damn sick at the same time. Captain took me to dinner that evening and told me it was ok. He even laughed and said, more than once, that we all take our turn in the tank. My turn just seemed to be coming around more often than not.

Take Away:

Just because you have "credit" at an establishment to purchase alcohol does not mean you should.

Chapter Thirty-six

Key to My Heart

June–July 2014

This was another pivotal month for Captain and I's relationship. Something that was not really needed tangibly—but emotionally needed by me—was finally received.

Love Letter to My Captain
June 16, 2014

Captain,

What a wonderful weekend! I hope you enjoyed your Father's Day and our weekend together. I know I did :-) I know you were disappointed that the weather wouldn't be nice enough for us to go to Tawas, but everything worked out perfectly. We were able to eat fish :-) and go canoeing and partake in some extracurricular activities.

Thank you for always being so good to me. I know you're always there, and I can believe in you. Thank you for the "key" It means so much to me. I'll probably never need it, but just knowing you're "all in" in our relationship makes me feel fabulous (and wanted).

I love you so so much, and you mean the world to me. I am the luckiest girl in the world!!! We have such a wonderful life, and I'm so grateful to have your love. I'll count down the sleeps till we're together again.

I miss you already.

Love you Sunshine-

You are My Forever and A Day - Your Princess

Yes, the key meant everything to me. For the record, Captain would leave the door unlocked when he knew I was coming up. I was never locked out, nor did I ever make any surprise visits up to Mt Pleasant, where I would need to get in the house without him knowing. Surprise visits are never good—I learned that lesson early on in my dating life.

Paul and I technically were not living together—although we were every weekend, more or less. He'd had a key to my home on Kozak before the Ridgeway purchase, but life is a little more laid back in Mt Pleasant. Captain never locked his car, either, so leaving the front door unlocked wasn't a big deal. He was giving me a key, though. Oh boy. Trust me when I say that when it came to my Captain, it was significant.

Love Letter to My Captain
July 6, 2014

Hey Sunshine of My Life,

Where do I begin? Thursday seems like ages ago since we received the good news. Thank you so much for being there for me and supporting me. Real-life stuff isn't fun sometimes, is it? You were there for me, and for that, I am thankful. I pray we have smooth sailing for a long time. Tawas was fun and restful, and you know how much I love just being close to you. Others say we "fit," and I agree. I also think we complement each other. You are the chocolate to my peanut butter, and I am the sweet vermouth to your Manhattans!

What can I say, Captain - you've been rocking my world for 4 1/2 years; let's keep it going! I can't imagine us being closer than we are now, but I know with our journey, I'll love you even more as the days pass. Thank you for being my MAN, and I still look at you in amazement, knowing you chose me!

Love you Captain
3sleeps

XOXOXO

Your Princess

At the end of the month, another surprise came. Well, it was less of a surprise and more of a life-can-be-cut-short-at-any-moment reality check. As a woman over forty, getting mammograms—or before forty if there is a history of breast cancer in your family—is recommended. My family has no history; however, history has to start somewhere, right? I am fortunate to say that, as of the writing of this book, I have not started the historical line of breast cancer. I did have a scare, though; luckily, it was just dense breast tissue. I'm grateful for my health and realize how blessed I am. I also recognize and genuinely support the women faced with this and their strength.

Take Away:

Be grateful for the time you have and the people you get to spend it with.

CHAPTER THIRTY-SEVEN

Captain, Columbus, and Cake

August 2014

Love Note to My Captain
August 5, 2014

My Love,

Time for sleepy sleepy!

Happy Birthday, Week, Captain-

Thank you for going out on the weekend with my friends. We really did have a crazy, silly, fun time. The GPYC is always a good time with Tom and Lynda.

Sweetheart, I want you to know how much I appreciate, love, and like you:) You are so special. I don't want you to worry about getting older, and I'm getting older too! But age is just a number, and as we go down this road, our journey changes- it gets better, and I fall more in love with you, not to mention you get more handsome! Oh la la…

So, I'm super excited to spend the weekend with my Captain and your Riki and Isaiah. We'll do a lot of laughing! OK, Captain time for me to wrap it up and hit the road. You get a check this week - yippee!

Love you forever and a day

XOXOXO

Trip #20 saw us hitting the road to Columbus, Ohio. Yes, by road, I mean literally—we drove. The question I asked Captain at the time was what counted as a trip for us—or should I say a trip I had written down on my little sheet of paper folded up in my wallet? Ultimately, we considered it a trip if we left the Michigan border!

In Columbus, we shared more bouts of laughter, great food, and spirits! It was another successful birthday—and one that did not end with me in the tank. We enjoyed spending it with Erica and Isaiah and also had an opportunity to see Isaiah's parents. As I've often said to my Captain, I would go anywhere with you, and I meant it.

The following weekend Sara and her boyfriend came up to Tawas. It was relaxing and fun and… included a trip to the emergency room…

Love Letter to My Captain
August 19, 2014

Captain -

I'm so sorry you're injured. I wish I could take your pain away. Thank you for the weekend, and thank you for working

*in the dream cruise. You went out of your way, and I appreci-
ate that. I enjoyed spending time with Sara and your yummy
meals! Thank you for supporting me in my "not smoking"
new world. I just want the best for us and to be at my best for
you. I love you so much and want our journey to continue for
a long time.*

*I hope you're ok for the next few days. I wish I could stay
and take care of you. I love you so deeply I could kiss you
everywhere!*

OK Lover, I am off on the road again - sleep tight, pain-free -

I Love You Forever And A Day!

*XOXO
Your Princess*

We made a one-day trip to Royal Oak from Tawas for the annual
Dream Cruise. I had decided to quit smoking a few days earlier. I'd
purchased a silly vape pen, which now I find out is probably worse
than smoking. It was not that tough for the first few days. My body
was used to smoking, and then I'd go home and not smoke for four
days or so and then come back and start again. I would go through
the withdrawal only to start back at square one and go through it
again the following week. It was stupid what I was doing to myself,
plus my daughter was getting married, and I wanted to be around a
long time for my kids and grandkids. We made our appearance at the
Cruise, enjoyed seeing family and friends, and headed back to Tawas.

That same weekend was an interesting trip to the emergency
room back in Tawas. Someone thought they didn't have to go, so we
had a vote; Captain was outnumbered. A chunk of the flesh between

his pointer and middle finger had been ripped off in a garbage dis-
posal accident. Unsurprisingly, Captain was in his usual good spirits
while being stitched up in the ER. It makes a great story to tell. The
pictures are pretty cool, too!

Love Letter to My Captain

August 25, 2014

Sunshine -

*I want to kiss you all over and make your boo-boo all better. I
love you so much and hate seeing you in pain.*

*Thank you for another wonderful weekend. Thank you for
being so good to Charles and allowing him to drive the boat.
He is getting older, and the time he wants to spend with us
will change. :-(. My little Brussel...*

*I also want to apologize for angering you the other night
when I sat on the couch and not next to you on the big chair.
I guess I was feeling a little left out like your phone was more
important, and I know that wasn't the case. I didn't do it to
upset you. I didn't know why I did it. I've never been accused
of being passive-aggressive, so I didn't know how to take
it. Maybe it seemed like that. I guess I was feeling sorry for
myself.*

*I know you have a great deal on your plate and are in pain,
so I am sorry. I never want to upset you. My love for you is so
strong it can't even be explained -*

Love You Forever and A Day My Captain

Xoxo
Your Princess

Authentic me again... When I tell you we never really argued, it is true. I am unsure if it was me conceding all the time or if I was starting it and then backing off. Either way, I was ok with that. I hate drama. I do not need drama. And when I think I'm being dramatic, I back off. However, Captain had called me passive-aggressive, which stung because no one had ever said it to me. He was probably right. We usually sat in his big reclining chair in Tawas together, and that evening I decided to sit on the couch by myself. Smartphones can be the demise of relationships, and I felt like the phone was taking precedence over whatever I may have wanted to say. Fortunately, it was resolved that evening.

On a side note, I have been told that I "bury" my feelings like an ostrich sticking its head in the sand—which, by the way, is a myth. I'm also sensitive—although I'm always trying to toughen up. It is just one of those personal things that is a work in progress.

Take Away:

According to *Psychology Today*, "passive aggression often stems from underlying anger, sadness, or insecurity, of which the person may or may not be consciously aware." Ok, I will agree with the insecurity part in my case, and I think we all suffer from a little passive-aggressive behavior from time to time. However, if you find yourself doing it more often than not to people, it's time to get some serious help.

CHAPTER THIRTY-EIGHT

Everybody Dance Now

September–December 2014

September meant the end of the summer and one of the final weekends in Tawas. It also meant football in the suite—Fire Up Chips! We added in something new this September, though. We decided we would dance for the United Way Fundraiser, Dance United. I was unsure what we were thinking, but it sounded fun. Captain and I loved to dance—we still do—and it meant dancing in front of people. No big deal.

Love Letter to My Captain
October 20, 2014

> *First there was "you"*
> *Then there was "me."*
> *And it's truly unbelievable*
> *You and Me became "We."*

So very grateful for the love you give to me. I often think about how crazy and fortunate we are to have this extraordinary love. I don't understand why God looked down on me and said I deserve you. We are so blessed!

What a wonderful few days we've shared. I always wish it was more. I'm having fun learning this dance with you - feeling a little tentative that I'll get it down, though.

I was wondering at this point if Captain and I could go up and freestyle it. We never had any problems dancing like that. Hell, I took a Zumba class once; I never went back.

Love Letter to My Captain
Oct 27, 2014

Hi Lover,

Where is my snuggle bunny?

Oh, how I wish we were lying next to each other.

As I close my eyes, I think of you and our special moments. What a lovely weekend we had, our dance adventure thus far has been fun! I know we will do great, and I realize it's for a good cause, but I'm still a little nervous. I know my Captain will be there to calm me, so that's comforting! With all this dance craze I keep forgetting we're heading to New Orleans! I am Super, Duper, excited to go to the Big Easy with you!

Captain…you are my everything… just need to tell you that again, and I love you very much! Thanks for being so handsome and so loving, and so precious. Thank you for the intimacy this weekend. It was wonderful!

Three sleeps – can you imagine that?

Three sleeps too many, but I'll take it

Thank you for your generosity.

You are in my heart

Team Murray and Provenzano

Forever and a Day!

We were matched up with a local dance studio and an instructor, Karen. We chose the music: C&C Music Factory's "Everybody Dance Now," and had six formal practices with a disco theme. When we could, we practiced at home in the living room at Greenbanks—the nickname for Paul's main house. Costume-wise, Captain looked like a million bucks, with a button-down purple and white striped shirt, silver and black vest, and black pants. Then again, he would have looked like a million bucks even if he wasn't dressed for the event. But maybe I'm a bit biased, haha. Luckily, it was around Halloween time, so I was able to purchase a retro 1970's sequined, abstract-designed dress with flared sleeves and a bit on the shorter side.

On the day of the fundraiser, a local hair salon, Side Door Salon, donated their time for the women—and men—to get their hair and makeup done. I brought my extensions, and we got all dolled up. As our time to dance was approaching, I was getting antsy. Captain had brought along a little flask with Crown in it. We each had a swig, and off we went to line up. The emcee introduced us and read the bios we had provided.

One of the questions was, "What's the craziest thing you've ever done?"

Captain answered, "Going up on stage in nothing but a diaper."

And I said, "Swallowing a live goldfish in college."

The crowd chuckled, and we got in our positions. Once we started dancing, it was fun, and then just like that, it was over. We only missed a couple of steps, not that anyone would have noticed it. Captain added another move I wasn't expecting: A dip at the end. Oh, that trickster of mine.

The emcee praised us for our moves—although Captain stole the show—and I was given a bag with a live goldfish in it.

"Not planning on swallowing this one," I assured the crowd.

Paul and I sat and watched the rest of the dancers, who were all great! In the end, everyone came back up on stage, and the winner was announced as to the most money raised. Drum roll… It was Team Murray and Provenzano! We even got a trophy. I remember going home that night and feeling fantastic. We did something we had never done together, and I felt so connected to my Captain.

P.S. The goldfish lived and went for a swim in the Chippewa River.

The day after, we were slated to get on a plane and head to New Orleans for the Business Valuation Conference, aka Trip #21 (November 7–12).

Love Letter to My Captain
November 13, 2014

Lover,

What a fabulous trip we had to New Orleans! Thank you for choosing me to go with you. I was still on a high from our

dance from the day we arrived till the day we left. How frick-
ing fun was that? I was so nervous, but we pulled it off - and
it looked great too!

I'm so glad we did it. It was for a great cause, and it brought
us closer. I couldn't have been happier with how it turned out;
it was perfect!

I love you, Captain, and we have only one sleep, so close your
peepers and know I'll be there soon.

I Love You Forever, and A Day

XOXO
Your Dancing Princess

New Orleans trip. Back to Bourbon Street, dining, dancing, and taking it all in. We did make some interesting side trips during the time we were there, though. One of them was the Swamp Tour. Seeing the trees growing out of the water and the wildlife, including the alligators, was incredible. There were a few houses, and our tour guide pointed out the bus stop for the school-aged children across the water, traveling only by boat. As beautiful as it was, I was grateful we had actual homes to return to, with driveways and all.

Love Letter to My Captain
November 25, 2014

Oh Captain - My Captain!!

You were such an all-star yesterday. Thank you so much for
everything you did for me. You can't even imagine how lucky
and special I feel when you're standing by my side.

Thank you also for going to the Rainbow Connection Fundraiser and for donating. You have such a huge heart! My Captain is everything rolled into one: strong, intelligent, powerful, kind, generous, empathetic, and so much more! There are moments of our journey when I stop and reflect on what a genuinely good guy you are, and then I stop again and wonder, why me?

I give you all my heart, loyalty, respect, confidence, and every-thing I am. I have so much to be thankful for, and you, my love, are the undeniable pinnacle of it all.

I love you Sunshine - sleep well, and I'll see you in one sleep!

XOXO
Your Princess

The Rainbow Connection fundraiser for children with life-threat-ening medical conditions stirred up old feelings from the past. My niece was diagnosed with leukemia back in December 2012. She was just four years old at the time. I remember thinking how unfair it was that a child so tiny and innocent could be dealt such a cruel card so early in life. I am happy to say that she is in remission and is a healthy, active, and beautiful fifteen-year-old.

Another Thanksgiving came to the Ridgeway house, and Captain was a big help. I still like to put him in charge of the turkey. Isn't that what most men want to do? Personally, I hate sticking my hand inside the cavity to clean it. The only issue we usually have is the big question: Is it done yet? Even though technology and the pop-up thermometer may tell you the turkey is cooked, it may not have that shiny, golden-brown, glistening skin yet. And if it isn't cooked?

Salmonella! Of course, I tend to overcook everything—not purposely. It just happens, haha.

Love Note to My Captain
November 30, 2014

Lover,

Thanksgiving is over. Can you believe it? Thank you so very much for all the help you gave me this weekend. I couldn't have done it without you. Thank you for taking me to urgent care also. You topped the list of things I am thankful for!

I'm sorry if I got a bit emotional the other night. I love you so much and I pray you'll always feel the same about me as we journey down the road. I'm getting older, and my age will slowly creep up. I am trying very hard to stay younger, fit, and beautiful for you, well and for me too :-)

Christmas is approaching, and I'm excited to spend the holiday with you. I Love You Sunshine.

Forever And A Day
Your Princess!

For the life of me, I do not remember why I went to urgent care. Usually, it was for UTIs.

Love Note to My Captain
December 8, 2014

Captain -

As you lay your handsome head to sleep on this, our 59th Anniversary Month, know that I love you so much more than the 1st, 2nd, 3rd, and all the other months up to today. I have been blessed with the most wonderful man in my life.

What a lovely weekend we had, getting ready for Christmas is so much fun with you! Thank you for sharing your holiday prep with me and for your generosity. I still can't believe this will be our fifth Christmas together, and it seems like just yesterday we shared our first. But our journey keeps getting better, with my love for you growing deeper.

Talking about deep, thanks for the intimacy this weekend :-) sharing of yourself inside of myself - I love it! OK, sunshine, three quick sleeps, and I'm back. Don't miss me too much. Just enjoy!

Love You Forever And A Day

XOXO

Despite admitting to it, there seems to be a pattern in my love notes, and I am not proud of it. I was constantly apologizing back then, and the reasons behind why I apologized were pretty insignificant most of the time. You know that saying, "Never go to bed mad," well, I felt as if I had to clear the air if something was remotely off when Captain and I were together. Then, I could go on about the rest of my week until we saw each other again.

Love Note to My Captain
December 12, 2014

Hi Honey -

We're on the Christmas countdown. I know we'll get all of our stuff done. We just need to take a few deep breaths. At least I do lol

I'm so glad you included me and Erica's graduation ceremony. What an accomplished young lady, and so sweet! But she came from you - so who could expect anything less?

I want to thank you again for loving me and accepting me. I love you so much and want you to be my one and only. Every girl wants the fairytale- no matter what age.

OK, sunshine, I'll try not to get so deep. I love you and appreciate you and am grateful for Match.com. You are my travelwithme365, and I love traveling the road of life with you.

Sleep tight my handsome Captain

Xoxo

Love,
Your Princess

Around this time, Paul's daughter Erica graduated from Michigan State University with a master's degree in Marketing Research. I was so happy to be included in these momentous occasions of his girls' lives. Plus, it was always fun seeing Erica, Isaiah, and Isaiah's parents, Floyd and Darnise.

Love Letter to My Captain
December 29, 2014

Hi Lover,

I can't believe Christmas is over. What a whirlwind and oh so much fun! I enjoyed spending time with your babies, plus Kevin and Isaiah. We sure did have the laughs! Thank you, thank you, thank you for my Christmas presents. I love my arrangement from Elliot's Greenhouse and the opportunity to get life insurance for myself so my children are taken care of. I cherish the card and the handwritten note the best —I guess you do love me. :-) XOXO, yes, I know you do!

Your generosity and ever-giving heart I have never known with any other human being. You are one in 1 million Captain. I am so … GLAD, ECSTATIC, HAPPY, and BLESSED you've chosen me!

Thank you again for allowing me to throw the St. Paul reunion party. I know it must have been a bit uncomfortable for you, especially since you had to sit through it and pay for it! Unbelievably fabulous, you are Captain!

Leaving Mount Pleasant is always hard, especially since I love you more today than I did when I closed my peepers last night. Enjoy your downtime because New Year's Eve is coming! I will celebrate the end of 2014 and ring in 2015 while looking forward to our continued journey.

I love you, Captain Paul "Claus."

Hehe
Xoxo

New Year's Eve was spent in Detroit with our friends Robert and Tina. We went to a Red Wings game and spent the evening at The Westin Book Cadillac! More adventures with them to come...

Take Away:

Try something new with your partner that neither of you has ever done before. It will bring new life to your relationship.

Chapter Thirty-nine

Family Time, Parties, and Aruba

January, 2015

Captain and I headed back to Mt Pleasant on New Year's Day, and I brought Charles up with me. He loved hanging out and watching movies in the sunroom, and he loved Captain's cooking.

Love Letter to My Captain
January 4, 2015

Lover -

Are you all tucked in your comfy cozy bed? Without me?? I hope you have sweet dreams and sleep well. What a holiday season it has been! Oh so fun. I hope you enjoyed yourself as much as I did and enjoyed spending it with me as much as I did with you.

New Year's Eve was fun and silly! 2015 brings our 6th year together on our journey, amazing! Amazing that you chose me and amazing that our love is so strong, that this journey has been so smooth, a couple of bumps, but really the ease of our relationship makes us perfect together. We fit.

I hope you have a wonderful productive week and when we come back together again we'll hug and kiss and be so happy! Well, I will. I think you may be too. Sunshine, thank you for being so wonderful and generous with Charlie. You two have a special bond, and I am so grateful. You rock my world Captain and I expect a great 2015 with my Love!

Your Princess

XOXO

We were back in Mt Pleasant the following weekend for Paul's office holiday party—well, post-holiday. These parties were always fun. The themes were unique and incorporated fun games. His colleagues at Robert F. Murray were always super nice to me, too. I enjoyed my time with them because they treated me like a person, not just another girl on my Captain's "Ferris wheel" of dating. That carnival had shut down!

Love Letter to My Captain
January 19, 2015

Lover,

Thank you, thank you, thank you for being so wonderful and understanding, and my ROCK!

Life can be crazy at times and navigating our way through becomes challenging for me. I am not as wise as my lover, and definitely not as calm. Sorry for bringing my crap to our relationship and having it affect my mood.

On a lighter note, thank you for a fabulous weekend and for coming downstate for our work gathering. Also for taking Tom and Lynda with us to the Red Wings game. I love you so much and I can't even begin to tell you what you've done to become the foundation to my world, and bring me to a better place making me a better person.

I will continue to love and respect you and appreciate you for everything you do. You are my heart. Next time we kiss we will be Aruba bound, how exciting!

Love You

XOXO
Your Princess

The destination for Trip #22 was Aruba's beautiful beach and desert landscape in the Caribbean. We went with Paul's friend, Joe, and his wife, Barb, whom I was also becoming close friends with. It is always fun to go on vacation with another couple. It adds a new dimension to travel and new stories to tell and laugh about later. Since we had an early flight to Aruba, we all chose to spend the evening at the airport. Captain and I picked up Joe and Barb on the way, and we headed down I-75 to Flint Bishop Airport. The next morning, the airport was so busy, and we barely got through TSA PreCheck and Clear. Then, Joe realized he had left a piece of luggage at the hotel, so he returned to get it. Luckily, he made it back to the terminal and boarded on time. I remember being so concerned that this trip was going south fast. However, it definitely wasn't Barb's first rodeo!

In Aruba, we stayed at The Rui, an all-inclusive resort on the adults-only side, with privileges to the family-friendly hotel next door. We had a beautiful corner room with extra-large sliding doors and balconies on both sides. The room also had a "help yourself" bar dispenser with rum, scotch, vodka, and whiskey. Now, as you know, that could get very dangerous for me. The beauty of it being all-inclusive was that we did not have to worry about tabs, tips, or the mini-fridge—all you needed to do was show up. The hotel provided entertainment, and one night the boys were coerced—well, not really; they pretty much volunteered—into going up on stage for a silly skit. In the end, Paul and Joe ended up dancing with their shirts off in sparkly vests and bow ties. They were good sports. I recall Barb saying, "*Dear God*," as their hands were in the air dancing to "Who Let The Dogs Out." It was a real hootenanny!

The trade winds on the island kept the atmosphere comfortable. We spent equal time at the pool, touring the island, and even headed out to the famous Madame Janette for an evening of culinary delights with the island's award-winning chef. Dining alfresco definitely made it that much nicer. We had perfect weather the week we were there, too. I had always wanted to go to Aruba, so I was delighted to check it off my imaginary bucket list and add it to my vacation trip list nicely folded in my wallet—it's still there, with frayed edges and all.

Captain's Valentine's Day Card to Me

To My Princess Forever and a Day

No ones loved me as much as you
Nor have I loved anyone as much as I do
I know in my heart our love will never quit.
Cuz we fit!!

Hugs & Kisses and a little more too!

Love Your Captain

Love Letter to My Captain
February 16, 2015

Nighter Nights My Love -

Thank you for the beautiful Valentines weekend together. It was special to me to have been able to feel so connected with you, in so many ways. I love you more this Valentine's Day than our first, I was only beginning to learn the depths of my PBM and his fabulous soul. As I look back I wouldn't change anything. Well, maybe the incidents with me and too much alcohol!

As you move deeper into tax season, I'll be supporting you from the sidelines. I know how important your work is, and I don't want to put extra pressure on you. I'm excited to try to make more money for you, and I'll head back with that goal in mind.

You are my first thought when I wake up and my last thought before I close my peepers.

I love you Sunshine forever and a day

Thank you for being so Wonderful

XOXO

Take Away:

Never ask the front desk at a hotel to hold only one of your bags overnight. You may end up forgetting it the next morning.

CHAPTER FORTY

Adding up the Son-in-Laws

Yep, tax season was yet again upon us, and our weekends were spent in Mt Pleasant. As tough as it was for my Captain with the workload, I loved "just hanging out." We had such busy lives in between; it was nice to decompress. That did not mean we didn't have fun—we had plenty!

Love Letter to My Captain
March 16, 2015

Goodnight Lover -

I'm sorry it was such a quick visit. Crazy/busy time now for both of us. I enjoyed our snuggles and our crazy, hot sex. Most of all just being in the same town with you is what makes me happy. Thank you for the Murray sweatshirt I liked wearing it, you're the fourth leaf to my clover!

OK sunshine sorry I have to run.

I love you immensely, and always will!

Thank you for picking me!

XOXO

Till our lips meet again

This is a little peck!

Captain was able to come downstate a couple of times during this period. One visit was for Autorama. This was an extra special one. My dad had his classic 1947 Mercury Coupe that he had restored and entered in the hot rod section. He was so proud of it, and rightly so. He'd spent so much time on it, and it was show-worthy. Now, we actually had a place to hang out with the car gang. That was a monumental year for Dad as he'd always wanted to bring a car to Autorama. Dream accomplished!

A couple of weekends later was Maddy's bridal shower. Of course, Paul had to come. However, he did not understand why because, as he said, "*Isn't this what the ladies do?*" I laughed and replied, "*Yes, but you're forgetting how my family works. My dad, uncle, sons, ex-husband, and you will be at a special table off to the side because how could we not have you there celebrating this monumental event?*" Captain, of course, agreed because he knew how much it was important to me—and it didn't hurt that we served alcohol!

Love Letter to My Captain
March 23, 2015

Hi My Handsome Captain,

I can't keep thanking you enough for all of the wonderful things you do for me. You keep giving and giving and I'm always amazed. Thank you thank you thank you for coming in for the shower, and also being so accommodating with the schedule, not to mention you treat Madeline and Cody so well. I think I know, no I do know, you are a gift from heaven. I just don't know what I did to deserve you.

BIG CONGRATULATIONS on your beautiful daughter, Diana and her soon to be-you're 1st son-in law- Kevin. She picked a nice guy, and one that I know loves her very much and will give her the world. What more could you ask for? So many exciting things happening in our lives right now. You, my Quality of Life Award winner:-) well, you didn't have to win an award for me to believe you're award winning material. :-) It's the icing on the cupcake. I'm glad I'll be there to share it with you.

So, for now I say goodnight.

3 sleeps till we're naked again with each other, and no, I won't be naked with anyone else prior. :-)

I Love You to the Moon and Back and a little further.

Forever and a Day -

Xoxo

Thank you for Rocking My World!

These were definitely exciting times for our families. We had a wedding on the horizon—in just a few months—and now another engagement! Kevin proposed to Diana in one of their favorite speakeasies, Please Don't Tell in Manhattan. They FaceTimed us right after. I will never forget Diana saying, "*I'm so excited for this life!*" It came right from her heart and was authentic, and as I said, "*It's something I'll never forget.*"

Love Letter From My Captain
March 30, 2015

Hi Lover -

Thank you for the fabulous weekend. It was delightful and relaxing. It felt so good to be with you this weekend. You are so wonderful and so successful, and deserving of your award. You are so humble and expect no accolades. God gave this earth quite a gift when he made you. He also gave all the other chicks before me the gift of you too. But now you're mine!

We're almost done with March. Can you believe that? Looking so forward to Cali honey and spending some downtime with my Captain. I'm sorry I can't make this love note longer.

I Love You Baby!

Xoxoxo
Your Princess
One Sleep

Yipee!

Captain had won Mt Pleasant's United Way Quality of Life Award for 2014. We were notified in advance, so Captain had some time to prepare a few comments. As I said, he was so humble and graciously accepted it while he thanked the community for being a great place to raise his daughters and have his business. He even included me in the speech!

The next day was The New Venture Challenge at Central Michigan University and reception. Again, Captain volunteered his time to judge—as he had done in the past. From all my conversations with him and what I learned, he was involved through the years, and the bonds he formed with the community and his friends were strong.

Take Away:

If you have the opportunity to get involved in the community, do it. Experiences and relationships make life that much sweeter.

CHAPTER FORTY-ONE

Two Top Shelf Margaritas and an Awesome Hand

Trip #23 catapulted us back to the desert. We flew into Palm Springs on Friday, April twenty-fourth, and were there through to Thursday, May seventh. We rented a sprawling ranch with a pool on a golf course. Diana, Kevin, Erica, and Isaiah were able to join us for six of the days. This was family time. It is generally lovely visiting family any time of the year, let alone when you have access to an outdoor pool and golf. Thank you to Paul's brothers, Dan and Peter, and Peter's wife, Lynda, for living in California.

The boys golfed, the girls shopped, we all barbecued, made cocktails, had dinners out and in, and enjoyed family time and plenty of card playing—euchre, that is. Captain tried to teach us another card game, but I never caught on. I recall one night when I had the best hand ever in euchre—although we had just returned from dinner and possibly had one too many top-shelf margaritas. All I kept saying was, "*This is the best hand!*" It was too bad I couldn't play it. It seemed I needed a Crown and diet first. In all honesty, Diana was trying to get me to drink water, and I decided to throw it over my shoulder, saying, "*I NEEDED a Crown and diet.*" Now, I have mentioned a few times about me imbibing too much. This didn't happen often, but when it did, it was something to be remembered—more likely the next day, as I wished I could forget it. Anyway, that evening, Diana poured me my requested beverage, and I thanked her. Of course, I didn't know there wasn't any crown it in. It wouldn't have mattered since the evening ended for me shortly after that. Thank you, Captain, for taking control and ensuring your Princess was ok. ;-)

Love Note to My Captain
May 10, 2015

Oh Lover,

So many sleeps together, I've lost count, but now I have to stop counting. It makes me a little sad. What a wonderful vacation we had. Thank you for taking me and for spending your vacation with me. Thank you for being my forever and a day. I'm sorry to have caused any issues between us on our vacation. I love you so much, and listening to stories about your past conquests is hard. Thank you for talking about it. I appreciate you and your genuine honesty because it's so important that we can communicate.

What fun I had with the kids, maybe too much fun that night! Thanks for taking care of me. As we move into the next month, I'll try to remain my happy fun loving self, and there's a bunch to do coming up. Please keep in mind the big day on June 19! Thank you for everything you've done for Maddy and Cody and all you do for my babies.

I still can't believe you're my Captain. I must have done some-
thing good years ago, and God knew we'd be together. We Fit.
I hope you have a wonderful week. I'll miss you, all of you. I
hope you golf well. I love your balls and putter. :-)

Oh, and one more BIG thing - Thanks for all the fabulous sex
we've had the last two weeks. It Rocked My World!

Love You, Bunches and Bunches!

Xoxo
Your Princess

Yes, there I go, apologizing again. When alcohol is involved,
one's empathy toward others declines because one will talk freely
when loosened up. I know Captain had a life before me, and I know
he visited Cali with other women. I do not need to know how they
"were" and what he did. It is irrelevant. So, here I am, listening to
one night of this banter, and I think to myself, *What the hell am I*
doing sitting here putting up with it? I could be back in Michigan with
my babies. Now, I will admit that I had had some wine, just enough
to let my Captain know I wasn't happy with the conversation. At
times like this, I wish I hadn't loved him so much. It's awful to say,
but I'm being authentic here. Captain changed my life. I knew it. I
also knew I couldn't keep bringing up the past—it was five fricking
years ago. My head knew better—although my heart was tender, and
the feelings of not being enough were always there. It was no one's
fault. It was something I needed to accept. Something I was willing
to adjust regarding my own thinking.

Love Letter to My Captain

May 18, 2015

Sunshine -

*How can I, I mean really, how can I thank you for every-
thing you've done and for loving me as you do. I shouldn't be
amazed since I feel I know you and your kindness and generous spirit, although I'm always amazed. It's not just what you
do. It's that you do it without any second thought.*

*So, thank you for making my birthday and weekend so special.
What a great day I had yesterday, and it was topped off by
you giving me one more sleep next to you! My bracelet is
beautiful, and I love it, and the necklace too. I love looking at
the jewelry you gave me and realizing how special each piece
is and that you put thought into giving them to me. I LOVE
LOVE it when people comment how beautiful my jewelry is,
and I tell them it›s from you and what great taste you have.*

*I mean, really, how lucky am I? I am the luckiest girl in the
world, and so many people know it. You spoil me so much,
and you know it doesn›t go unappreciated. I hope you understand that my love for you goes so deep that no one outside
of us can ever imagine or realize it. I know people (friends,
family) may think it's silly how over the top my actions are for
you, as in the PBM and the nails, but I don't care. I'd always
do it and will continue because we "fit" and are meant for
each other.*

*I hope you have a wonderful few days, and I'll count down
our sleeps. The next few weeks are going to be crazy. Thank*

you for understanding and accepting my random bouts of "puddling up."

I love you Captain

Forever in a day

You are my everything.

I'm lucky, the luckiest 48-year-old around

XOXO

P.S. Loved sharing your manhood. :-)

Captain does give the best gifts. But, of course, it helps when you have a great jeweler in town. Thank you, Silverburg Finer Jewelers, and Steve, for the excellent customer service and unique jewelry pieces.

Love Letter to My Captain
May 25, 2015

Lover -

Thank you so much for the wonderful holiday weekend and for allowing me to bring Charles! He loves Tawas, as you already know.

I hope the next month goes smoothly for us, as we have so much going on. I pray the excitement and memory-making will only bring us closer. You have been so understanding and giving throughout this whole process. I pray one day that I can do something so wonderful for you to show all of my appreciation, in the meantime, you have my heart and all of its love.

Again what a wonderful weekend. Thanks for the "romp." I definitely needed that — Enjoyed it and hope you did too. Ok, Lover, I must close this love note.

Have a wonderful week, and I'll miss you -

Sealed with a kiss.

Your Princess, 4 Ever & A Day!

The wedding day was approaching, and there were final dress fittings, payments, and other wedding preparations.

Take Away:

If you are ordering jumbo margaritas, especially top shelf, stop at one—if you want to keep your sh*t together, that is.

CHAPTER FORTY-TWO

Mourning and Celebrating All in One Week

Love Letter to My Captain

June 14, 2015

Hi -

Well, it's almost here. I can't believe it! Excited, as you know, although tempered with sadness. Thank you so much for coming down to go to the funeral home with me. It meant so much. I'm still in shock. I feel terrible for Anne Marie and the girls.

Thank you for always being so lovable and loving me back, even when I'm such a girl. The next week is going to be a whirlwind. I'll try not to get too emotional if you'll try to be understanding.

I Love You to the Moon and Back again, and I am so grate-
ful we are together.

Xoxo

On June eleventh, life changed again. The husband of one of my closest girlfriends, Anne Marie, passed away suddenly. It was devastating. Charlie was such a good guy. Our families had become very close, with our daughters being good friends. It was such a shock. I still remember Anne Maire's daughter, Katelyn, calling me to say that her dad had a massive heart attack, and they couldn't bring him back. That was hours after it happened. I still don't know how she made those phone calls. The next day, we went to see Anne Marie and their girls, Katelyn and Gabrielle. There were so many tears and so many memories that flooded back. They were married for twenty-nine years. How is it that one day you are married, and the next, you're a widow? My poor friend buried her husband on Monday, June fifteenth, at Saint Michael's Catholic Church. We returned to the same church for Madeline and Cody's wedding four days later. Katelyn was a bridesmaid at the wedding, stayed for pictures at the venue, and went home before dinner. In all their grief, I could not believe this family was still kind enough to think of Madeline and us and even apologize that they couldn't stay. The character of my friend and her girls speaks volumes.

We each had our own stories with Charlie. My dad was close to him and took his passing hard. They both shared a love of cars and had engineering brains that could fix anything. He and my dad would work on cars in my dad's back garage. My brother, Doug, would tease Charlie and say he was the son my dad never had, as my dad's sons did *not* share an affinity for cars. The Whites were at many family parties and, to this day, continue to be. We'll never forget Charlie and everything he did for us, especially when he came to my rescue after the rolling garage door literally fell apart one morning as I opened it—not good. Many, many memories of a truly giving family.

Love Note to My Captain
June 21, 2015

Captain –

Wow, Wow, Wow!!!

Is it really over? What a crazy last few weeks it's been. Thank you for EVERYTHING!!! And I mean EVERYTHING!!! You know there is no way to thank you enough for being so generous, giving, kind, and AWESOME, and everyone knows how lucky I am to have you in my life. If I ever were to write a story with a fairytale ending, it would be my life right now. I couldn't have dreamt of a love story like ours has been. I'll always wonder how and why God blessed me with you.

I hope you didn't think I was too emotional. I try to keep it together. Thank you for loving me unconditionally and my babies. Your heart is so big, growing with the love you give and outpouring to those you care about.

Now, it's time for us to have some fun and be the wonderful in-love couple we are. It's time for me to focus back on us and work to bring in funds. I'm excited about Traverse City and the many more good times ahead. I love you Captain!

I hope you know how much I do...

Love you always...

Forever and A Day
Your Princess

The wedding was perfect! It was also extra special because Madeline and Cody were getting married sooner rather than later. I wanted my mom and dad to experience their granddaughter getting married and the thought of them one day becoming great-grandparents. Of course, I broke down in tears when I saw my girl walk down the aisle. Madeline looked beautiful and happy. They were surrounded by family and friends who witnessed the vows and celebrated their matrimony with them. It was a lovely reception. Madeline put in so much effort, and it showed because Cody had assisted from afar, as he was still in New York. Everything was perfect—from the delicious meal to the dancing and spingione (Sicilian pizza) midnight snack. From what I could tell, the guests enjoyed themselves, and it was great seeing many of our loved ones all in one place. Additionally, the epic guests at Table Eight will forever live on. You all know who you are. ;-)

Love Letter to My Captain

July 6, 2015

Hot Hot Stuff -

We just spent our sixth 4th of July together. Can you believe it? Thank you for making my fireworks go off! I love our journey, and I love our love story. Thank you for always loving me and taking care of me. I love you to the bottom of the deepest sea and higher than the highest star.

It was all in the "kiss" and still is!

Love you, baby,

XOXO
Your Princess

It was Captain's birthday again! This year, we celebrated his sixty-second in Tawas with Sara, her boyfriend, Erica, and Isaiah. Boating, tubing, grilling, and more card playing mixed in with a few bottles of wine.

Love Letter to My Captain

August 10, 2015

Lover -

*I hope you had the bestest (I know bestest isn't a word) birth-day yet. I think every year should get better and better, just like you***

What a grand celebration, you are my favorite person to celebrate anything with – especially your birthday! He he seriously, that's the truth, but I want to thank you for always being my Captain, loving me, and understanding the situation with my kids. Sometimes it gets complicated when it comes to financial issues, and I appreciate your honesty and want you to understand I never take you or your generosity for granted. I understand your position and apologize if I cry sometimes; I can't help it.

Well, baby, four sleeps and then it's another birthday celebration for you, and cars, lots of cars.

I love you more than you'll ever know. Thank you for the fabulous sex and for the sensational time!

You so turn me on – my man in the yellow pants.

I love you, Captain, Forever and a Day.

The Dream Cruise was coming up the following weekend, and my family would celebrate Paul's birthday at Cindy's house on the prior Friday evening.

Love Letter to My Captain
August 17, 2015

Lover -

Big, big thanks for staying the whole weekend! I'm such a lucky girl. I love you so much, and I hope you enjoy the dream cruise this year and your birthday celebration! I hope I'm the one you always choose to spend your birthday with every year.

I can't believe summer is coming to a close. Where did it go? I apologize for the lack of Tawas time this year and thank you so so so much for investing time and money in the big wedding of this year.

Thank you for the super hot sex. You are such a turn-on to me, as you already know, and the best Lover! Again, how did I get so lucky? You smell good too! 😜

So, in closing this love note, there's no need to tell you how much I hate this part of leaving, but I will again... I HATE THIS PART!!

I'll countdown the sleeps, my love, and miss you. I'll work on my productivity for you because bringing money to you and us feels so good.

I love you Captain

You are forever mine and always in my heart.

Love you bunches

XOXO
Your Princess

Take Away:

Take one day at a time, enjoy the little moments, and know everything happens for a reason.

CHAPTER FORTY-THREE

Road Trip

Love Note to My Captain
September 14, 2015

Sweetheart,

Thank you for the beautiful vacation. Thank you for pampering me. Also, thank you for letting us visit Madeline and Cody and for picking up the tab. You were so kind and generous. How did I get so lucky? Being with you is so easy. It just flows. I hope you feel the same way. I'll miss you this week. I hope you have an excellent shareholder meeting and fun playing golf. I'll be busy at work trying to make and keep deals together. Please be a good boy Tuesday evening. I would be devastated if our love wasn't strong enough. Sleep tight Captain.

Love you

XOXO

First, I cannot remember why I asked Captain to be a good boy on Tuesday evening. It must have been one of those after-hours business events, and since my Captain looked so damn hot in a suit, I wanted to gently remind him he was a taken man. Of course, I think I wrote it playfully… Maybe I didn't! Anyway, I am here writing this book, so whatever I was worried about didn't happen.

Trip #24 was a good old-fashioned road trip with snacks—yes, I have become my parents! We headed to the Poconos (in Pennsylvania) on September 9. It was an eight-hour car ride, and it poured rain for about three of those hours. So, I was a bit nervous on the winding expressways with the windshield wipers at full speed. Captain was cool as a cucumber, though.

I had always wondered what the Poconos was like. Growing up, I would hear stories about couples going there for their honeymoon and taking pictures in oversized Champagne glasses. Our resort was nothing like that. In fact, it was the opposite. It was nestled back in the woods and considered a luxury destination spa. Captain and I like luxury and spas—especially with massages. However, we did not know this place was a retreat resort spa known for "heightened levels of relaxation and well-being." They offered different classes for the mind and body, and the tone of the whole resort was quiet and restful. When we first walked in, Captain started playing with the singing bowls—which I assumed were there for guests to interact with. Either way, I never really know what kind of shenanigans my Captain may pull. Looking back, we did have a beautiful room overlooking the woods, spent some time by the water, ate delicious meals, and thoroughly enjoyed the spa. We didn't know what we were in for but rolled with it. The craziness would ensue soon enough when we left two nights later to drive into Manhattan. Now, that was an experience…

When we reached Diana and Kevin's apartment, we found a place to park on the street, another huge win. This trip was extra memorable since I could see Madeline, too. She and Cody had packed up a U-haul and driven to Manhattan two days after their wedding. Cody was in medical school—although now married, he couldn't stay in his current housing. So, they rented a cute little apartment in Washington Heights, and Madeline was coming back to Michigan in mid-September to finish her last semester of college and then study abroad. They planned it perfectly. Cody would take a couple of weeks and join Madeline during her study abroad in Rome.

Back to Manhattan and the trip… After staying with Diana and Kevin the first night, they walked us to the subway and explained how to get to Washington Heights to see Madeline. Captain and I looked and felt like a couple of tourists. To make things more awkward, I was carrying a large box of requests Madeline had asked for as she'd forgotten to pack them before leaving Michigan, and it was hot out, especially in the subway. What Paul and I didn't know at the time was that the trains change on the weekends. They run on different tracks—or something like that. So, our E became our A, or we were supposed to be on the A that was the E. We had a few minutes before the train came—although we were still unsure—so we waited for the next one. Of course, cell service is not the best underground, so the text messages weren't going through when we tried to contact Madeline. After a while, we had to ask a nice couple how to get to Washington Heights. To this day, I still don't know how we successfully got there; I'm just glad we did. Again, it's something to laugh about now. I was so happy to see where the kids were living, though. It made me feel so much more at ease. Madeline and Cody's apartment was small but perfect for them. It was also a relief to know that

Diana and Kevin were only a phone call away if Madeline needed them.

We spent the next couple of nights having fun with all four kids. We took a fun walking tour of the speakeasies in Manhattan, tasting the interesting craft cocktails. Then, we dined in Little Italy on the street during the Feast of San Gennaro festival. Tidbit: This celebration started in 1926. It has grown to an eleven-day festival. Those Italians sure know how to party. I have to admit that I proudly represent that percentage of my heritage. All in all, the trip was delightful!

Love Letter to My Captain
November 2, 2015

Good night my one and only Lover. May you slumber with visions of me and Manhattans, he he. Thank you for the fabulous extended weekend. I get so spoiled knowing we have so many nights together, and then I have to leave. Luckily I'll be back soon.

I hope your week is manageable. The holiday season is approaching, and I'm looking forward to Thanksgiving with all the kids. Lots of laughs will be had and a few hands of euchre. We have to establish our lead again! I love you Captain!

Thanks for being my everything

Love you so much
XOXOXO

Paul's kids and their significant others came for Thanksgiving in Mt Pleasant. It was always fun when the kids were all together. I loved sitting around the big dining room table and catching up. We would crack open a bottle—or a few—of Cabernet and break into a euchre tournament or play some sort of group game. The evenings were always full of laughter, and this particular Thanksgiving was no different. On Thanksgiving itself, the house was buzzing with preparations. At one point, everyone was out of the kitchen, and I noticed Captain outside on the back patio with Sara's boyfriend. I didn't overthink it, but Kevin came into the kitchen and said, "*Do you know what's happening? Did you hear?*"

I shook my head and replied, "*No, what?*"

"*He's going to propose tonight.*"

"*What? Really?*"

"*It's supposed to be a secret.*"

However, this secret had clearly worked its way through the Greenbanks house, just like the scent of the cooking turkey.

When it was time for dinner, we all sat at the table, including a few extended family members who had joined us that year. Captain got up and said he was going to choose who would be saying grace. He did a shortened version of Eeny, Meeny, Miny, Moe and landed on the soon-to-be-engaged gentleman. Sara's boyfriend said the prayer, turned to her, pushed the chair out behind him, and got on one knee. Well, you can figure out the rest... There were hugs and congratulations and, of course, a photo op! The Thanksgiving dinner tasted much better that year, and the conversations flowed with questions fitting for a newly engaged couple.

Love Letter to My Captain
November 29, 2015

Lover,

Can you believe this weekend is already over? It was such fun with all the kids around, and I'm so thankful for you and that you've included me in your life with your family. I am so blessed, and what a fantastic proposal in front of the family. You now have two daughters who will be planning weddings! How exciting!

I love you, Captain, and I am so excited to have you in my bed next! Also, I am super happy to be getting on a plane with you and leaving my life in your hands, well my destiny, that is... XOXO

I love you more than you know

XOXO Forever and A Day
Your Princess

Take Away:

Do not take the subway in New York on the weekends unless you live there. It is just too confusing.

Chapter Forty-four

Florida, Minus the Flu

Trip #25 was to Fort Lauderdale for another conference for my Captain. We stayed at the Margaritaville Beach Resort, and the weather could have been a bit warmer. We were not shoveling snow or wearing winter coats—although some locals seemed to pull out their winter gear when the temps dropped. I am assuming their blood is thinner down there. Hailing from the Mitten, as some call Michigan, sixty-five and cloudy in December would bring out shorts on some people.

After the conference, we jumped in our rental to head over to the other side of the state to visit Bruce and Sue again. I remember driving across the Everglades with the "Beware of Alligator" signs and fencing. I was also looking for the endangered black panther or maybe a black bear. I didn't see either—although it probably would be random to see an alligator sitting at a fence watching traffic unless you were Lyle The Crocodile.

As always, we enjoyed our stay in Cape Coral and made our trip to the local fish restaurant in Cortez, Star Fish Company. The soft-shelled crab sandwiches are the best!

When it opens at ten a.m., there usually is a line outside. This is an outdoor-only walk-up-to-the-counter-and-order restaurant. The seafood is extremely fresh, maybe even caught that same morning. Just remember to bring cash, as no credit cards are accepted. Captain always says I'd love to see their books.

Love Letter to My Captain
December 14, 2015

Hi Sweetheart,

Thank you for being "the one" in my life. I keep repeating the same words, but they are so true. My world changed the day I met you, and I never realized it could be so awesome and I could be so happy.

Your generosity has reached far beyond me, though, and you've touched so many others in my family and helped in many ways. Thank you for letting us go in on the computer for my parents and helping with all the Christmas gifts. Christmas will be different this year, but I promise it will still be special. I'm so happy we got the extra night together, and I am so glad I made it through Saturday night. You almost lost me!

Sleep Tight
Know my heart is with you!Love You Captain

Your Princess

Since the kids came home for Thanksgiving, they planned on spending Christmas with their significant others' families or back in their own towns. Paul and I planned to be downstate for Christmas Eve and Christmas Day, two long days for my Captain. How would he hold up?

And what happened on Saturday night? I'm not one-hundred percent sure—although during our dinner, which included packaged rice, my jaw on my right side and my neck puffed up and felt numb yet tingly. After some googling, I assumed I reacted to the MSG in the rice. After the Benadryl, all I could do was wait. I was breathing ok, so I didn't panic. Captain was mildly concerned, but we both figured I'd wake up the next day and be ok. Probably not the best move going to sleep, but who said I make good decisions? Wait… deciding to date my Captain was the best decision I'd made in a long time.

Love Letter to My Captain
December 20, 2015

Well Captain,

I'll own it. I am weak. I didn't realize how involved this would be, but let me tell you how grateful I am. I am holding onto the belief that it worked and, in time, my vision will come back. I'll tell you I am a little scared, though. Thank you for putting up with me, my worries, and my needs. I couldn't ask for a better Captain. You are my everything. You know I would do anything for you and care for you in a heartbeat.

It's going to be a crazy few days. I hope yours are relatively quiet and you are productive. Thank you again for taking so much time out of your schedule to stay with me and care for me. I'm sorry I'm such an expensive pain in the butt. Thank you for loving me through it all.

Close your functioning eyes (haha) and drift off to sleep, knowing no one will pester you tonight... Lol...

Forever and Day ... Love You

XOXO
Your Princess

On December seventeenth, I had Lasik surgery. I did not think I would ever be a candidate for it, as my astigmatism was atrocious. I had the CATz custom Lasik courtesy of my Captain. That is a lot of C's... haha. I was concerned since, after the surgery, I had to go home with bandage lenses over my corneas. That was pretty uncomfortable. I wasn't the best patient for my Captain. I just wanted to lay there with my eyes closed. In addition, my vision wasn't as clear as it was supposed to be. I kept telling myself I would be ok, but secretly, I wondered if I had made the right decision.

After four days, the lenses were removed. What relief! My vision didn't get better, though. I could navigate life normally, but my distance vision wasn't the best.

On Monday, December twenty-first, Madeline came home from her study abroad in Rome. I was so excited to hear all of her stories. We even went to the airport and held welcome signs. There were two different areas in the terminal that she could have been arriving from, and yep, you guessed it, we were upstairs, and she was downstairs. It was like rats chasing after Cheetos as we scrambled down the escalator, each with our portion of the "Welcome Home Madeline" sign, and arranged ourselves correctly in line. After realizing my circle

"Home" sign was upside down, what else could go wrong? Well, we saw Madeline through the crowd in her Santa hat. So cute, by the way! The exuberant embrace between her and Cody was so touching. By now, I had flipped my "Home" sign correctly, haha, and she noticed Charles, her dad, myself, and Joseph. I cannot take the credit for the idea; it was all Cody's.

We headed to dinner at PF Changs, and while I was sitting there with all my babies and their father, I remember feeling so grateful because my children were happy, and we were all together.

Christmas Card From my Captain
December 25, 2015

> *To My Bright-Eyed Princess,*
>
> *You are the Best Thing That's Ever Happened To Me.*
>
> *I'm so lucky to have you in my Life*
>
> *To Us - Forever!*
>
> *Captain Loves you Forever and A Day!*
>
> *Love,*
> *Paul*

I love the way Captain signs his name—Paul. The P starts at the bottom, swoops up to form something that looks like the eye on a needle, comes back down, spins off to the left, high and wide, then heads back to the "eye of the needle," leading with another downward slope to form the closure of the P and finishing with a confident upward sweep! It is strange, but I love watching him do it. It's rhythmic and graceful, yet so self-assured. Have I mentioned how much I love this man?

We spent the holiday with my family: Six hours on Christmas Eve at my sister Cindy's house and nine hours on Christmas Day at our house on Ridgeway. Captain was a big help and a trouper.

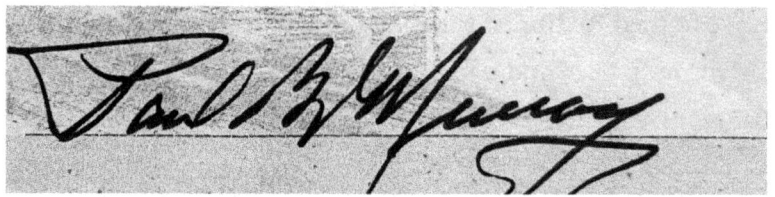

Take Away:

If you want to make your significant other happy, do the family parties, the holidays, and drop-bys. Life goes quickly… then your loved ones are gone. 💔

Chapter Forty-five

Vision of the Seas… How Appropriate

Love Letter to My Captain
January 3, 2016

Hi Lover!

Well, the holidays are over, they went by so fast. Can you believe it? Thank you for making it so special. I had a wonderful weekend with you and love sharing my sleeps next to you. 2015 was a wonderful year spent with my Captain, and as we enter into 2016 I know it will be equally as fabulous and I'll fall deeper in love with you. You are deep in my heart and I wish I would have found you sooner.

I love you Sunshine.

Sleep tight

Xoxoxo

Another year was over, and a new one had just begun.

Love Note From My Captain

January 24, 2016

Dear Princess,

Thank you for remembering my love note and for the artistic picture.

Can't wait to share another journey with my Lover. Hope your day is going well and the same for this week.

Nice job in making Pa & Dubs 60th special for them. (I saw the Devonshire Update). Sorry I can't enjoy today's playoff games with you.:-(

Love You Forever And A Day,

Your Captain

My parents' anniversary was on January twenty-eighth, so we celebrated a few days early at Picanos—an Italian restaurant in Troy. Sixty years was quite a feat, especially these days. My siblings and I tried to make it special since my mom's health was not the greatest, and we didn't know how much time we would have with her. You can only be on oxygen for so many years. Mom had PAH (pulmonary arterial hypertension), which affects the arteries in the lungs. The blood vessels in the lungs thicken and become narrow, making it harder to breath. I had never heard of it before she was diagnosed. I did learn, though, that there is no cure, and it is always fatal. My mom was in a support group that included younger people—even a nineteen-year-old at the time—and was enrolled in a clinical trial drug. However, it only helped for a little while.

My mom used to email all of us kids, even if we had talked to her that day. The subject line always read *Devonshire* (the name of their street) *Update*. I always enjoyed the Devonshire Updates; you never knew what she would email about. This one was written on Jan 15, 2016, at 4:30 a.m.:

> *As I work around the house at this ungodly hour, I thought about Madeline's upcoming birthday.*
>
> *Will she be flying home for the event? I don't think her funds permit it. If she will fly in, let me know so that I will not mail the birthday card to Manhattan. Our baby. I love her so much, that wee little girl scooting under the garage door so she could have the garage to herself, and then slipping in the puddle of oil on the garage door. I actually had to use cleanser to get it off of her body, a bath was not enough!!!! Or the time she slipped her tiny finger in the detergent cup on the dishwasher and tasted the stuff prompting me to call poison control. I would make a nest for her on the sofa and she would get in to take her nap. I could go on and on because they are such fun memories. All three of my darlings are special and I love them so very, very much. Grandmother's are supposed to love them.*
>
> *Unfortunately, I allowed them to sip pop or coffee, which is something I would not do now. Back then it was hit or miss. Oh well, enough of the nostalgia. It's too bad that my health doesn't warrant driving Charles and the other three little people to do special things or to go out to lunch. Everything must be planned days in advance anymore.*

I guess I've been on the subject of the kids too long. Now to get back to my business of taking pills—ha ha ha, and treatments.

OK my child, that's about all for the day. But, did you watch the Debate? At least they are making some sense of it now. I still prefer Rubio of all of them!!!!!!! He and Santorum do put their heart and soul in their convincing arguments. Unfortunately, Santorum would not allow any other religion to practice in peace, so he doesn't have a ghost of a chance. It's unfortunate that I will not live long enough to watch Rubio rise in the Republican Circles.

That's it for tonight for the second time. Goodnight and I love you. Your Mom, XXXOOOXXX

My mom was ever the realist. Boy, do I miss her. I would love to get just one more Devonshire Update.

Love Letter to My Captain
February 7, 2016

Lover –

As we transition into this next work week I'll realize again how fortunate I am to have you as my Captain. What a fabulous trip/cruise we had. How lucky was I to wake up next to you all of those days in a row! I enjoyed our new adventures together, as it makes us grow as a couple. What a beautiful journey we have.

I'm going to miss you so much this week. I'll have to get back into my Ridgeway groove.

I love you Captain with every fiber of my being, forever in a day

Your Princess
XOXO

Trip #26 was a cruise on the Royal Caribbean. We flew into Tampa on Friday and boarded the ship on Saturday. There is something exciting about seeing that big ship in port, knowing you are about to get on it, with exciting adventures awaiting. Our stops were Key West, Belize, Costa Maya, and Cozumel, with a day at sea. Like the other cruise we went on five years earlier, we ate, drank, shopped, and were entertained. And, of course, got off on the islands. However, there is always a bunch of shopping one can do on the boat. But I digress… One of the highlights was when we were in our cabin and out at sea. We turned on CNN to see if Sara was on. She was! It was fun for Captain to see his girl on the campaign trail as one of CNN's political coresspondents.

We enjoyed the islands, but unfortunately, the water became choppy, making it impossible to stop at Costa Maya. In fact, the pools were drained, and I noticed little brown paper bags taped to the handrails of the stairways. Then I figured it out: Thankfully, I didn't need one of those bags, but I was smart enough to head over to where the staff were distributing sea sickness patches.

Captain purchased a pair of cowboy boots in Cancun. When we arrived back in Tampa to disembark, we were held back. Since the boots were made of crocodile skin, the authorities said they were on the endangered species list and not allowed to enter the States. I think they just wanted the boots, though, as they were super cool. As we waited for someone who had to talk to someone—who could tell us we were ok to get off with our boots—we learned a bit more about cruise ships, specifically how many people die on cruise ships and where they are stored. Interesting how conversations can go… Let's just say that I wouldn't want to die on a cruise ship. By the way, the boots got the green light to come home!

Love Letter to My Captain
February 21, 2016

Damn!

I feel like I just blew into town and now I have to go! Super quick weekend, but not lacking a great romp in the hay. You are an awesome lover and I am so so lucky to benefit from it.

I can't believe February is almost over. I guess that's what happens when you're happy and in love! I'll look forward to sleeping next to you again. I feel so safe when we are together. Little skittles, sleeping at the foot of the bed just doesn't cut it, although he is darn precious.

I hope you have a week that's not too stressful. Keep your feet on the ground and your ass off the floor lol. Really, please be careful. I love you way too much for this journey to end.

You are my Rock Captain

Love You Bunches

Sleep tight

XOXO

Your Princess

February came to an end with the annual Autorama car show and a trip to Mexican Village, one of my favorites. Tax season appointments for Captain were filling up, files were piling up, and the miles on the car were going up. However, I wouldn't have changed a thing.

Love Note to My Captain
March 7, 2016

Hi Lover -

Roses are red

Violets are blue

I give you financial grief

But my heart is so true

I'm glad you're on this journey

For there's no one I'd rather be with

So cheers to more excitement, new experiences and deep love on the eve of this, our anniversary

Love you my handsome Captain

XOXOXO

Love Letter to My Captain

March 21, 2016

Hey there good looking –

And no I'm not going out hookin' because I am tookin'

You have all of me sweetheart and I am yours completely, I pray our bond gets stronger and stronger.

Thank you for the lovely weekend, sorry I spent so much money :-(but I am your honey :-(. I love cooking for you and taking care of you.

I hope your week doesn't bring too many twists and turns and door slams :-(always know I'm thinking of you and trying to make your life easier in whatever way I can.

You look so incredibly hot and handsome today. I still can't believe you're mine!

I love you Captain from Mount Pleasant to the moon!

XOXO
Your Princess

People who knew about my background in accounting would often ask if I would work for Captain one day at the practice. I would laugh and tell them, "No way!" I could not handle him being my boss and telling me off if I made a mistake with any number. Nope, for me, the key to a great relationship is: I'll do my thing, and he can do his thing—which may or may not have included a random door slam, haha.

On March twenty-fourth, my dad drove me back to the eye center for an enhancement to my lasik. I was nervous but hopeful. Cindy, my sister, was dating a new guy, Leon—who is not new to us anymore—and she mentioned to him the issues I was having with my eye. It turned out he had the same doctor, and apparently, after the doctor did a touch-up surgery for him, Leon's vision was 20/20! So, here I was, staying positive that the same thing would happen to me.

On the car ride back home, I remember having the pain again—although I didn't need the bandage lenses. Dad took me back to their house, and Mom tucked me in on the couch and asked what else she could do for me. "How about a shot of whiskey?" I replied. And with a smile, she went and poured me one. Yep, my parents were pretty cool. After the shot, I fell asleep, and four hours later, I woke up and read the time on their cable box perfectly. I was so relieved!

Love Letter to My Captain
March 26, 2016

A Tisket a Tasket

What a shame you can't get into my basket :-(

Hope you had a nice and relaxing Easter Sunday. I'm sorry I wasn't here to take care of you. I love you and wish you a calm week, if that's possible.

Stay Handsome My Captain

Love you

XOXO
Your Princess

The following day was Easter Sunday. I headed back downstate and let Captain handle his business.

Take Away:

There is no place like home. I am so thankful for having amazing parents.

CHAPTER FORTY-SIX

A Self-Fulfilling Prophecy

Love Letter to My Captain
April 11, 2016

Wow! We never seem to have unexciting experiences do we?

I want to thank you for coming downstate this weekend, to share the events of "all things Irish "and the many hours of family time. I hate taking you away from your work and what's going on now, especially at this critical time. I can't wait for tax season to be over, for you, and a little for me.

Thank you for the heart to heart conversation. I've never met anyone like you and I guess I wonder sometimes how could you really want me? I gave you all of me, with all my heart and have been and will continue to be so loyal and an open book.I regret that I'm so authentic with my fears and concerns. I wish I could just stuffed them and not care, but I tried and I can't.

I'll never be like anyone in your past, but I will be me, imperfect, but with a commitment to being the best I can. I pray that's good enough for my Captain.I guess everything that happens in our journey is meant to happen, and there's a gift in every situation, sometimes not to be revealed right away. So lover, have a great week and hopefully sweet dreams of lovely thoughts and fabulous sex (with me)! I can't wait for Austin. I'm super excited, trip #26!

I Love You Captain

Forever And A Day

XOXO
Your Princess ❤

Love Letter to My Captain
April 15, 2016

Captain,

I hope I'm your first "journal" entry post April 17th....hehe

It was a super quick overnighter, but thank you for letting me bring the kids up and taking us to dinner. I pray this stress won't be too much these next couple of days for you. My heart and thoughts will hold you close. You are my superman and the glue of Robert F Murray. I have to keep reminding myself of all of your responsibilities because you handle them so well and don't show it to me. You are so smart and so intelligent and so confident in everything you do. I am so blessed to have you as my Captain. You have rocked my world and I continue

*to fall deeper in love with you as the days pass. I can't wait to
see you again.*

I'm so excited about our trip!

I love you forever and a day!

Your Princess
XOXOXO ❤

It was impossible for me to go a weekend or an extended period
of time without seeing my Captain if he was in Mt Pleasant. There
were times I made the trip up and back in one day. It was doable—
although I was younger then. :-)

On Sunday, April seventeenth, we celebrated Madeline's graduation from Aquinas College and Cody's birthday. I love having parties.
My mom was a great host, and my sister and I picked up the love of
entertaining.

Love Letter to My Captain
April 27, 2016

Captain,

*Another tax season and vacation wrapped up! I hope I wasn't
too much of a burden these past few months. I have to keep
reminding myself how much responsibility you have, because
you handle it so well and leave it at the office when we're
together.*

*Thank you for the wonderful vacation. I really enjoyed Austin
and being with the kids. They're all so much fun. I hope you
were able to unwind and relax.*

I am aware that the "newness" of our relationship may have changed into a "comfort" level, but please don't let it become something that's just assumed or taken for granted. I seriously give 110% and still make you my Captain in every aspect of my life and I do it because I love you, and wanted you to know that.

I know my looks have changed and I'm getting older and I can't compete, nor do I want to, with other women. I guess I'm just mourning the PBM that was always so crazy about me. What can I do differently? How have I changed or added to this?

I don't want to bring you stress or drama, but I also don't want our relationship to become stale or have you grow tired of me. It would have been easier for me just to bury it and not risk upsetting you, but you've always told me not to gunny-sack. I value us, and want us always to communicate. You are the love of my life and I want to preserve that, while feeling that you're crazy about me too.

I love you Captain

Forever in a Day

XOXO

It is funny how when you worry about something, it may never happen—although maybe you have brought energy to the "thing" and actually believe it, even though that "thing" may not have happened, or maybe you misread it. Or is seeing believing?

Trip #27 took us to Austin. Captain and I met Sara and her fiancé, his parents, and Erica and Isaiah. Sara was getting married the following year in Austin, so she invited us to a tasting event at her future venue. Erica and Isaiah were also living in Austin, so we stayed with them. Captain had just come off tax season and could finally catch his breath. We had fun checking out Austin and spent time on Rainey Street bar hopping and dancing.

My Captain appreciates beautiful women. I know all men look, and that is ok. I mentioned this earlier in the book. It's human and natural. Women do, too. I believe we conceal it, though. However, Captain does not. He's a turn-the-head–at-the-neck looker. It was so frustrating when it would happen. As my friend Tom would say, "Carol, you don't want to be with someone boring." Oh, Tom, you were always so right. I haven't figured out if my reaction to Paul appreciating other women's beauty was insecurity/jealousy or me just feeling sorry for myself.

Relationships take work. No one wants to be taken for granted, nor do they want to experience the waning of a relationship. I realize all relationships will eventually end "the honeymoon phase" or "I'm being on my best behavior" phase. I wasn't ready for it yet. Captain was so much a part of me, yet at times, I swear he didn't know I was standing right next to him.

I was grateful to go to Austin. It was my first time, and yes, I waited for the bats to come out from under the Congress Avenue Bridge at sunset. It was such an amazing and unusual sight.

Take Away:

Boys will be boys, and if the behavior is unpleasant, say something.

Chapter Forty-seven

The Seventh Step

Love Letter to My Captain

May 8, 2016

Hot, Hot Stuff!

Happy Happy Anniversary!! The train keeps rolling, and what a wonderful trip it's been. :-) Thank you for my gorgeous Mother's Day flowers. They're beautiful like your heart. I am the luckiest girl in the world. Thank you for picking me, and "cleaning me up"…lol…surgeries, botox, fillers… not letting me live under a bridge…and everything else!! My heart belongs to you. Please don't ever forget that feeling and the love from when we first met. I pray you never take me for granted and my loyalty to you. You still and will always be my Rock Star!

Love You Forever and A Day!
Xoxox

Love Letter to My Captain

May 16, 2016

Captain,

Guess What??

I'm super nuts about you! Yes it's true, there's no one but you, you are my sun, my moon, my stars in the sky, and everything in between!

What a great weekend lover. I really really enjoyed it. Thank you for making me feel so special. Thank you for being so hot and lighting my fire, all I have to do is look at you. I love our little adventures, I guess I am not the only one who gets wet.. hehe.. So glad you didn't drown, Ah..the dangers of mushroom hunting. I would have given you mouth to mouth.

Thank you for being the breadwinner. I'm always amazed at how intelligent you are and how you make such smart decisions. You really, really, really are very unique – and you are MINE! Hallelujah!

So as the trees bud and the flowers bloom, may our seventh spring/summer season bring another fabulous chapter in our journey together. I am forever grateful for you, your kindness with my family, your generosity, and the way you kiss me tenderly.

I Love You Captain!

XOXO
Your Princess

We headed to Tawas again on Thursday, May twenty-seventh, for the Memorial Day weekend. It was the beginning of our summer season there, and when we saw the gang from the marina and caught up with everyone. It was always an exciting time... Although, this year, we would experience loss on the seventh step.

Love Letter to My Captain
May 30, 2016

Awww Sweetheart –

Again I'm so sorry about the loss of your little Pedro. I'm glad I was there with you both, he was so special to me also. You are so strong and made such levelheaded decisions. I'm glad you're my Captain. No I'm ECSTATIC you're my Captain!

I hope you have a relaxing couple of days and you golf great tomorrow! Thank you for being so giving with Charlie and allowing him to drive the boat, you can tell how much fun he has. My two favorite "C"'s!!

I Love You Captain from my PBM's on my toes to my PBM's on my thumbs and everywhere in between. You are my heart and my soul and my Silver Fox. I Love Our Journey Together!

See you in 3 sleeps!

Captain's elderly Jack Russel, Pedro, had been having episodes of passing out or seizures. One time, we were at Ridgeway on the deck, and I remember him falling straight over. Captain jumped up, but

Pedro wasn't responsive and didn't seem to be breathing. Captain told him he loved him and all that other stuff you say when you're with your beloved pet at the end. I guess Pedro heard because he picked up his head and looked at Captain. It was sad, and yet Pedro was still bluffing with us. He loved attention, even so much that he sometimes sat and raised one of his front paws, insinuating it was hurt. We would leave the room, and then he'd have the other one up when we came back—silly, lovable Pedro.

Pedro had a good life. He wandered the property and the banks of the river at Greenbanks and played in the Bay at Tawas, catching balls. He was smart and knew how to escape when he and Sully, Paul's golden retriever, were contained, leaving only enough room for him to get through. That evening in Tawas, I remember giving him one of my chicken strips. He ate it and curled up underneath the reclining portion of the couch. Captain always said that when something happens to Pedro, Sully would let us know. We went upstairs for bed, and Sully followed. This wasn't unusual.

When I headed downstairs in the morning, I noticed little Pedro lying across one of the steps; it was the seventh step. He must have passed sometime during the night. We felt so sad. Captain wrapped him in a blanket, and we tried calling a few local vets to see if we could get him cremated. Unfortunately, that wasn't going to happen in Tawas on a Sunday of Memorial Day weekend, so we decided to pack up and drive back to Mt Pleasant. Charles and I took Sully, and Captain did the drive back, just he and Pedro. Remember the box freezer I saw when I met Paul? Poor Pedro had to stay there until Tuesday.

Love Letter to My Captain

June 5, 2016

Hi Sunshine,

You are the light shining at the end of a tunnel. You light my path and are there guiding me along my way. Thank you for bringing sunshine into my life. We have so much fun together and you make the serious times in life "doable". I'm never worried as long as I know my Captain is there.

Thank you for the nice relaxing weekend. I really enjoyed planting the flowers with you. Your yard looks fabulous and I'm glad you have a beautiful retreat right outside your door. I hope you have a stupendous next few days and an even better few days after that- when we're together.

I Love You Captain

You are my Forever and A Day! ❤

Take Away:

When your significant other has a pet, sometimes you see into their heart in ways you did not expect.

CHAPTER FORTY-EIGHT

The Euchre Trophy

Love Letter to My Captain

July 11, 2016

Goodnight Lover –

Just to be clear, you are my one and only "winning" golfer, and everything else. What a lovely weekend and how fun it was to be on your arm Friday night. You make me look good. :-) You are by far the most handsome man I've known and I still can't believe you've chosen me. Please keep me and love me, and share that ever giving, loving heart with me as you've been. I'll always try to keep you happy and love you with everything I have. It's been a fun summer so far and I believe we'll continue to enjoy it! Thank you again for your generosity and taking care of me. It's been an awesome 6 1/2 years and it will only get better as our journey continues. Counting the sleeps till you come to Ridgeway!

I Love You Captain With Every Bit of Me!

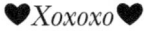*Xoxoxo*

Captain golfed on a league in Mt Pleasant and played in different outings. I would say he was a great golfer, but I do not play, so my expertise is limited. I have tried it, though—and I usually start cussing when I can't hit the ball, ha ha. I've always wanted to play golf with my dad, too; however, by the time I finally asked, it was too late. Dad decided to put away his clubs as his health was declining. I regret how much I waited. It is beautiful being out on a course. It's so tranquil, scenic, and green. The opportunity to see my hot Captain swing a club, showing his prowess and power, was just priceless.

Love Letter to My Captain
August 1, 2016

Thank you Captain for being the love of my life. Thank you for making me smile and telling me I'm beautiful. I feel so special to be your gal, I hope you feel as proud as I do that we are partners! I am excited for your birthday and our trip. It's so special to see the babies, well, adults now lol. We are so lucky to have the ability to do all these wonderful things together.

Thank you for opening up my world. I love you immensely for so many reasons, not just because you're so handsome and super smart, but because you have such an unending spirit of giving. You're a fabulous man, Paul Benjamin Murray, and an experienced one at that...hehe. I'm glad for so many reasons, but most importantly to be able to call you mine! XOXO

I Love You Captain
Your Princess

Trip #28 took us to Washington D.C. for Captain's birthday celebration. The girls, including Madeline and Cody, met us there. Captain and I and Madeline and Cody had rooms at the Hotel Washington, and Diana and Erica stayed with Sara. The Hotel Washington has some of the best views of D.C. from its rooftop bar, VUE. We indulged in cocktails, had spirited conversations, took a boat tour while sitting on the top deck while it was only one-hundred-dred degrees that day, and, of course, played euchre in the hotel lobby. Madeline and Cody ended up taking home the trophy, which is about five inches tall. It is a fine, golden plastic cup with handles mounted on a stand and sharpie writing on the plaque that states **MURRAY EUCHRE CHAMP**. Side note: This is a coveted trophy. In 2021, Sara had it proudly displayed in her and Nick's penthouse apartment, along with her Emmy, for breaking news for CNN's exclusive coverage of the raid and arrest of Roger Stone.

The balance of August was filled with Tawas weekends and the annual Woodward Dream Cruise.

Love Letter to My Captain
August 29, 2016

Hi Lover,

What a nice couple of nights in Tawas. Thanks for the great sex! I love when you kiss and touch me, it's electric. Like I said I still get that great "oh my gosh" feeling when I look at you, as I did back when and I pray I still catch your eye!!

Have a great couple of days, and try to relax at night when you're back home. You have so much on your plate. I'm sorry if I forget sometimes.

I Love You Captain so much, you'll never quite grasp it, but try!

XOXO
Your Princess

Take Away:

If it is one-hundred degrees and you think a boat ride will cool you down, avoid sitting on the sun deck while on a ferry boat that goes thirty miles per hour!

CHAPTER FORTY-NINE

Family Means Everything

September, 2016

We took one of our last few trips to Tawas for the season. Back home in Mt Pleasant, the football games were beginning, and we were entertaining again. The fall colors were always beautiful, and the road trips up I-75 gave me a chance to see the changing seasons in all their glory.

Love Letter to My Captain
September 5, 2016

Lover,

Sorry for being such a spendthrift. I'm trying really hard, but sometimes it just doesn't work and I go negative. Thank you so much for letting me take the boys to Cedar point. They really did have a great time and I enjoyed spending time with Charles.

I know we are a team, but you always have to bear the burden of me. I'm sorry for that. I know we have an unconditional relationship in regards to me being able to work "full-time "and bring more to the table. Thank God you're so smart, successful and make great decisions! And thank God for loving me the way you do.

Thank you for inviting Cindy and Leon to Tawas. It was nice to see them happy and relaxing. Tomorrow starts the beginning of regimentation, back to school year schedule! As crazy as it sounds, I like it! Not many years left of me taking care of Charles and getting him to school. I know the next couple of years will go by so fast.

Thank you also for helping me with the invites to the party. I want this to be special for Dubba, she deserves it. We'll have fun! Super excited for the wedding I have to get my dress!

Love You xoxox

Diana and Kevin's wedding on October first in Colorado Springs was only a few weeks away. It was such an exciting time, and our plates were full, as my siblings and I were also planning an eightieth birthday celebration for my mom the weekend after we were coming back from Colorado. Now, Captain will be the first one to tell you how good I am at spending money—although he'd also tell you I spend it on others, events, or obligations, and, at times, myself. I did end up purchasing a dress for Diana's wedding… But it was on the clearance rack at Lord & Taylor, less than $100, and I loved it!

Love Letter to My Captain

September 12, 2016

Goodnight my beautiful lover,

Thank you for the fun weekend, it always goes by super fast.

How I love being in public with you and to be able to be on your arm. I'm such a lucky gal. I'm sorry I've been so expensive lately, with the wedding and now my mom's party, I know it gets to be a bit much! I hope you don't harbor negative feelings about that and love me less.

Sometimes I sit back and realize how blessed I am in all aspects of my life. As of today, right now, both my parents are alive, my kids are happy, and I am in a fabulous relationship that allows me to live in a great home, drive a nice car, and live well! Really well, but most importantly I found someone who I can be me with and who I love so much and loves me back. So I'll take today and be grateful and live in today. I'll try not to think about what my tomorrows look like and realize that whatever they hold – you'll be by my side to hold me.

I love you Captain and realize how busy and stressed you are. You do handle it all well though. I hope you have a good week and enjoy the next few days that Erica is here. She's such a sweetheart, thanks for the fabulous ribs, oh they were so good! Yum

I love you sunshine forever and a day and then some!

XOXO
Your Princess!

♥

As I type this, I remember writing that part about my parents being alive. I am so happy they were a part of our lives together for as long as they were here. They loved my Captain.

Love Letter to My Captain
September 19, 2016

Sunshine –

I wish I could be laying beside you to take care of you and just be there, when you had a rough day, which I know you had today. I'm glad I was able to see you at lunch today! You're so handsome and I still get all googly eyed when I see you!

Good luck this week with the retreat and the draft. I'd always retreat with you and you are forever my first pick!

I love you Captain. Soon you will gain a son-in-law! I'm so excited for this wedding for everyone!

Love you Captain

XOXO
So much!

*Thank you for a great weekend and thank you for coming
down on Thursday night to see Joe play!*

You are My Rockstar!

My son, Joe, was in a band that performed at Saint Andrews Hall
in Detroit. Even though we are the "parents," I believe we can be
cool sometimes. I will always support the kids in their musical and
creative endeavors. Captain also had the annual Robert F. Murray
Shareholder retreat, and the Detroit Red Wings ticket draft with the
guys who held the combined season tickets. It was going to be a busy
week for him.

Love Letter to My Captain
September 25, 2016

(Written on a columnar worksheet)

Hi Lover,

You're in my column- lol ....♥

*I am so excited for the wedding and to travel to a place I've
never been with you!. You're such a special man and I'm so
lucky to have met you. I give you my heart and everything
else. I wish I had more to give you, and I know that I could
never repay you for everything you've done for me, but give
you all the love I can and continue to treat you as the love of
my life and the Captain at my Helm! We have such a blessed
life, and I can't believe I'm your Princess, yes I still can't
believe it! OK my handsome, tan man and hot hot stud, two
sleeps and then I see you again!*

Love you baby

XOXO

♥

Take Away:

There are moments in life when everything is perfectly in line and you are happy. Cherish those moments.

CHAPTER FIFTY

Wedding Bells and Trip #29

Captain came in the evening before we flew out. We had this tradition of going to one of our favorite restaurants, J. Baldwins, the night before we would travel out of town. We'd have a cocktail and a bite to eat, sit at the bar, and talk about the upcoming trip. I loved every part of preparing for these trips while the anticipation would build.

We stayed at The Mining Exchange in Colorado Springs. It is a boutique hotel built in 1902 as a stock exchange for local mining companies. There is even the original safe on the fourth floor that is now being used as a housekeeping closet. The lobby was charming and comfortable, and the alley attached was intimate. We spent time in both visiting with family and friends. Kevin's parents hosted the welcome party at their beautiful home. It was great to meet all of Kevin's family, and his parents, Keyes and Carol, were so welcoming.

The wedding was held at The Pinery at The Hill and it was simply lovely. Captain spoke about Diana when she was a little girl and included a cute video of her with a bug—hence her nickname

Nannerbugs. It was a joyous event, and the happiness on Diana and Kevin's faces said it all.

Love Letter to My Captain
October 4, 2016

My Captain,

You gained a son-in-law this weekend, and a really good one also! What a fabulous time we all had and with no drama.:) Your little girl was just beautiful and of course you know you were the most handsome man there, my Silver Fox! Everything came together perfectly and we have great memories in photos/ video documentation! Thank you so much for making it possible for my kids to come. You're always so generous and inclusive.

I'll say it again and again how lucky we are to have such a blessed life and family, but I know it's not just luck, it's what we put into it. You have done such a great job as a father and it really, really shows. You've amassed great success in business and your family. You've done it right Paul Benjamin Murray!! 😄

I'm so blessed and grateful to have met you and to be allowed into your world. You could have picked anyone, and you chose me. My heart is so full of love for you. Your speech at the wedding was just perfect. The video clip really topped it off. You looked so handsome up there and spoke of your Nannerbugs with such tenderness. Erica did a fantastic job also. Those two are close and share their little cat squeaks lol. Sara looked beautiful and spoke her reading like a true professional. She's just so good at what she does! It will feel like a blink of the eye and then it will be her turn. It was such a great weekend.

I love making memories with my Captain. I hope I made you look even better than you did by being on your arm. Lol I wanted to look good for not only me, but for you. I wanted you to feel like even more of the silver fox than you already were, if that's even possible hehe

I could keep going on, but I better wrap this up. I love you Captain and I'm so happy for your Diana, and her new hubby, Kevin. Well we'll make many more memories along the journey.

Love you forever and a day Captain

Thank you for making me your Princess

XOXO

♥

Love Letter to My Captain
October 24, 2016

Hey there Love of MY Life and Captain of My Ship –

What fun we've had the past few days. I think I'm getting too old to keep up with such an arduous party life… I love spending time with you, it never gets old. Thank you for letting me shop for Maddy and Cody, they're good kids and they really appreciate the boxes we send and the support they get. You give so much of yourself and your treasures that the laws of the universe, can only keep giving back to you tenfold plus.

You are an amazing man, Paul Benjamin Murray, and I'm lucky to share in this part of your life journey with you, our journey...

I hope you have a good week and please don't get too stressed. It's not good for your heart, or your head. Sleep tight lover, and see you in a few days.

XOXO
Yours Forever and a Day
Princess

Mt Pleasant was my "playground." At times, it would seem as if I was on my own special vacation from the stressors of my life downstate. This particular Saturday, we had the Robert F. Murray wine tour. We all boarded a bus and headed up north to Traverse City to see some of the local wineries and distilleries. That meant sampling—a good deal of sampling! I wish I could say it was the only day of imbibing that weekend; however, that would be shamefully untrue.

Friday evening and Sunday were spent with friends, cocktails, and cheer. Sometimes, I would need to go back home to dry out! Remember, I had never led a lifestyle like this before I met Paul. I was loving all of the new experiences and camaraderie—although it often came with a price the next morning...

Take Away:

Always eat when you drink! And when you drink, the optimal word and action associated with the evening's festivities should be "pace."

CHAPTER FIFTY-ONE

The Speaker, the Student, and the Swamp

Love Letter to My Captain
November 1, 2016

Goodnight Sweetheart,

We've been so lucky to have so many sleeps together lately. I love sleeping next to you! What a great weekend and fun day yesterday. You must be so proud of Sara! I mean really, she's following a presidential candidate! You can't get much better than that! You raised all of your babies to be remarkable adult. Of course, it wasn't just luck. You spent the time with them, they're so lucky to have you as their Papa.

Can you believe we're going on our 30th trip! Yikes! I guess you really do love me :-) I'm so excited since you know how much I love to travel with you. I hope you have a great couple of days and will be together again into sleeps! Thank you for being my Captain and being so good to my babies. I'll have another check for you when you come back :-) sleep tight my love

XOXO
Your Princess

♥

We were heading to Nashville again for Trip #30. This time, it was just Captain and I, and we were staying at The Gaylord Opryland Resort and Conference Center. I love this resort! Captain had the annual Business Valuation Conference—although, as usual, we added a few days for sightseeing. Now, firstly, if you ever get the chance, stay at the Gaylord. It is just beautiful. The resort's interior is filled with lush greenery, lit up beautifully in the evening, and you can stay in a room with a balcony overlooking the breathtaking views. Secondly, take a swamp tour; it was amazing, and if the weather permits, the General Jackson Showboat Dinner Cruise on the Cumberland River is very entertaining.

As this trip was in 2016, it was a presidential election year, and we had filled out our absentee ballots in Michigan prior to leaving. The evening of the election, though, was a long night. Finally, around one a.m., we turned off the TV. The next morning, I woke up to a text from Charles, sent earlier in the middle of the night, announcing who won the presidency. National events—or even world events—always seemed to happen when we were on vacation. Of course, we were on vacation a lot! I know; I am a lucky gal, and I appreciated every trip.

During Captain's conference, one of the speakers took a liking to him. Paul told me she would call on him and share small talk. I was not threatened per se—as I knew he was with me—

she never knew his relationship status. So, when the conference was over, she invited him to spend the rest of the day with her. Basically, he said he had plans already. However, why do men do that? If a woman is asked the same question, I would venture that their reply would be "Thank you. It's very kind of you, but I'm in a serious relationship." Right? Do men want to leave their options open? Are they being kind? Do they feel their answer is true, so it's appropriate and good enough? Maybe I'm in the small minority who need that affirmation. Or maybe I'm so in love that I wanted to share it with anyone who would listen. Why should I expect someone to be so crazy in love after six years? Was I asking too much?

Love Letter to My Captain
November 29, 2016

> *Goodnight Sweetheart,*
>
> *-Wow-Wow-Wow-*
>
> *-So many days together in November-*
>
> *And you didn't even tire of me- (I think)*
>
> *My Love, My Heart, My World-*
>
> *Does that scare you?*
>
> *I'm sorry, I just love you so much and can't even imagine my life without you. I hope I am not too much of a burden. I know I'm an impulsive shopper, talk too much, and overly sensitive and cost you time and money! I do have some good qualities though. :-)*

Thank you for sharing Thanksgiving with me. I am so thankful for you and our relationship. I never mean to bark at you – I didn't think I did. I always want to be able to talk to you and not gunny sack. I'll try to approach it in a different way when I need to talk to you.

One more day in November and then Bam December! Another holiday season and cheer! I know it will be an enjoyable one, so much to be grateful for and appreciative of. I'm so excited your babies are coming in, we have such fun with all of them. You are a blessed father, and rightly so with the guidance and upbringing you gave them.

So sunshine, sleep tight and enjoy your heating pad tonight. I know you'll be sharing the bed with another blonde, but I am OK with that one. :-)

I love you Captain

See you in three sleeps
XOXOXO

After Pedro passed, Sully came into his own. He did not seem to miss Pedro much as now he got all the treats and could sleep on the bed with Captain!

The holidays came and went as quickly as they usually did. We spent New Year's Eve at Ridgeway with my kids and their dad. Captain made a nice dinner. One of the many qualities I loved about him back then was that he never said no when I wanted Ludovico to share time with the kids at parties or get-togethers.

Take Away:

Sometimes, we just need to believe in things we cannot hear or see. We have to go with our gut and believe all things happen for a reason.

CHAPTER FIFTY-TWO

A New Me

Love Letter to My Captain

January 2, 2017

2017!!!

Wow Captain –

A new year, a new chapter of our journey together. Can you believe this is our 7th year? My love for you just keeps growing and growing. I've been so blessed by all your generosity and unselfishness, I can never repay you. I have such a charmed life and you gave me that!

I pray you're still as infatuated with me l as I am with you. I'll never ever forget the beginning of our journey together and falling so deeply in love with you.:) As I think back I know I am the luckiest girl in the world! I pray I'm always enough for you . I'll never be a 20 something but I do have a huge heart and will always love you and do what I can to take care of you. My heart belongs to you. :-) ♥

Thank you for helping (in all ways) for my dad's car guy get together. You know I love entertaining and how much my Dad and my Mom mean to me. Thank you for always understanding. I hope you have a good week and I'll count down the sleeps . I love you forever and a day and then some.

Xoxo
♥*Your Princess*

During Christmas and New Year, I invited some of my dad's friends and their spouses over for an evening of fun, food, and conversation. These guys were my dad's car-gang group. They would meet every Saturday morning for breakfast, attend car shows together, help each other out on their classic cars, and, all in all, were good friends. I loved how they would check on Dad. Later on, in life, after Mom passed, they were so caring; they'd call and stop by. These were good guys, and when one would pass away, it was a painful reminder that we're only here for a short time. My dad outlived a few of them, and I can imagine them now, gathered together someplace beyond the stars…

On January eighth, Captain and I celebrated our anniversary. I remember being chided by friends about the seven-year itch. Even though I didn't believe that to be true for us, we weren't married, so it was still in the back of my mind.

Captain gave me a card on our anniversary (Jan 8, 2017) with a picture of two squirrels that looked like they were dancing. The printed front said: *It takes two to tango.* Inside, Captain wrote: *Didn't we do that already?*

He also wrote:

I'm so lucky you're mine.

Love You Princess
Captain

Love Letter to My Captain
January 8, 2017

7 years Wow!

In seven years you've given your heart to me along with your means. You gave me the gifts of a flat tummy, big new knockers, a car, a house for me to live in, helped with my daughter's wedding, new and improved peepers and so so much more financial support for myself, my babies and my extended family. I could never thank you enough. OMG, did I mention all the trips- all 30 of them! I've lived an unbelievable existence these past seven years and all because of you. Oh... also the investment accounts for the kids, and the investment in Charlie and in Joe. The list could go on and on. I'm amazed that you would do all of this for me!! You did and continue to support me. I never take it for granted and many nights before I fall asleep, I thank God for you and recall how wonderful you've been to me. The other nights I probably just fall asleep too quickly to finish my prayers.:) You are always in my heart. As you enter into your busy season I pray you'll be somewhat relaxed and allow yourself to destress or I'll suck it out of you! Hehe

I love you Captain

You are my everything and everything I have and what I am today is because of you.

I Love You Sweetheart.

Xoxo
Forever And A Day
F.A.A.D.

Captain really was all in financially. As I mentioned earlier, he paid for Charlie to go to Florida for the modeling/entertainment opportunity. For Joseph he fronted the money for his band to build a sound studio in one of the member's basements. They formed an LLC and made monthly payments to Paul until he told Joe he was going to forgive the loan. By this time, only two members were left in the band who were carrying the load that four used to. The boys were ever so grateful, and so was I. Captain said, "Joe's a good kid, and he's shown that by making the payments for the years he did."

Love Letter to My Captain
January 16, 2017

Captain –

Yahoo!

Get me out of this zoo of crazy coldness!

Take me to the beach and show me your manhood!

So excited about our 31st trip! What a wonderful way to start 2017! I'm excited to spend some time with you and work in a bit of your real estate investment work-:)

Thank you for the nice, relaxing and snuggling weekend. I love knowing that when I'm here and you come home from the office I can take care of you. I hope you enjoy it as much as I do. I'll say my prayers and continue to thank God for giving you to me and I'll pray you sleep well without me. :(

Oh Baby- see you in I think 4 sleeps back in Clinton Township. I hope you can still come down. I love you sunshine so much!

Thank you for giving me what I've never dreamed possible.

Love you Forever and A Day!

Xoxoxo

For Trip #31, we flew off to tranquil Captiva Island, Florida. We stayed at the South Seas Island Resort and rented a cool Mustang convertible to get around in. The weather was lovely, and we had a view of the water and enjoyed our downtime. We bathed in the sun during the days and walked the beach at sunsets. I looked into what the resort offered, amenity-wise, and they had a yoga class that I decided to attend one morning. Now, I am not very coordinated when it comes to sports—although since I was thinking about getting into better shape, yoga was probably the most non-sport thing I could do. Little did I know that the class I took was a bit more advanced, and I should have snuck out the back door after it started. My gut told me to, but my head said, *Oh, you'll embarrass yourself. What if someone notices you leaving?* After I heard the crack and felt the pop of my baby toe, though, it only cemented my poor decision-making qualities. After class, I walked back to our room. As my toe began to swell and turn purple, I thought, *Who breaks their toe in a yoga class? Unbelievable.*

The heels I wore when we took a day trip to Cape Coral so Paul could meet with his business partners were another poor choice. I mean, come on. What on earth was I thinking? I had a broken toe and was wearing high heels!

Take Away:

Keep wearing the heels—when you don't have any broken bones in your foot, that is— because most men love a woman in heels… Plus, a little pain is worth it to feel sexy.

CHAPTER FIFTY-THREE

A Wedding, a Graduation, and Another Diagnosis

Love Letter to My Captain
February 27, 2017

Captain –

Love of my, love of my life – got that? That's a lot of love XOXO thank you sweetheart for coming downstate this weekend and going to Autorama. It means so much to me that you took the time to spend with my dad and family at this time when you are so busy also. Thank you for not minding that I went to Joe's gig without you. Cindy and I had a great time. It was enjoyable, but would have been better with you there!

I hope your week isn't too taxing (I made a funny) and I hope you sleep great tonight I can't wait to see you on Thursday, that would be only three sleeps. You are my world Captain and thank you for letting me be a part of your world.

XOXO

Sleep Tight Baby –

Love,
Your Princess ♥

My son's band, Sun Tribe, played at St. Andrews Hall again on that Friday evening. I remember when my older brother played there, and my parents and their friends would go see him perform. The circle of life goes on.

Love Letter to My Captain
March 20, 2017

Lover –

Sleep tight my handsome Captain. I'm sorry I'm not here to curl up next to you. Thank you for spending St. Patrick's Day with me and sharing our first "Mount Pleasant "Uber ride. It's always so much fun going out with you. I'm grateful to be on your arm knowing you're mine. How quickly time goes by-and what an enjoyable journey this has been. I'm getting excited for Austin, the wedding and New York for the graduation. So much fun to be had!

Thank you always for your generous spirit in supporting me, and since I have such a sucky credit score:(and you're aware of it) you still love me!

That's amazing-xoxo

I love you honey. Have a great week and sweet dreams!

Love You Forever and A Day!

Your Princess

Uber had finally gone live in Mt Pleasant. We had been using it downstate for a while, and it was invaluable for late-night and/or airport runs. Before I drove up to Mt Pleasant, I dropped off a crock-pot of corned beef and cabbage for my parents. I loved cooking or bringing them food. It seemed I was always on the road or gone, so when I was able to help, I did. Thank you, Cindy, for always helping out when I couldn't.

Love Letter to My Captain
March 26, 2017

Sleep like a Baby Captain- Because you are my "Baby" forever! (And then some). What a fabulous weekend. I'm sorry you didn't feel the greatest, but you looked Hot as F—k!

Thanks for picking me to share your life with.

I hope you have a decent week and know that before you know it- I'LL BE BACK! (You thought I was going to say tax season would be over.... :) lol)

Ok Lover, sweet, sexy dreams and sleep well!

Love you Captain –

Xoxo
Your Princess

Love Letter to My Captain

April 13, 2017

My Calculating Captain -

*Thank you thank you (in advance) for taking care of yourself
these last few days of tax season! I won't be here to tuck you
in or snuggle with you (Sully will do that) so I'm asking you
in advance to take some deep breaths and try to take it all in
stride. We have such a fun couple of weeks ahead of us and
then May! Then boating! Then… And then… You know our
journey. Have a good sleep and please be good to yourself
these next few days. I love you Captain, you are a part of me.*

Love you so much!

Forever and a day and then some!

Your Princess

I was back downstate during this time, focusing on my work,
family, and new exercise routine. After my toe had healed, I figured I
would have a go at yoga again. Unfortunately, I have a habit of going
all in or nothing. I added cycling, boot camp, and TRX (Total Body
Resistance Exercise) to the mix. I was feeling fabulous—until the
pain started in my right elbow. It wasn't bad at first, just kind of a
dull pain. One morning, though, I woke up and went to get a coffee
cup out of the cupboard, only to find that I didn't have the strength
to pick it up and hold it in my hand. That was a shocking way to start
the day. I ended up googling it and learned that I likely had tennis
elbow, which may make it difficult to grip an object. Plus, I vaguely

remembered my mom had a bout of it once before. Time to set up another doctor's appointment!

Once the orthopedic surgeon saw me, I was sent in for an EMG (electromyography) to be sure I didn't have any nerve damage. This test wasn't so much painful as it was irritating, and the fact that you're just waiting for the tech to push the zap button can probably be likened to sitting at the top of the hill on a roller coaster waiting for that moment when you go over the edge. The anticipation is the same—although you probably shouldn't scream as loud in a doctor's office! Luckily, there was no nerve damage, and a cortisone shot would do the trick; in fact, it made for instant relief. I remember the doctor telling me that it wasn't the most pleasant injection, but hey, I was in pain, so a bit of pain now for the long haul was totally doable! In fact, by this time, my other elbow was acting up. Two injections plus one visit equals one happy Carol. Life went on, and I vowed only to allow myself five-pound weights or less when I was using my arms, not only because I didn't want any more flare-ups but because I didn't want to hear my mom say again, "I told you that you're older now and shouldn't do that." It was never in a contemptuous way, though. I call it simply being a caring mother.

Take Away:

Your physical actions can be harmful to your health. No good deed goes unpunished.

CHAPTER FIFTY-FOUR

Cowboy Boots and Longhorns

Love Letter to My Captain

April 25, 2017

Captain –

Well that was a whirlwind dash to Texas and back. Did that just happen so quickly? All I can say is thank you so much for carrying the load for my babies (and +ones) for Sara's wedding. Your generosity is so unbelievable. You look so handsome, not just at the wedding but basically all the time. I have to say that you looked especially hot in that suit of yours with your cowboy boots.

I know I spend a great deal of time telling you how handsome you are, and it's true, and I want you to believe this. In addition to your outward handsomeness your heart is HUGE. I swear the mold was thrown away after you entered the world. I am so blessed to have you as mine, I can't believe it at times how lucky I am. Without you I don't know how my life would be? I wouldn't have traveled on 32 trips, lived in a beautiful home, drove a new car, had tummy tuck surgery and corrected vision, was given jewelry, clothing and shoes? You've helped pay for my daughter's wedding, support my family, assisted extensively with my parents, and Charles... Joseph... Madeline...I could go on and on. The money you've invested in these kids is unbelievable. I'm crazy to say but thank you God you went through all those women and waited for me. Timing is everything and I wouldn't have been ready for you until you appeared on my computer screen. Plus, I hope by these other relationships you realize what you wanted and when you were ready for it. So, now you are all mine! To wrap this up, I never take for granted how fortunate I am and how lucky I feel to be on your arm and in your heart. Congratulations, another successful wedding. You are so blessed to have the best three daughters who love you so deeply and appreciate you!

I love you Captain forever and a day

Sleep tight!

XOXO

Again, Captain's generosity for my children went above and beyond. He paid for their flights to Austin and hotel rooms. Sara's venue was The Wild Onion Ranch in Machaca, Hill County, Texas. It was such a beautiful location, especially with the longhorn grazing as a backdrop. Sara looked stunning. Her dance with her father was nothing short of movie-worthy. Lovely, delicate, flowing, and graceful are just a few words to describe how they swayed to "The Way You Look Tonight" by Frank Sinatra.

It was a season of marriages: Madeline in 2015, Diana in 2016, and Sara in 2017. Erica was the last of our daughters, and then we had a break before Joseph and Charles would be up on deck. Or maybe the next couple to get hitched would be Captain and I? Only time would tell… I knew, though, that I was loving every minute of this journey. It wasn't just our journey; it was living our lives with our children and being a part of their life events. It was a perfect time in our lives.

Take away:

You never know how others are affecting your life until their presence goes away. The bad times do not last, and neither do the good times. They are just replaced.

CHAPTER FIFTY-FIVE

Pivotal Moments

Love Note to My Captain
May 1, 2017

Goodnight my Love –

Another weekend blew by, crazy, huh? Our journey is going way too fast. I am loving every minute of it and spending my life with my Captain. May… Wow… Busy month and the start of summer season, what interesting events will happen this season? I know we'll have a blast whatever happens.

I'm so looking forward to New York. I'm sorry I cost you so much money. I am trying to get business going. I feel good when I can give you checks, it makes me think that even though it's a tiny contribution, it's still something. I hope you have an awesome week lover, I'll miss you. Can't wait to kiss that handsome face of yours again!

XOXO

Your Princess

Love you bunches ♥

It was going to be a crazy month. Not only were there birthdays to celebrate and Mother's Day, but we were headed back to New York for Madeline's graduation.

Love Note to My Captain
May 8, 2017

Hi there my Handsome Prince -

I am writing this looking at your beautiful sculpted legs, I love your body! I look at you in awe and wonder sometimes why you are with me, but then I realize our love is so much deeper than appearances.

It seem to be such a quick weekend but I don't take for granted the sleeps I do get with you. I'm sorry I injured my back and made it a little harder for us. Thank you for being my Captain and taking care of me. You are the love of my life forever and a day, end of story...

I'm so excited about NYC and traveling with you. We always have such a great time. Our journey gets better and better – like how a sandwich gets better when you cook it in the sandwich maker! :-)

You are my Rockstar! Thanks for f———-g me this weekend – I absolutely love it!

I'll miss you Captain

XOXO
Your Princess

Trip #33 to New York was to celebrate Madeline and her graduation, a Masters of Nursing (with honors) from Columbia. My Madeline is driven and unwavering; she finishes everything she sets her mind on. At the time of writing this book, she is a nurse with two children and a third on the way. That makes three children under three years old by age thirty!

Mother's Day this year was celebrated in New York. Diana and Kevin were still living there, so we included them in our celebrations. We stayed at the Park Central Hotel, within walking distance of Central Park. Joseph and his girlfriend, Charles, and Ludovico flew in a day after us. We had three days until her actual graduation. We went to the Solomon R. Guggenheim Museum for one of the days. They had "America" (a golden toilet) on display by the artist Maurizio Cattelan. The toilet was replaced in a restroom with a fully functional replica cast in eighteen-karat gold and available for the public to use. The artist's intention was to provide an extravagant, luxury experience that would usually only be available to the top one percent of the population. The Guggenheim elicited the American dream of opportunity for all, and Charles took the opportunity:-) How often does one get the chance to sit on a Golden Toilet?

After visiting the museum, we met Diana and Kevin in Chinatown for dinner at one of their favorite restaurants. It was lively and fun! We shared great dishes and conversation. I don't believe we pulled out the euchre cards here—although they had been out many times prior on this trip.

A few hours before dinner, I had been waiting to hear back from my parents regarding a doctor's visit my dad had with a lung doctor. I am not sure why I wasn't more concerned at the time; I guess I was convinced Dad couldn't have any issues because he was strong and taking such good care of my mom. However, I was wrong. It turned out that he was diagnosed with interstitial lung disease, specifically IPF (idiopathic pulmonary fibrosis). On the foundation's website, the definition of IPF is:

"Idiopathic pulmonary fibrosis (IPF) is a progressive and generally fatal disease characterized by scarring of the lungs that thickens the lining of the lungs, causing an irreversible loss of the tissue's ability to transport oxygen. IPF ultimately robs a patient of the ability to breathe."

Unfortunately, eighty percent of people with IPF die within five years of diagnosis, and fifty percent of the time, it is misdiagnosed. Dad had been dealing with what we thought were heart issues— which sometimes caused coughing—for two years. Was he already past two of the five years? Did he only have three years left? This news was devastating. I attempted to put on a good face during the dinner in Chinatown, knowing that I couldn't change anything. I would wait for more information before letting the kids know, though. Later that night, I cried myself to sleep. Now, I had two parents with lung diseases. Both were different but one-hundred percent fatal without a lung transplant, which wasn't an option due to their ages.

It was sunny and warm the following morning for Madeline's graduation. I sat during the ceremony, thinking about my girl and her fortitude in getting through these last eighteen months in a 590 sq. ft apartment with her husband, both studying fervently; she for her masters, and Cody in medical school along with his masters in public health. The circle of life: I had my parents "winding" down, and my children were accomplishing their life goals and heading towards creating their own families. It was the way it was supposed to be. That's the funny thing about life; it keeps going, and everything always changes.

After the ceremony, we took pictures at Fort Tryon Park, near Madeline and Cody's apartment. The spring flowers were in bloom, and the trees were green.

That evening, we had a delicious dinner in Little Italy, complete with abundant red wine and toasting.

The following day, I turned fifty years old. I spent the morning and a good part of the afternoon in a U-haul truck while the kids loaded it up. Obviously, on the streets in New York, you cannot leave an open moving truck! As it was, though, Joseph's car window had already been broken into, and he was parked on the same street. And since the police acted like it happened often, we were extra cautious. Most of the apartment was getting packed up and sent back to Michigan with Ludovico and Charles for storage in my basement. The kids would spend a couple of months living with the bare minimum until Madeline would come back to Michigan, and Cody would begin his externships—the first one being in Boston. You may think all this sounds like an awful way to begin a birthday; however, it wasn't. I was with my babies, and I had time to sit and think about everything I was grateful for and how blessed my life was.

Once the truck was fully packed, I returned to the hotel and we got ready for an evening out with Madeline, Cody, and Diana, seeing *The Lion King* on Broadway.

Two days later, I was back home at the Ridgeway house and visited my parents. It was tough as it was the first time I had physically seen my dad in person since his diagnosis. I remember vividly getting out of Captain's Shelby Mustang and seeing Mom at the front door to greet us. Dad was sitting inside at the counter. I hugged him and cried. He teared up, too—although I know he was holding back. We all sat down like we always did when we visited, but this time felt different. Mom was now the one seemingly in charge and telling my Dad she was there to take care of him despite her limitations with her lung disease. Plus, she was on a timeline as well. Captain and Dad got talking about cars and Dad's younger days, which seemed to lift his spirits. My dad then wanted to show me where he kept his important paperwork in the basement. The file box was stored in his workroom on a shelf behind a suitcase. However, when he pulled it out and we exited the workroom, he broke down. I had never witnessed these emotions pouring out of my dad, so I just held him and cried, too. I thanked him for being a great dad and everything he did for us. But then I realized he was still there, alive, and we had to focus on doing what we could to give him the best quality of life for the time he had let—along with my mom—including researching stem cell treatments to help him. It was a tough visit, and one I knew I had to face with courage and optimism, even when, sometimes, the heart and emotions take over. Thank God my Captain was there to support me.

Love Letter to My Captain
May 29, 2017

Goodnight Sweetheart!

Thank you for the beautiful memorial weekend in Tawas. Thank you for taking me to Camille's on Friday night, I really enjoyed our night out. I appreciate all the support, love and understanding you're giving me and continue to give me throughout this phase of my life. I pray I can become as strong as you and get through as best I can.

During this time that my family is going through this I want you to know I'm not minimizing your decision to sell Tawas after the season ends. I understand the emotional ties and I am grateful I was able to spend time in our journey here. I'll represent you with excellent service "special" service none of my other clients get... Lol... I hope you have a really good week and an enjoyable one. Looking forward already to Friday night when I can sleep next to you again

Love you forever and a day

Xoxox

Tawas was Captain's playground. He loved it there and sharing it with his girls, especially after his divorce. It was their special place. The years go by quickly. He now had two daughters married and all were living in different states.

My dad's eighty-fourth birthday was on June fifth; we celebrated it at our house the weekend before. We also included Charles, since we had not had a chance before we left for New York to celebrate his birthday. Dad and Charles were more than just grandfather and grandson; they were buddies and alike in many ways. For example, Dad would only speak after he read the room or listened to everyone so that he knew exactly what he was going to say. Charles is like that, too. I was relieved to see my dad in better spirits for this birthday. We were in the process of researching the stem cell procedures and had lined up some additional testing for him to make that happen.

Love Letter to My Captain

June 11, 2017

Goodnight My Love -

We fit like a glove

We are like two doves

I think it's true love!!

Thank you for the beautiful weekend. I'm sorry I was so late getting up here Friday night. I felt cheated that I didn't get my "full-time" with you, but then I thought of the individuals in the car accident, which was why I was late, and how they felt, were they even alive? We have more journey to go and theirs were possibly uncertain.

Thank you for being so cheerful always, one of the many many reasons I love you and fell in love with you. I wanted to thank you again for my gift of vision. Without Lasik I still would be dealing with contacts and glasses and always worrying about not seeing in the middle of the night. Now I can see how handsome you are all the time! I hope you have a great week and enjoy the beautiful flowers in the yard. You are my heart and my love and we are fabulous together.

Love you baby!

XOXO

We were bound to have delays with all the driving we did between Mt Pleasant and Clinton Township. It always saddened me when the expressway shut down due to an accident because I knew what it meant for the parties involved. I always thanked God for our safe arrivals. Luckily, Captain and I had not been involved in an accident heading back or forth—at least up until now in 2017.

Love Letter to My Captain
June 18, 2017

Goodnight Sweetheart -

Happy Father's Day again to an exceptional dad. You are so loved and respected and I'm so fortunate that I am in your world. I love you with all my heart and want the best for you. This means me loving you 100% and liking you too! I wish I could keep my feelings in and not let stuff bother me, but I can't. I only want to ask that you understand my soft heart and tender feelings. I know that you (and men all over the earth) look and think thoughts when they see "other" women. But, if at all possible, (it's tough when they're verbalized) keep them in that handsome head of yours. It just makes me feel less beautiful in your eyes. I know it's not right to say remember when, but I know you didn't verbalize words like that before. Maybe it's comfort, and that's OK, but it still stings to hear words/sexual comments from the man that I love and who loves me say them. So, I'm glad we're still game to work on our relationship when needed. I don't want to become cynical and complacent.

*Thank you, thank you for helping out my folks. I don't know
what we'd do without you. They are so appreciative. I hope
you enjoy your week and our flowers. I hope you find out
who that little bugger is who's eating them.*

Have a great sleep Captain!
Love You!

Xoxo
Your Princess

It exposed itself again. It was either my insecurity or the lack of
filter of my boyfriend, but I hated it when this stuff happened. I do
not yell, scream, or storm off; I recoil, feel sad, and wonder if this
happens to everyone. I learned, though, thanks again to my dear
friend Tom, that men who are leaders, executives, and entrepreneurs
usually have higher levels of testosterone. Of course, this is not a
fact, so please don't think this is a verified and tested truth of science.
Captain never wanted me to "gunny sack," so I told him when I felt
these feelings. I guess I could have kept them to myself—as some of
you might be thinking—and not been crazy and nagged him, just be
grateful. However, this was a relationship. The material things and
experiences wouldn't mean anything if I wasn't living authentically,
knowing I could sleep at night and letting my peace be known. Sure,
I was taking a chance at Captain saying, "I don't need this anymore.
Look at everything I've done for you," but it was a chance I was willing to take. For the record, Captain never said anything like that to
me.

Since my dad and mom were now ill, Paul set them up with an
attorney who specialized in Trusts. He also accompanied them and
paid for the financial side of things. My parents were so grateful,

and Captain was grateful for them. I recall him thanking them for having me. Yes, underneath that shell of masculinity, there was always tenderness.

Take away:

Always stay true to yourself and your feelings.

CHAPTER FIFTY-SIX

Almost, Thankfully Not

Love Letter to my Captain

July 9, 2017

Sunshine of My Life –

You are such a good guy, thank you so much for coming downstate for me and missing a beautiful weekend in Tawas. You are definitely the Captain of my life, Happy 7 1/2 years together! How time has flown by, I love being able to call you my Captain and the fact that we met on match, and "we fit". I am excited to continue our roll and what new adventures we have planned. Thank you for your patience and grace in my checks not coming in lately. They will again, I promise.

Enjoy your beautiful yard, driveway, flowers, TV, birds, and everything! Just don't enjoy the hot tub with any other chicks except your daughters! lol

Love you to the moon and back and then some, sleep well this week and I'll be counting down till we're together again

I miss you already

XOXO
Your Princess

For all the times I mentioned his comments about other women and teased him about having other women around when I was not there, when it truly came down to it, I trusted my Captain and always looked forward to more happy times together.

Love Letter to My Captain
July 31, 2017

Hey there Handsome Lover,

Thank you for the stellar weekend, you were an all-star considering 2/3 of it was spent with my family. I know you love and care for them, and I also realize that it can be "a lot" for you. Yesterday was so cool, my dad was so impressed and happy. Thank you so much for adding this into his life. Thank you for all you do for my parents, I don't know how I would blaze this trail on my own. You are so intelligent and have the ability to make them feel at ease. You are truly the most brilliant and perceptive man I've ever met. I'm so glad you're mine.

I love you with all my heart and look forward to Thursday and our encounter.

Xoxo
Your Princess

During this time, our hopes of moving forward with Dad's stem cell treatment were no longer an option. Another CT scan showed a larger fibroid that could grow if they injected the stem cells. We hoped the process would regrow normal cells—although we had not viewed it as feeding the fibroid to get larger. My dad decided to give up and just wait it out. Our primary physician, who sees many of us in the family, did not want Dad to do this, though. He gave us a contact from the University of Michigan's Pulmonary Clinic. Fortunately, we got an appointment and enrolled in a clinical trial. This meant visits to Ann Arbor, extensive breathing tests, and more than a handful of pills to be taken daily. Dad was such a trouper. He did everything he could. He said that if it does not help him, at least it could help someone else in the future. We were told that he was being given the drug, not the placebo, and I had to believe it since the pills would make him nauseous. Now, I had two parents on two clinical trial drugs and was so grateful. Not everyone gets these medical opportunities to spend more time with loved ones who are very ill. We were supportive as long as they wanted to continue in the studies.

Another birthday for Captain was around the corner. This one would be spent in Tawas with Sara and her husband…

Love Letter to My Captain

August 7, 2017

Goodnight Sweetheart,

When you wake up tomorrow you'll be another year fantastic! A new year of opportunities, adventures in a new path into our journey together. You get better every year! Thank you for the fabulous weekend we had such a nice time with the kids, sorry I purchased so much food, I do that sometime. Lol

I hope you have a great week and I look forward to next time and more lovemaking! I love you Captain, you are my heart. I hope you have a fantastic birthday!

Love you bunches

XOXO
Your Princess

Isaiah gave me the well-deserved nickname of "snack lady." Ask any of Paul's kids, and they probably will agree. My kids already knew this fact. My sister Cindy and I learned this from my mom: If you are having company over, taking a road trip, visiting someone, or have to bring food, you can never have enough snacks!

Love Letter to My Captain

August 22, 2017

Goodnight Lover,

As of the Time I am writing this I have no idea where our housing future is headed. I do know how much I love you, how much you mean to me and know that you make the decisions that are best for us. At the end of the day all that matters for us is being together I pray that our health holds up and we can enjoy many more adventures. Thank you for everything you've done for my parents and my family, you are one in a million! I still can't believe you were sent to me. I am so grateful. I love you Captain you are my rock and I believe in your guidance and decision making.

Love you bunches

XOXO
Your Princess

A few days earlier, we had viewed a home on a canal in Chesterfield Township in a subdivision named Lottivue. The house had an inground pool and a basement. I knew Captain loved the water, and I did not want to purchase a home without a basement. It is tricky to find full basements by the water for obvious reasons. We were not really "looking" for a house; however, our friends Russ and Cara lived on a beautiful, private canal in Harrison Township, and every time we visited and went boating with them, we would always talk houses. Then again, Russ was also a Realtor®, so it was basically impossible not to talk about houses! Anyway, Paul and I seriously considered buying a house on the canal. My only real concern was the distance from my parents, yet the place would have been great for entertaining, and they could enjoy that with us for the time they had left. After all, Mom and Dad were still mobile, had oxygen, and could walk and leave the house. So, Captain and I inspected the house on Friday, went on a Dream Cruise on Saturday, and viewed the house again on Monday. By the following weekend, we had put in an offer and had it accepted with a pending inspection.

As awesome as the place would have been, unfortunately, the inspection uncovered issues the current owner had yet to address, so we did not proceed. In truth, though, I was relieved. There was just too much going on at the time with my parents. I also had a nagging feeling that I wanted to be a homeowner again, but as Paul and I weren't married, he would be the one with the name on the deed, and I would just be living there without him most of the time. It just didn't seem like the right thing to do. From a real estate point of view, I know both of us could have been on the deed without being married; however, I didn't want that. I wanted to be husband and wife when we moved in permanently together. It was my dream and desire.

Take Away:

As a Midwesterner, I love having a basement. It is great if it's finished for parties or unfinished and a storage area for your "stuff" you really don't need. I have heard that the less stuff a person has, the happier they are. What happens when you get rid of that stuff, though? It makes me unhappy to think about...

CHAPTER FIFTY-SEVEN

Spinning Wheels, Circus Tents, Christmas, and a Special Letter

September–December, 2017

I was so excited to go to Cape Cod. I had heard how beautiful it was, and it just so happened that Captain had a conference he could attend there. Madeline flew out with us for Trip #34, too, as Cody was in the middle of his externship at Cambridge in Massachusetts. We flew into Boston, rented a car, dropped Madeline off at Cambridge, and headed toward the water. We stayed at the Sea Crest Beach Hotel on Cape Cod in North Falmouth. Our room had a balcony facing the beachfront, with beautiful white sand and mists of water that permeated the air. Even though my hair didn't always love the climate, I loved Cape Cod. We went on a twenty-five-mile bike ride and viewed the beauty of the homes, trees, and waterfront. The undulation of the trails was just enough; I wasn't going to give up. Now, Captain has always had strong muscles in his legs. Bike riding for him was not an issue. Me, on the other hand—well, I was surprised I did so well, and I even included a picture of myself in a helmet on Facebook. That was the real win!

Madeline and Cody joined us on the weekend for an evening. While we were there, a wedding was held on the beach, and we watched people set up the tents. We jokingly laughed that we might crash the wedding and have a cocktail. The music from the DJ was loud enough for us to hear on our balcony, so we had our own little dance party. Before you know it, we were being cheered and motioned to join the party. That was a fun night!

The rest of September was spent at football games and Captain's annual Shareholder Retreat.

October brought birthday celebrations for my niece, Chloe, my mom (who turned eighty-one), and Charles. I relished more than ever the time I could spend with my parents. I knew we were moving toward being on "borrowed time."

Love Letter to My Captain
October 22, 2017

Hi Cutie!

I bet you're snuggling with Sullivan right now, the other blonde in your life lol. Thank you so much for coming down-state this weekend and thank you for talking openly with me about the change is going on right now with you. I want to be here to support you and being the best, healthiest version of yourself. We have so much fun when we are together and I want to continue down that road! There is so much to look forward to within the next couple of months. I'm so grateful for what we have today and for what you've done for me in my life. You are so giving and never ask for anything in return. I love you Captain with my everything and all that I have to give.

You are my forever and a day.

Saturday, October twenty-first, was Sweetest Day. Cindy and Leon invited us to dinner at The Caucus Club in Detroit with them. Earlier in the day, I set up a massage for Captain. This was the day Captain decided to stop smoking. This is funny because when I first met him—I laugh about it now—his profile said, "trying to quit." I believe every smoker is trying to quit, and that is what I told him the first time he lit up. To be honest, though, he did ask if I would mind. And then you know what happened to me eight months later... the corruption! I know he did not force it in my mouth, but I was happy he was finally quitting. It took him four years after I quit. I never nagged him about stopping; I would just tell him I wanted him to be around for a long time. The masseuse knew he had smoked his last cigarette and gave him a massage that would release the toxins. I'm sure it helped, and to this day, I have never witnessed him smoke another cigarette.

In October, we went to the Red Wings and CMU games, celebrated another McEvoy birthday for my sister-in-law, Monika, attended a Robert F. Murray client appreciation night at Bucks Run, and enjoyed a surprise retirement party for Paul's sister, Mary Beth. Our lives were nonstop! We were fortunate to celebrate with family and friends and share good times and laughter.

Right around the corner was Trip #35—back to Vegas from November 11 to 16. We stayed at Caesar's again for another AICPA Conference. After the conference, we had some fun and saw the show *Absinthe*, set up in its own circus tent outside of the hotel, and entered what looked like a phone booth. What a great show. We also visited the Shelby Factory. It's all things Carroll Shelby, and it was neat to see Captain's Shelby Mustang there—or should I say one like it? Captain drove one of the new Mustangs back to our hotel and "opened her up"—I guess that is what you call it. The rep said that's what they are made for!

Love Letter to My Captain
November 20, 2017

Hey Baby,

Can you believe we've had 10 sleeps together? Now we have to break our streak. It was a fabulous trip to Las Vegas, thank you for always treating me like a princess. I'm so fortunate you love and respect me so much. You could've picked anyone and you know that and you chose me. Thank God! Thank you for the intimacy this weekend and in Vegas, my lady parts love it when you touch them and when your manhood enters me! 😆

As we proceed into the holiday season I'll be grateful for all the blessings I have and how appreciative I am of my life. I feel bad for those out there that don't have someone to love, and whom they can feel secure with. You are in my heart and I thank you for taking care of yourself for us.

I love you Captain forever and a day and then some

XOXO
Your Princess

The following Thursday was Thanksgiving at the Ridgeway house. The holiday hosting went as follows: Cindy would have Mother's Day every year, Easter was a toss-up between Monika and I, Monika would have Father's Day, I would have Thanksgiving, Cindy would have Christmas Eve, and Monika would have Christmas Day—for the record, Monika is my brother Doug's wife. We would always celebrate Doug's birthday, and usually their twins, Aiden and Ethan, on Thanksgiving as their birthdays are in November. We would sing to Doug with a pumpkin pie—I'm not even sure if it was his favorite—and the twins would get a cake. Of course, we were stuffed when it came time to sing, but what the heck? Who is counting calories on Thanksgiving Day anyway?

Love Letter to My Captain
November 27, 2017

Hey Baby –

Thank you for the lovely weekend and spending Thanksgiving with my family. I know sometimes it's grueling, so I appreciate all you put up with. I love you and would always do anything for you and always put you before myself. I'll always put you on a pedestal and continue to praise how wonderful you are. Thank you for loving me. I'm not perfect, but try to make your life enriched by doing what I can. I hope you have a great week and I look forward to seeing you again, in just a few sleeps.

Love you baby

XOXO

Mom was getting frailer, and Dad was starting to have other issues unrelated to his lung disease. I feared we were entering the beginning of the end, but I wasn't sure for whom. All I know is that I was sad. When I would go to my parents' house, I'd try to bring positive energy, be silly, and tell stories to entertain them. Their lives had become a series of doctor visits, so getting together with family was more important and precious than ever.

Love Letter to My Captain
December 11, 2017

Hi Captain,

I'd like to start this love note by telling you again... "You are the love of my life... My Captain, my everything... " Sorry to give you all that responsibility, that title, that all inclusive integral part of my life that you've become... But I know my Captain can handle it!

What another great weekend. I love being with you and sharing the holiday season, for me, is one of the best parts. Thank you, thank you, thank you for allowing me to Christmas shop. I don't know what I'd do without you, not just financially you know, but the whole picture. As I leave you, I leave a piece of me here. I'll miss you but will put my big girl pants on and do what I need to do. Thank you for sharing your intimacy with me, not just the fabulous sex, your heart. But, you know – the sex is fabulous!

OK sunshine I'll end this and countdown to sleep! Love you forever and a day!

XOXO
Princess

As Christmas approached, I felt even more grateful. I wondered how many Christmases we would have in Mt Pleasant, and how many my parents would be alive for downstate…

Love Letter to My Captain
December 18, 2017

Goodnight my Captain,

Thank you for the beautiful time we spent together this weekend. It was perfect! A BIG thank you for watching the Sound of Music with me. I know it wasn't tops on your list, but I so did appreciate it. Doe a deer… A female deer… Ray… A drop of golden sun… You are my sunshine! Music makes me happy so I'm glad you put up with my singing which isn't the greatest.

Countdown to Christmas – can you believe it? I'm sorry I spent so much money lately. Thank you for being understanding and letting me do/give all these things/presents. The best gift I get is you every day in my life. My handsome Captain turned my world upside down eight years ago and it's never been the same. I could not have dreamt of a more fabulous life. I love you Captain to the moon and back!

Forever and a day and then some

XOXOXO

Your Princess

Love Letter to My Captain
December 26, 2017

Lover - My Christmas Gift-My World-..so much more...

Thank you for making this Christmas so special. Thank you so much for my beautiful necklace, it's just so sparkly and gorgeous. And, thank you for the beautiful love letter. It came from your heart I treasure it. I'll be reading it many times. What a fun, exciting weekend we had. I know there was a great deal of family time for you and I want to thank you for handling it so well. Like you said time will be changing, thank you for being alongside me so I don't have to go through the bad times alone.

Not only do I carry you on my fingernails (PBM) but you are always with me. Your presence is in my heart making me feel so loved always. I hope the end of the year is it not too stressful for you, please, please stop to breathe and relax. I love you so much and like I said before you are the best Christmas gift ever.

Love you Captain

XOXOXO

I loved it when Captain would write me a love note or letter. Inside my beautiful Christmas card was a folded yellow-lined sheet of paper. On the card, he wrote:

"Thank You For Picking Me"

I'm The Luckiest Guy In The World

Love You Forever And A Day (plus he drew the face of a cute little devil)

Love, Your Captain

Love Letter From My Captain
December 25, 2017

Dear Princess,

You've made my life so special and the best I ever imagined! Thank you for loving me, taking care of me and always thinking about us.

2017 was a great year and we have so much to look forward to. Our lives will be changing as we grow older together and our children start having children! I hope you still love me as I grow "FAT". I'll try to reverse that trend. I'm sure you will make a wonderful grandma and can't wait to be a grandpa with you. I'm looking forward to our Christmas trip to Grand Cayman. Maybe this weekend we can look at schedules and activities? Thank you for being my princess. I hope your Mom and Dad enjoy this holiday. I think of them often and you and how kind and generous you are with your time and help.

I love you forever and a day!

Your Captain ❤

Take Away:

Family is wonderful. Travel is wonderful. A handwritten love letter from my Captain is wonderful.

Chapter Fifty-eight

Life Changes

January, 2018

We rang in the New Year with Rob and Tina in Detroit. We had gone to a Red Wings Game, dinner, and then the Casino. We stayed at the Greektown Casino Hotel, now named Hollywood Casino at Greektown. We laughed, and all had such fun.

The following day, Captain and I headed home to Ridgeway. Then he went on to Mt Pleasant. Who knew what 2018 would hold?

Love Letter to My Captain
January 1, 2018

Happy New Year Lover,

Thank you for spending 2017 with me. Another great year, a great deal happened: A wedding, A graduation, A 50th birthday, my Dad's diagnosis and you quit smoking. My heart grows fonder and my love for you increases. This year marks eight years, wow, incredible! Through all of this you still love me, even though I'm a few pounds heavier and all lol

I am so excited for our trip, we'll have so much fun with the kids I'll try really hard not be worry about my mom. I can't change it. So worrying won't help. It will be nice to lay in the sun and be warm.

I'll miss you these next two sleeps, you'll be all alone and I know you'll be just fine. Thank you for always loving me and for your generosity. You are the best lover, and you are meant for me. We fit, I love you Captain! XOXOXO

In the middle of the night on January first, I received a call from my dad. When the phone rings in the middle of the night, you know it is not good. The ambulance was on the way to pick up Mom. She was having trouble breathing and was extremely weak. The phone call also woke Madeline, and I remember looking at her and saying, *"I think Dubba is going to pass away tonight."* Dubba was the name my kids called their grandma. Madeline assured me it was going to be ok, and I was going to be ok. I was always worried every time I got a call from Dad. I remember how happy I would be to see a Devonshire Update email from Mom. Loving a parent comes with the realization that it will be painful when they are no longer here. My head knew this; my heart wasn't ready for this process. Through the years, even my Captain knew how close my family was and how much my parents meant to me. He would try to cushion the inevitable by lovingly reminding me that, in time, things will change.

Fortunately, that evening, my mom survived. Her oxygen levels were low, and they found out she was anemic. We were leaving for Grand Cayman to meet Captain's kids to celebrate their family

Christmas together, as they had not come to Michigan for the holidays. So, here I was wondering if I should go. In the end, my parents insisted I should, but when I left Mom, I told her not to pull any funny stuff while I was gone. She replied, "*I won't die while you're gone, honey.*" It was sad and yet comical. My mom was such a realist.

Love Letter to My Captain

January 12, 2018

> *Hi Lover -*
>
> *You're back in your own bed tonight and must be so happy to snuggle with Sullivan. What a wonderful vacation with the kids. More memories to store in the banks of our lives. They really enjoyed the time spent with you, you're such a good Papa. I'll make this short and sweet and save the rest of the gooey love story for the next letter.*
>
> *Thank you for taking me on vacation and all the support you've given me with my family situation and your generosity. Paul Benjamin Murray you are one of a kind, and I love carrying you on my thumbnails:-)*
>
> *Love you Baby*
>
> *XOXO*

For Trip #36 to Grand Cayman with the kids, we stayed in a vacation rental on the water. The views were lovely, there were great restaurants and beaches within walking distance, although we had rented a car. The plan was to pick up the kids as they came in—although, for some crazy reason, we ended up with a five-seater when there were seven of us. For the most part, we made it work, even though I was chided yet again for the amount and size of my luggage. This was—and is—still a problem of mine, not the chiding, of course. One particularly funny incident was when a random bull decided to charge at the car from the side of the road. Luckily, we avoided impact (especially happy were Sara and Erica, as they were positioned in the hatchback part of the rental, basically the trunk). It was a story that no one would ever believe unless they were there. No kidding around; the bull was larger than our car!

Snorkeling, scuba diving, kayaking, sandcastle building, and several hands of euchre filled our days on the trip. Meanwhile, I tried not to worry about home and Mom; however, I was only half successful. It was such an emotional rollercoaster at times. Learning to be present is a skill that I have continued to develop. If I was consumed with thoughts of my mom, I was missing making memories with the kids and my Captain. For instance, the time Erica and I were euchre partners, and she decided to call me on "the shell phone" next to her because a shell was the original cell phone—the wine was clearly getting the better of us, especially when I answered her on my "shell phone." Now, we lovingly refer to each other as shell sisters.

Love Letter to My Captain
January 14, 2018

Sunday Funday Captain or Sunday Sexday…:)

What a whirlwind holiday season it's been. It went by so quickly thank you again for spending the holidays with my family. The road is becoming bumpier as we go in regards to my mom and dad. I can't deny that I am a bit scared, and apprehensive as to this upcoming year. I pray that I don't

*become too emotional or irrational. I've never been down this
road before. I know you'll be there holding my hand and my
heart.*

*Thank you again for the beautiful necklace you gave me for
Christmas. I always love jewelry you know :-) I am so so glad
I did not lose the bracelet coming home from Grand Cayman.
I would've been devastated. Thanks for letting me tag along
on the family trip. I know your babies really enjoyed the time
with you. They are so lucky to have you as their father. I am
so lucky to have you as my Captain. I'll pray one day that
I can call you my husband and wear the "badge" of Mrs.
Murray. I pray you want the same thing also. Part of me did
get a bit concerned when you asked what I would do after
Charles graduated, if you weren't planning on marrying me.
My heart sank. I pray I read too much into. All right Captain
enough heavy stuff. My gut tells me you're an honorable man
and love the shit out of me. Hopefully I'll see you Tuesday.*

XOXO

*Love you forever and a day
Your Princess*

I never pressured Captain to marry me. In truth, I let things grow
naturally because it really is all about the journey and not the destination. We would randomly have conversations like this—usually
when we were having cocktails or sharing a bottle of wine. In my
heart, I believed that Captain was one-hundred percent sure about
becoming my husband. It was just a matter of when. With Charles
still in high school, both of my parents ailing, and Paul not ready to

retire, there was just no reason for him to leave Mt Pleasant yet, and I was not leaving Clinton Township. I guess I should have just stopped asking, and we should've just stopped talking about it, but it seemed the thing to do as we had been together for so many years. From the outside, it was probably a no-brainer; I am sure people looked at it like Captain had a great deal to lose—or should I say put at risk—by getting married again. He was so established, and I was just this gal from downstate who did not have much to her name but had a heart as pure as gold.

We celebrated my parent's sixty-second wedding anniversary on January twenty-eighth at their house. It would be their last anniversary together. Mom was hospitalized again on February sixth and came home on the February tenth. The doctors were trying to find where she was losing blood and why she was still so anemic. Scopes of all sorts were ordered, and transfusions were given.

Take Away:

As hard as one tries, one cannot stop time, and we only have a certain amount of it left.

CHAPTER FIFTY-NINE

Packing Away Memories

Love Letter to My Captain
February 18, 2018

Hello Handsome and Goodnight Handsome –

I'm sorry I'm not there to kiss you goodnight and bring you your coffee in the morning. I really do love taking care of you. You do so much for me and I wish I could do more for you. Thank you so much for coming downstate this weekend to attend Charles's program with me. It's so good to support these kids, he's growing so fast he's going to be a full-fledged adult soon. He's a cutie :-) I'm glad he's not chasing tail yet, as you would say like you were in high school, lol. I hope you have a good week and try to not stress too much. I can't believe I only saw you for two quick sleeps and we're back again to our other lives. Makes me sad sometime.

I love you Captain and pray you love me like you did the day we met. :-)

I was losing my mother, and Dad was also ill, so I knew every-thing was going to change and was desperately trying to take one day at a time. I was so consumed by what was happening that I even worried about Paul getting tired of my emotional rollercoaster. We each had so much going on. Another tax season was ramping up, and all I seemed to do was cry…

Love Letter to My Captain
March 18, 2018

Hey there my Rock Star C.P.A. (Captain, Perfect, Always)

Another seemingly quick weekend, but alas – a productive one. I'm so glad I can help you. I know it's not much, but a bit of a contribution to the household. Thank you for being my Irish Lad. You sure are a cute one, I think I'll schedule you in for next St. Patrick's Day to be my good luck clover. He he I've scheduled you in for the rest of my life, you're stuck :-) I hope that's ok, have a good week at work and I'll keep you near in my thoughts and pray you aren't too stressed.

I love you baby forever and a day and then some!

Loving you always

XOXO
Your Princess

Love Letter to My Captain
March 25, 2018

My Hot Shot Boyfriend –

Love, love, and kisses and many, many wishes that you are feeling back to normal in the next few days. I know this is crunch time and I also know that it takes a toll on your body. Please try to take care of yourself. I wish I could be there to wait on you, I'll be back soon! :-)

Thank you for allowing the boys to stay here this past weekend and thank you for being so good to my son, and allowing me to be a cool mom, well, I probably didn't look too cool standing on the sidelines at Centennial Hall, but you get my drift.

I love you Captain and I love everything about us

Hugs, Kisses and Forever wishes

Your Princess

XOXO

Joseph's band at the time had a gig in Mt Pleasant at Centennial Hall. Captain stayed home as the time for their band to go on was later than our bedtime, haha. I was probably the oldest at the concert, but that was ok. After all, age is just a number, right? Captain was gracious enough to let the band stay at Greenbanks, though, and who wouldn't want to hang out downstairs in the theatre room?

Love Letter to My Captain
April 1, 2018

To my "Honey Bunny Easter Bunny"

Thank you for the great weekend, I always love pulling into the driveway, knowing I'll be seeing my Captain soon. I love, love, love the way we interact and can be talking or just laying next to each other in each others arms. I've never felt so comfortable with anyone, yes... We fit!

It was so much fun going out to dinner the other night with Joe and Barb at Camille's, lots of laughs and much-needed wine. I hope your week goes well and your staff is on top of their work. I know the buck stops with you... And if they don't get it done right, then my PBM has to bat clean up - hopefully that won't happen too much this week. Know that I love you and think the world of you.

Sleep tight my Snuggle Bunny

Love,
Your Easter Chick

Lol

Captain spent Easter in Mt Pleasant. April fifteenth was just around the corner and Paul had to wrap up before the tax return deadline. Our family celebrated at my brother's house, and I remember how feeble my mom looked, I knew it could possibly be here last Easter with us.

Love Letter to My Captain

April 8, 2018

Hey Lover,

Quick but fun. I'm so sorry I'm leaving you so early, one sleep doesn't cut it. Thank you for understanding my desire to improve my skills and get better at my craft, to eventually bring you more checks! I love bringing you checks :-) I hope you feel better honey, get lots of sleep and keep your face out of burning candles.

I love you bunches and more than bunches

XOXO

Your Princess

I remember a great deal; however, I cannot remember why I would tell my Captain to keep his face out of burning candles… Oh well, it is good advice anyway!

Love Letter to My Captain

April 17, 2018

Goodnight Lover –

I'm here. I'm gone. I return and I go back again.

Which end is up?

One day this silly stuff will change into you having me all the time:-). Can you imagine that? Thank you for the love, snuggles and fun we had together these last couple of days.

Thank you for letting me share your second-to-last tax season with you. Please keep an eye on your tree guests, maybe throw some treats out there for them. Who needs the BBC network when you have GRC, Greenbanks River Creatures. I know, I'll stop now.

I love you to pieces!

Xoxo
Your Princess

Love Letter to My Captain
April 19, 2018

Goodnight my Accounter –

Well, tax season is done! You made it through, and we made it through :-) thank you so much for including me in your party. It makes me feel special. Glad I could be a help with the pics and the taxi service… He he

You are my one and only captain and I still can't believe you're mine. Who knew you would fall for some chunky girl in Sterling Heights. Thank you for making me feel beautiful and understanding my insecurities. I'm excited for the warmer weather and I can't wait for our next trip. I love traveling with my Captain. It's always an adventure.

Love, hugs, kisses

And much "misses"

(Like missing you on my part)

XOXO
Your Princess

During this period, when I was back downstate, I was spending a great deal of time with my parents. My sister and I frequently went over to their house, whether it was to bring dinner, clean, or take one of them to a doctor's appointment. My dad was "holding"—if one could call it that. He faithfully took the medication from the clinical trial, even though it made him sick. He loved Mom so much that he said he had to be around to take care of her. She was his gal.

Captain decided it was time to officially put Tawas on the market. The decision to sell came quickly after Erica told him she was moving to Austin with Isaiah. Captain says he remembers the moment we were on the boat with them anchored in the bay. It was the end of an era, only to be replaced with new memories in a new era. The kids were so busy with their lives now in different states. It was getting more difficult for them to fly in, drive two-and-a-half-hours to Mt Pleasant, and even further if they were headed to Tawas. I was sad because I knew how much my Captain loved the water. At least he still had a river at Greenbanks.

Love Letter to My Captain
April 22, 2018

Goodnight Handsome Man with the beautiful hands!

I think we accomplished a lot this weekend. As usual, it went by so quickly. I'm sorry I arrived in Tawas so late on Friday, I hope my work on Saturday made up for it, lol! I know it saddens you to think about not having Tawas. Such great memories were made there with you and your girls and the other kind of girls, ha ha. I have to say though that my babies and I really did get to enjoy it also. We'll have fun memories and Charlie will never forget driving the boat. Thank you for making that opportunity a reality for him. We have other great places in Michigan to discover and I'm excited to take some new journeys with you.

I love you Captain with all my heart and will miss you this week. I hope it's productive for you and you get to relax a bit post tax season. Enjoy the sunshine this week

I love you forever and a day and then some

XOXO
Your Princess

Captain had a log book, or guest book, placed on the wall in a beach-themed holder. Guests who would visit Tawas typically would write something in the journal. I even did the first time I went up there. Paul told me stories of other girls writing in the book and past girlfriends ripping out the pages. He would just laugh. I had no desire to go looking through the pages. Why would I want to purposely make myself feel bad? We all have history—although it seemed I did a better job of keeping my history just that… history! Then again, Captain was in a small town, and history is always harder to pack away in small towns.

Take Away:

If you date a man fourteen years your senior, who is educated, charismatic, successful, intelligent, at the top of his game, and not to mention, fuc*ing hot, your mind can definitely go places it shouldn't. And regardless of whether your man's past girlfriends live within a five-mile radius, in the next town, or in another state, one should never let their guard down.

Chapter Sixty

Sadness, Joy, Gratitude; The Last Summer

Love Letter to My Captain
May 6, 2018

Lover –

Another weekend that flew by, it was so nice having you back in Clinton Township. It was especially nice when we made love in our Ridgeway bed. Thank you also for hanging out with Cindy and Leon. I know it was a late night, and we did pay for it on Saturday. I hope you enjoyed your massage and pedicure. It makes me happy when you have these little treats. I hope you had a wonderful relaxing Sunday and are enjoying your chicken barbecue dinner. I wish I could've been with you today.

I'm looking forward to the rest of May, we have some fun stuff on our calendar. I'll turn another year older and I hope that means you'll love me even more… Thank you for our journey and all the trips we've taken, and adventures we've had together. I've had such a fabulous life with you. You've given, done, and taken me places where I could never have been, had or experienced without you. I am so grateful and blessed. I love you Captain so much, and I am the luckiest girl in the world.

Love you forever and a day!

XOXO
Your Princess

Mother's Day was approaching, and I was hesitant since, in my heart, I knew this was probably the last Mother's Day we would have with Mom. Cindy's brunch was wonderful, as always. We took photos like we always do—although we definitely took more this year. I think my mom even was aware of it. She was such a good sport. At this point, she did not engage as much as she used to. She was always the conversationalist and fun. However, now, we were the ones trying to get her talking and lift her spirits. Charles had just turned seventeen, so we also celebrated him, and it always made Mom happy having the grandkids around.

Love Letter to My Captain
May 14, 2018

Hey Lover –

Thank you so much for my beautiful Mother's Day flowers, you always know how to make me feel special. Thank you for spending the weekend down here and everything you've done and continue to do to help with my mom and dad and my babies.

Yesterday was a rough day for me, and obviously for my mom. Thank you for understanding my crazy mood swings during this time, I realize this is all part of life but I can't help to think about never talking to my mom again. I guess it will be a learning process that I'll have to go through.

I hope you have a fan-tabulous (lol- my tabulator) week and are able to hit some balls or at least head out on the course. You're so hot when you swing and hit that ball… Love it… Sexy and Powerful…

Thank you again for being everything to me, I can't imagine this life without you.

Sleep tight lover

XOXO
Your Princess

Forever and a day

We were closing in on Trip #37. This time, we were heading back to the city that never sleeps. Cody was graduating with his Doctorate of Podiatric Medicine from the New York College of Podiatric Medicine with honors.

Love Letter to My Captain

May 20, 2018

Hi Love of My Life,

We have an exciting week and weekend coming up. I can't wait to spend time-days on end with you. I love to travel with my Captain and I'm excited to see Diana and Kevin. It'll be great getting the Provenzano's and the Ingram's together with the Murray's. I can't believe we are over half done with May? And lest I forget, my beautiful, crafty birthday card and the ensuing cosmetic procedure. I'm super excited! You spoil me and I am so fortunate. I love you to pieces!

You are my forever and a day

XOXO

So excited to get on a plane with you on Wednesday!

The birthday card Captain gave me read:

Every little bit of me loves every little bit of you…just the way you are.

It was very sweet—although the years were beginning to show on my face, my neck primarily. I called it my "turkey neck." Years ago, my mom had an envelope that she called her "facelift fund" with a heap of twenty-dollar bills in it. I don't know if she ever truly meant to use it for that, especially since every time the grandkids were over, she would slip them money from the envelope. Mom looked great, though. She didn't have a turkey neck like I did!

Paul's card had been personalized with cut-outs of women's necks and upper bodies, with a picture of my head and face. On the other side of the card were three pictures of turkeys and their sagging necks. It was very creative, and low and behold, Captain's gift to me this year was a facelift—or as I called it, a turkey lift, haha. I was so excited to get the work done and tell my mom about it.

P. S. She smiled when I told her.

Love Letter to My Captain
May 28, 2018

My Love,

Fresh back from NYC and I am so sad to see you go home. Although I have to say we made such great memories and had lots of laughs. It was double the fun with Diana and Kevin. Thank you so much for making it possible for us to go and see Cody graduate. I'm so proud of these kids. Trip #37 in the books!

Looking forward to traveling with my Captain, whenever and wherever that may be, next time. I am the luckiest girl in the world and I let everyone know it. Now to get more listings sold, especially 915 W. Lake when you're ready for it to go. Maybe we'll get to go up there sometime soon.

I love you Captain and I'm looking forward to seeing you Wednesday at Greenbanks!

Sleep tight my love

XOXO
Love your Princess

Cody's graduation ceremony was at nine a.m. at the Lincoln Center the day after we arrived in New York. It was sunny and warm, and I felt so fortunate to share this day with him, Madeline, Charles, Ludovico, and Cody's mom, Patty. After the ceremony, we went to Tavern on The Green in Central Park. We spent some time taking pictures at the fountain, recalling when we did this a few short years earlier. These kids were no longer kids; they were professionals.

We stopped at The Boathouse for a refreshing beverage and returned to our hotel, The Empire. The hotel had a great rooftop bar that we always frequented when we stayed there. Tasty cocktails, sun, fun, and, of course, euchre! Diana and Kevin even joined us a couple of times. We are so fortunate to have the children we do. How did we get so lucky?

Take Away:

If you're going to wear heels in New York, keep a pair of flats in your bag. Central Park in heels is really no "walk in the park."

Chapter Sixty-one

Caught Between a Rock and a Hard Place

Love Letter to My Captain

June 18, 2018

Hi Lover –

Bam!! That was quick, where did the weekend go? Thank you for coming downstate and for the party, I could not have had the party without your help, both physical and financial. Thank you for being an awesome cohost and for letting us get the deck done. I hope your Father's Day was enjoyable, I know you would've liked to have been with your babies. You're coming back in a few days and I can't wait! I'm sure I'll be able to give you my undivided attention! I'm excited for Diana and Kevin to come in, we'll have fun. Laughs, Euchre and a bottle or two of wine, a perfect combination for my perfect Captain!

Love you Bunches & Bunches

You are my heart!

Xoxo
Your Princess

The previous weekend, we had celebrated Father's Day at Ridgeway. My mom was able to come—although she was quiet. Joseph brought his new girlfriend, Margie, and introduced her to my parents. I was happy she was able to meet them. I didn't know how much longer we would have Mom with us.

Diana and Kevin had a wedding to attend in the Detroit area, so they stayed with us, too. The four of us went out golfing together. I tried—and I will always keep trying, despite golf not quite being my forte. I do love being on the course, though.

Love Letter to My Captain
July 8, 2018

Hey Lover,

Thank you for the beautiful extended holiday, we had five sleeps together. Sorry I had to leave on Friday for the day, but I came back :-) I wouldn't miss an opportunity to sleep next to my Captain.

Happy 8 1/2 year anniversary. I can't believe how fast time is going. I guess it's because we're happy and life is good. I'm so grateful for you and everything you continue to do for me. I'll continue to bring checks in, even if it's not regularly, at least you have my sparkling personality...hehe.

Life is such a blessing and I am blessed to be on this journey
with you. Please take care of yourself when I'm not with you,
I want to have the opportunity to spend as much of our lives
together as we can.

I love you with all my heart

XOXO

Forever and a Day
Your Princess

Fourth of July was spent in Tawas and then at Mt Pleasant for the weekend. I headed home on Sunday to get ready for the week ahead.

On Monday morning, my dad called me. Mom was back in the hospital. My heart immediately sank again.

Cindy and I headed to Beaumont. It was a rough stay for my mom. She was at the point where it was challenging to do her breathing treatments with the trial medication. Since it was a special machine for that drug, the hospital did not have the equipment needed, and we would end up having to bring it in and teach the nurses what to do. The shifts were always changing, too, making it virtually impossible for everything to run smoothly. Plus, by this time, Mom's pulmonary arterial hypertension had advanced, and we knew it was harder on her now to do the treatments. She spent the next thirty-five days between the hospital and rehab center (nursing home), as she was losing her ability to walk. It was heartbreaking.

Love Letter to My Captain

July 22, 2018

Goodnight Sweetheart,

I wish I was laying next to you right now. I feel so safe in your arms. Thank you for going to the nursing home with me, it's so sad and depressing. I know we didn't get to spend too much time together this weekend and I'm sorry about that but we will make it up. My life seems to be made up of doctors, hospitals and the nursing home. It's sad to see my mom in this condition she is in. And this is the way life goes...

I am excited for Erica and Isaiah to come in next weekend. She's your little Tawas girl, she loves it so much. You'll have fun with them, I'm bummed I'm going to miss two of your home cooked meals! I love you Captain and I hope you have an awesome week. My heart is always with you. I am the luckiest girl in the world to be called yours! Thanks for making that happen.

Hugs and kisses

Forever and a day... And then some

Your Princess who loves you and proudly wears your PBM's.

Love Letter to My Captain

July 30, 2018

Goodnight Sweetheart,

Another month down the calendar. How quickly July went! It was a beautiful weekend with my Captain. I'm so glad Erica and Isaiah were able to make it up to Tawas this summer, they're so much fun. I'm sorry if it seems or feels I have abandoned you a little. I'm so preoccupied with this new phase of life. Taking care/guiding/being there for my Mom & Dad. It's the uncertainty of everything that gets to me. I know no one knows their future, and I realize the decline and passing on are all part of life, but damn it's hard! Thank you for being by my side and helping me and thank you so much for always being willing to call my folks and talk with them.I have been blessed to have you and to have you know my parents when they were healthy. That means so much to me.

I am super excited for the birthday trip! My Captain gets better every year, and definitely more handsome! Thank you for allowing me to share the last almost 10 birthdays with you. I'm not sure how my week is going to go, I'm sure it will be taking care of more personal matters than my real estate life. I do have two appointments this week though. In addition, I just listed a home in Saint Clair Shores and that may have some action this week. Thank goodness for work, as it takes my mind off the present situation even if it's just for a few minutes. I promise you I won't always be like this, I'll adjust to the new norm at some point. Please be patient and tender to me. I hope you have a fabulous week and some fun squeezed in there. I'll miss you honey.

XOXO
Your Princess

I tried to be happy when I was with Captain; however, what was happening at home with my mom was always on my mind. She was safe at the rehab center, and I knew nurses and aides were around to help her. When I would go and visit, I'd take her for a wheelchair walk outside in the common area where there were flowers and container gardens. They also had a large glass bird enclosure, and we'd watch them flitter around. Mom was always an animal lover... The number of strays we took in through the years could verify that!

Captain's birthday was coming up, and we had planned a trip to D.C. to celebrate his sixty-fifth. I was hesitant to go—although my dad assured me I should. Mom was stable, he was ok, and Cindy and Doug were around if needed. My greatest fear—again—was my mom passing when I was out of town.

Love Letter to My Captain
August 6, 2018

Hi Baby –

It's your birthday week! DC is around the corner and we get to be with the kids. I'm so excited. I know you really need this break, thank you for putting up with me and all the family issues going on right now. You are a fabulous, generous, kind and tender man and I am so lucky to call you mine! I hope

you are able to get what you need done this week before our
trip. Know that I love you forever and a day and then some!

XOXO
Your Princess

We left on August ninth for Trip #38 to the nation's capital. This time, we stayed at the hotel Mason & Rook. We had a great time with the kids. We ate extravagantly, had great conversations with craft cocktails, visited the cigar bar, and walked into a surprise birthday party for Captain in our hotel room. The kids had even put together a book of Tawas memories for their dad. It was so precious and thoughtful.

We came home on August thirteenth, and the next day, Dad and I went to pick up Mom and bring her home from the rehab center. She was still having difficulty walking, but with our assistance, we could—or thought we could—take care of her. My dad hated the thought of her in the nursing home, even though, at this point, she was in what was considered the rehabilitation unit. For the next fifteen days, my mom was back at home and more at ease. But when you are at this phase of winding down—Mom called it—things can change quickly… and they did.

A short time later, we visited the family physician, who encouraged us to look at options for my mom, such as having someone come in, or trying a different setting for her with additional help, and not necessarily a nursing home. The days were manageable with my mom; she would rest and sleep, but she kept trying to get out of bed and walk at night. She needed a walker but would hop out of bed and just start walking. We always had to be on high alert so she would not fall. Cindy and I took turns in the evenings. It was tough. One night, I heard Mom get up, so I jumped off the couch in the other bedroom and ran to make sure she was ok. I started to feel dizzy, and everything around me was turning black. I lay outside the bathroom on the floor, hoping to still be able to watch my mom. Dad was up by now, and I think that is when we realized we had all given it our best shot. We could no longer do this alone.

Love Letter to My Captain
September 3, 2018

Captain,

It was so nice to be back in Mount Pleasant. A much-needed escape from what's happening downstate. Thank you for being so understanding and flexible during this stressful time. The thought of losing my Mom is so hard for me, but I know I have to accept it. Loss is part of life. It sucks though. Thank you for being by my side through it all.

We have some exciting stuff going on in our lives. It may be stressful, although I know my Captain always makes decisions that benefit us and thinks through them, to avoid the possible collateral damage. Whatever happens we'll be together, for that I'm sure. Your guidance is a blessing in this crazy life of mine. I'm super excited for our next adventure together, whatever that may be I love you forever and a day.

My former mother-in-law was living at a place called My Doctors Inn. It was a senior/assisted living residence. They had one, two-bedroom, and studio apartments. We visited it and made the very hard decision to transfer Mom there. She would have her own room, and staff were available all night. Dad could also go and stay all day if he wanted to, have meals with her, and then go home and sleep through the night without worrying. It sounded like an ideal situation, but, in truth, it never got easier on the heart. Mom seemed to enjoy being there. At least in the beginning...

Love Letter to My Captain
September 11, 2018

Lover,

Where do I start? There are not enough words in the English language to express my love and gratitude for you.. You keep letting me improve myself and to get better and better for you and us as a couple. I know it sounds all mushy and every-thing, but I really, really do believe we were meant for each other. Of course, you just had to wait till I got out of dia-pers... Lol. Timing is everything and I believe we met at the time we should. We've had so many cool experiences that have brought us closer together and laughter, silliness and even a few tears.

Collectively, we've married off three daughters, net two and more marriages to come. It's interesting to think about Joe and Charles and how their love lives will play out. This coming year is so full of changes, my gosh, I guess we eat the elephant one bite at a time, fun stuff!

Thank you for going to Ann Arbor last Saturday night. I don't get to spend that much time with my Joseph so it was great to be able to have him and Margie cook for us, and make us cool cocktails. I love hanging with all our kids, each and everyone is so different.

Thank you, thank you, thank you for my neck/mini facelift.
Bye-bye turkey neck! Let's hope we like the results!

I love you so much my Captain. You are my heart and soul
and my everything. Thank you for being you and for loving
me.

XOXO
Your Princess

So, you might be wondering why I went ahead with the cosmetic surgery when all of this was going on. However, it had been scheduled—although I was going to reschedule—and my dad insisted I see it through. He said, "We have to continue with our lives because Mom would want that." Again, he noted that she was safe and he would be ok. The recovery period would be seven days, and at least we had FaceTime. There was that part of me that also knew how much Mom had always wanted the same surgery, so I thought about how she would be happy knowing I was getting it done—in a way, it was for both of us.

Love Letter to My Captain
September 16, 2018

Hi Lover –

It's me, your stapled up girlfriend who looks like her ears were
just sewn on… Lol. Thank you so much for coming down-
state again for me. By next weekend I should look a great
deal better, at least with make up on. Sorry it was a bit boring
here, I love being able to snuggle next to you even if I can
only touch your arm. The next few months into the end of the

*year sure will be busy. Looking forward to traveling with my
Captain again oh how I love it so, you have so much pressure
on you now. I hope I'm not putting any more on than you
already have. Thanks for being my Captain and everything
that goes with it.*

*I love you Forever and a Day and I can't imagine my life
without you. I pray we'll always be as happy as we are now, if
not more. Congrats on getting Tawas under contract!*

XOXO

*Love,
Your Princess.*

Captain left, and on Monday, my dad took me to get my staples
removed. My parents were always there for me, Paul, and my kids.
You didn't even have to ask; they would know you needed help and
insist on helping.

After the surgeon's office, we went to My Doctor's Inn. I could
not wait to hug and kiss my mom, touch her skin, hold her hand,
brush her hair, and just sit there with her.

By this time, Mom had been there for a few weeks, and there had
been a few falls. One was bad enough to send her to the hospital. We
became unsure whether this was the right place for her after all. It
was so hard on Dad not having her at home. He kept saying that he'd
made the wrong decision.

On September twenty-third, we left My Doctor's Inn with my
mom and brought her back home. Dad kept saying how he should
have never taken her there in the first place. But who really knows if
a decision made is the correct one? You use the information available

to you at the time and hope you made the right decision. If not, you pivot and try again. We had tried, and now, we were going home. This time, my dad decided to get a couple of caretakers to come in and help during the day. We were going to try the nights again and see what happened. We could always add more hours on.

Love Letter to My Captain,
September 23, 2018

> *Goodnight Sweetheart,*
>
> *Thank you for the great weekend, sorry I had to leave early today. I'm hoping you had a nice and relaxing Sunday. Thank you for taking me to Ascend. It was fun to go out and forget about life for a while. I'm not sure what these next few weeks will bring over at Devonshire, I pray they will be somewhat uneventful and my Mom and Dad can get into some sort of a rhythm in their daily life. Something tells me that won't happen though. Thank you for understanding what I'm going through. I love you Captain with all my heart and appreciate how you always step up to the plate, even when they're not your family or your responsibility. You are the greatest!*
>
> *I love you bunches and forever and a day!*
>
> *XOXO*
> *Your Princess*

Soaring Eagle Casino had just opened a new sports bar, so Captain and I thought we would check it out. Do not get me wrong; I am not a big gambler. However, I loved going back to the Casino because it would bring back fond memories of our first weekend back in 2010 when I started falling in love with this wonderful man. I remember Paul out on the floor dancing to the Cupid Shuffle. Be still my beating heart!

Two of the most poignant moments in my life were watching Mom sign her hospice paperwork and, eighteen months later, seeing Dad do the same. It was surreal. I realize hospice is there to support the process of passing—and it surely did for my parents—and sometimes, people "graduated" from hospice and went on to live longer than expected, but seeing my parents sign that paperwork… They were just so brave and ready to move on. They both lived full lives and now seemed content. It was me who had to make peace with this final stage.

Love Letter to My Captain
September 29, 2018

Mr. Handsome,

Happy Saturday! Hope it was a good day for you today. I wish I could have been there with you and did fun Saturday things. Thank you for including the girls on your shareholder retreat trip. It was nice to get away for a couple of days. I tried to be present and forget my worries for a few. I'm glad I had some time with my Captain. I enjoyed our little side trip through the tunnel of trees, it was beautiful and thank you for that I I'm not sure about next weekend, I guess we'll figure it out.

I love you forever and a day and appreciate you so much, thank you for being my Captain.

XOXO

The shareholder retreat was in Bay Harbor in Petoskey. This, more than likely, was Captain's last time, as his planned to retire the following fall. I was a wreck leaving my parents. I convinced myself that nothing would happen to my mom for those three days I was gone, and Cindy would be there with Dad in the evenings. I would take over once I came back downstate. And, again, Dad told me to go.

Take Away:

You cannot physically be in two places at once. I made a decision and knew what the consequences could be. Again, we make decisions with the knowledge and information available to us at the time.

CHAPTER SIXTY-TWO

Will I Ever Be the Same?

October, 2018

I left Captain that Saturday morning, which incidentally was my son Joe's twenty-third birthday, and headed to my parents' house. I spent that evening there with Dad and the next seven nights. My sister had gone home to get some sleep; however, I ended up calling her the next morning, and she, too, would spend the next several days there with me. One of the many benefits of hospice is the medication they provide to allow patients to be pain-free and relaxed. Of course, the dilemma is… when is one at that point? We had never experienced this before, so the guidance from hospice was invaluable. The last thing we wanted to do was have Mom in pain. We ended up getting a hospital bed for her and put it in the family room, across from the kitchen. We wanted to be around her, and she loved entertaining, so this was our way of having her where she loved to be. By this time, we were down to one caregiver, who came in for a few hours during the day, as Mom was bedridden. Even though we were there, it was nice to have someone else to ask questions to who had been down this road before.

I write still with the heaviest of hearts... Mom passed away on Saturday, October sixth, at approximately nine p.m. Hospice told us that sometimes our loved ones will not pass if we sit with them or watch them. We, of course, didn't want to leave her side. That day was cold and rainy. Madeline, Cody, and Ludovico came by around eight p.m. and brought our little dog, Skittles, whom Mom loved. Skittles jumped right up on the hospital bed and curled up. It was like he knew what was happening. My dad was on the couch talking with Ludovico, Madeline and Cody were at the counter, and Cindy and I were in the kitchen feeding them all. Cindy had whispered in Mom's ear earlier in the day that she was making a chicken. Mom even squeezed her hand when she told her. We all understood at this point that Mom could not eat and wasn't talking anymore, but the squeeze of Cindy's hand told us she was aware. Cindy also wanted the house to smell like the home-cooked meals Mom would make because we knew it was getting close to her time. A few minutes before the 8:59 p.m. alarm on my phone went off, reminding us that it had been two hours and time for her medication, I had gone over to her, like I had many times, kissed her head, and told her how much I loved her. However, within those few minutes of being away in the kitchen, something had changed. Cindy and I lowered her bed, and there came a final exhale. Mom had passed when we weren't looking. I was devastated at first because we hadn't been there with her. Then I thought about it and realized it was her choice. Being a mother, I am not sure I would want my kids to witness my death. Would it be something gruesome? Tragic? Or a comfort for them? My mom was so selfless; she died as she had lived. The rest of the family gathered at the house and said their goodbyes. My heart broke when my dad crawled into bed next to her, held her, and cried. These are the moments that stay with you forever.

Captain had spent the day in Tawas working on emptying the furniture out of the condo. As the day went by, I remember hoping that he would head downstate to be with me; however, he had no way of knowing she would pass that night, either. When I called him, I just cried. I mean, I knew losing my mom was inevitable, and I should have been relieved that she was finally free, but the sheer finality of it still hits you right in the center of your heart. Thankfully, Captain headed downstate the next day to spend a few hours with Dad and I.

Three days later, Mom would have turned eight-two years old. We gathered at my parents' house that evening and sang to her on a chocolate bumpy cake, one of her favorites.

Two weeks later, we held a celebration of life for her. It was lovely, and Ludovico eulogized her, as she had always asked him to do. Even though we were divorced, he was—and still is—a large part of our family.

Love Letter to My Captain
October 16, 2018

Lover,

Thank you for inviting me to Sara's speech. I am so glad I was able to come up here for it. I know how proud you are of all your girls. You and Sue did a great job raising them, and they know it. Sorry I couldn't go with you to Tawas today, thank you for picking up the pace so we could close sooner than later. I love you and thank you for steering my ship, our ship, and my life and always making the best decisions for us.

I love you to pieces and forever and a day… And then some-sleep tight my love!

XOXO
Your Princess

Sara was asked to speak at The Women's Initiative Luncheon in Mt Pleasant that year. She flew in from D.C., where she was working for CNN as a political correspondent. She spoke of her years growing up in Mt Pleasant, the tight-knit community, the opportunities she had, and how it helped her in her career—among other things. I was still raw from my mom's passing and remember thinking, *How can my life be "normal" again? I'll never have another conversation with her, and we spoke every day.* Life was never going to be the same.

Love Letter to My Captain
October 22, 2018

Hey Lover,

Now you only own two homes! Isn't downsizing great lol seriously, we've come off of my mom's funeral luncheon, a baby announcement, and a sale of your summer home. Life keeps changing, and all through it I have grown to love you more. Thank you for being by my side during this time with my mom and helping my dad out also. I love you so much and I'm so glad my Mom grew to know and love you also. I'm going to miss her so much. 😞 *Have a great couple of sleeps and I'll see you on Thursday for more fun. I love you Captain you are my forever and a day!*

XOXO

Earlier that day, Captain and I were in Tawas at the title company closing on the condo. I headed home that evening, knowing these chapters of my life kept closing. You cannot hold onto time, but you can hold on to memories… And we would be making new memories after Madeline and Cody announced they were having a baby, due the following June! On the evening Mom passed, Madeline told my dad that she was pregnant with his great-grandchild. It was a bitter-sweet moment, and I am glad she could share it with him.

Love Letter to My Captain
October 28, 2018

Hey Lover,

Another super fast weekend flew by, I can't believe how fast time is going! It seems to fly even faster when I'm with you. Thank you for including me in the client appreciation event for Robert F Murray, and for letting us pamper ourselves at Pure Vitality. You take such good care of us. I'm the luckiest girl in the world. Even though I'm headed downstate today I'm already looking forward to seeing you again. Five sleeps and I'm going to count them down! I'm working on getting used to my new norm, without my mom, and I'll try to remain happy, but please understand if I get a bit weepy sometimes. I'm so fortunate I have you and you're such a great support system for me and my dad, another reason I lucked out. I hope you have a great week and these pillows work out well you are always in my heart. I won't see you on Wednesday so I'll say it now…"Happy Halloweenie" and now keep your weenie tucked away! Lol

Love you Sunshine

Xoxo
Forever and a Day!

We tried out one of those float tanks. It was a unique experience and very relaxing, which is exactly what I needed. And for the pillows... Well, I'm sure My Pillow Guy is a great marketer, but I'm not a fan. Maybe we will try Giza sheets next?

Take Away:

A number of years before Mom passed, I wrote her a thank you letter for being my mom. It was cathartic knowing she had read that letter years before, and I found it tucked away in her drawer. Writing your thoughts of gratitude not only makes your loved one feel special; you will find peace knowing you held nothing back.

Chapter Sixty-three

Try to Keep It Interesting, and Hide the Sorrow

Love Letter to My Captain
November 4, 2018

Goodnight Sweetheart,

Thank you for coming downstate this weekend and "buying into" the wig. It sure was fun wearing it out. You think I like the attention, in reality I like the attention it brings to you. I like doing things like that for you. It keeps our relationship exciting. I love adventures with you.

Thank you for picking up the difference on Friday at Andiamo's. Family time is good for us now, especially my dad. Thank you for being so good to him. Will have our good days and bad days. I'm so excited about our upcoming trip to Austin and the excitement that will follow with Isaiah and Erica. I'm so happy for them. They're going to make a great team as they go through life. Talk about teams, thank you for including me in your team in life and in 'coupleship". I'm so happy in our relationship. I hope you always feel you can talk to me about our relationship if there's something that is bothering you. I don't want us to bury anything.

I love you sunshine for all my life, you are my forever and a day and then some. Thank you for being my captain. I'm looking forward to this coming weekend already!

XOXO
Your Princess

I decided to purchase a long-haired, auburn-colored wig. It was not meant to be worn out in public, but Captain loved it, so I wore it when we ventured out to Partridge Creek to see a movie and catch a bite to eat. It was comical, actually; I received several compliments, and not one person asked if it was my real hair. I broke out in laughter at one point as Paul kept putting his arm around my shoulders, and he almost knocked it off my head a few times! It was so fun to have a few laughs after everything I had been through.

Love Letter to My Captain
November 12, 2018

Goodnight my Lover –

I'm sorry I'm not laying next to you right now, I'm sure your other blonde is with you though. Thank you for the great weekend, I really enjoyed being out with you and being at home snuggling. I know I may not be a barrel of fun at times, I'm still so sad. Hopefully in time I'll learn how to be sad and still enjoy life. Thank you for always loving me, the way I am and always being my Captain. Thank you for all the support, financial and otherwise. I love my teammate – two is better than one.

I love you Captain

XOXO

Love Letter to My Captain
November 19, 2018

Hey Lover,

Thank you, Thank you for being such a trooper this weekend and outlaying all the finances for everything we did. It really was a fun weekend and luckily we made it through without any catastrophes. I can't even begin to know what my life would be like without you thank you for coming into it and being the best boyfriend ever!

Maybe one day you'll realize, even though I know you already do, how eternally grateful I am for you. I say this because I can't even put into words how I feel. So, I hope you get my eternally grateful vibes.

Looking forward to our next month and a half- all the fun we have planned. Our journey is the greatest!

Love you Captain

Xoxo
Your Princess

Thanksgiving was in a few days. It would be our first holiday without Mom. We placed a picture of her from a previous Thanksgiving in a heart frame next to my dad, in the place where she always sat at my dining room table. I tried to keep myself busy to avoid the pain that I was feeling, but I still felt it. We all did.

Love Letter to My Captain
December 2, 2018

Hey Lover,

My man who has the "icky siki" going on. 😴 *I hope today was a better day for you. I'm sorry I had to leave so early today. I hope you had a relaxing day watching the Lions play, or maybe you just turned the TV right off.*

I hope by staying in today you're feeling better. I love you so much and hate it when you don't feel well. In just a handful of days will be in the warmth of Florida, at least I hope it's warm. OK lover, have a goodnight's rest and I'll see you in five sleeps!

Your Princess
XOXO

P.S. Thank you for the beautiful poinsettia.

Trip #39 was scheduled in early Decemebr. Captain had another conference. We stayed at The Westin in Fort Lauderdale. I knew getting away would be good for us as I had not been the most "present" girlfriend. We enjoyed our stay, though, and I called Dad every day to check in.

Love Letter to My Captain

December 16, 2018

Hey Lover,

Thank you so much for always being so generous, with me and my family. I sure am lucky you love me and enjoy my company. I really believe we are perfect together.... except for that thing about having to have a home in lower Michigan I keep insisting on......Seriously, it's really, really important to me and if things change then I'll let you know. I know you're the decision-maker, so I really need to stress how important it is to me. Please please, please take it into serious consideration. I couldn't move away full-time. I know we'll travel and that I can understand, but taking me away from lower Michigan would be devastating. I would die on the vine.

Xoxo

Captain and I had the "what if" conversations about marriage, housing, and future winters as he was due to retire the following year. After losing my mom, the glue of our family, there was no way I could move out of the area. Dad needed us—my siblings and I—Charles was still in high school, Madeline was having a baby, and my life was here, at least for now. At this time, I also insisted that if he wanted me to move, it wouldn't be a good idea to propose. The challenge with long-distance relationships is that when they become no longer long-distance, one party must make the move. It is almost like playing chicken... Who is going to move first?

Christmas Card from My Captain
December 25, 2018

Dear Princess,

You are My Forever and a Day.

I'll Love you Forever and Couldn't Imagine Forever to Be without you!

You are my Princess-

Love Your Captain

I spent Christmas with my family and then flew out to Austin on December 27 with Captain for Trip #40. Isaiah had planned to propose to Erica on December 28 in Fredericksburg, Texas. It was a surprise for Erica, and even more of a surprise when her and Isaiah's family emerged to congratulate them. While in Fredericksburg, we did some really cool things, like attend a polo match—unfortunately, in the rain, but what the heck? I had never been to a polo match!

After a couple of days, we headed back to Austin and celebrated New Year's with the kids.

Take Away:

One can travel, keep busy, preoccupy themselves to run away from grief, or try to pack it away and bring it out later… However, it did not work for me. I am a terrible actor.

Chapter Sixty-four

Something Unexpected

Love Letter to My Captain

January 3, 2019

Wow,

What a ride that was, a holiday whirlwind sprinkled with an engagement! How fun that trip was to Texas. A great family time. Thank you for including me in your life and for being so accommodating with my family. I know at times it can be overwhelming. Thank you for my Christmas presents you are always so good to me. I love my pearls and can't wait to wear them.

So this is the beginning of the final full-time tax season for you. I hope you enjoy it and it's not too stressful for you. I'll do my best to be aware of a stress level and try not to cause you any more. Thank you and thank you for being my HOT, HANDSOME, and SEXY Captain, and for the 12 sleeps together!

Love you forever and a day

XOXO

The holidays were over, Erica was engaged, and we returned to our other lives. I was looking forward to the new baby, and we started planning for the baby shower. I kept thinking, *I wish Mom was here. She would be so excited, and we could talk about the upcoming birth.* It would take a lot more time to heal.

Lover Letter to My Captain
January 27, 2019

Hey Lover,

Four sleeps till you're back in my "mount" Ridgeway bed…
He he…. I say mount because maybe I can mount you… Lol

Seriously, well I was serious about that. Pretty soon we will be in sunny warm Key West I am so excited. I better start planning my outfits, you know I'm such a girl. It will be nice to get out of the cold and to have our skin exposed to some sun I'm looking forward to us being together for so many days in a row. I love being with my Captain, whether it be hanging by the pool, at the beach or out on the town, it's so much fun! I feel so special being on your arm. You are my hot, handsome Captain and you mean the world to me. You have changed my life irrevocably and I'm so glad for Match. Here's to our future, in our journey as it continues down the road of the unknown.

Love you Captain!

XOXO

Trip #41 was back to Key West. We were there from February first to sixth. This time, we stayed at the Almond Tree Inn. It was a sister hotel to Orchid Key Inn, which we stayed at in 2011.

Captain and I love the laid-back lifestyle of Key West. Appropriate footwear is flip-flops or other flat shoes, but you know me by now— unless I was at the pool or beach, I was in my heels, baby! The day we went parasailing was the only exception as we walked to the marina. I know; what the heck was I thinking? An odd thing was happening to my Captain on this trip, though. Whenever we walked long distances, the back of his leg would tighten up, and he would have pain that would not go away, even after stretching. After researching it on Google, we—mostly me—decided that Paul needed to have it looked into. Little did we know that in February 2019, this would begin a medical journey for him that would change his life.

Love Letter to My Husband
February 11, 2019

My Lover, My Heart, My World,

Thank you, thank you and really thank you. Captain, I can't tell you what my life would be without you in it. I shutter to even think about it. You and I have grown deeper in love through the years and sometimes tears. We've had mostly ups and only a couple of downs. Without miscommunication, we can't grow and I realize I haven't been grown-up enough to open up to you and speak my thoughts. Thank you for always listening and taking me seriously.

I don't know what I'm going to do sleeping alone after 11 sleeps together. You become such a fixture in my life, especially when we get to sleep next to each other. I know we still go our separate ways during the week, non-vacation, so it's especially difficult to leave when we've been together for an extended period of time.

I know I have to leave though to be able to see you again. Key West is fun and relaxing. I am grateful we were able to get away. You're my perfect travel partner! I hope you have a good couple of days and I'll count down the sleeps till I get to see you again.

Love you bunches!

XOXO

The following Thursday was Valentine's Day. Captain was coming into town that evening for a doctor's appointment the next day. Little did I know everything I hoped for, wanted and waited for would arrive so unexpectedly.

Love Letter to My Captain
February 17, 2019

Dear Fiancee,

OMG! I can't believe I'm saying that! How exciting this weekend was. Thank you for making me your future wife. Thank you for making my dreams come true! My ring is so beautiful.

I'm so blessed you love me so much and you really planned this, the ring shopping, and picked it out with so much love. You asked my dad and got down on your knee how much more can a girl ask for?

Our journey continues and our love grows, and so many ways. I sometimes sit and think of all the fun, crazy times together and just smile. It's something I hope I never stop doing. Along with all our memories past we continue to make future memories. I'm glad you switched doctors, we have to keep you healthy. You are my heart and I love you so. I can't wait to be Mrs. Murray!

You are my everything. Thank you thank you for loving me!

Your future wife,

XOXO

Yes, that hit me totally out of the blue. He had placed a card on the coffee table, and we were just chatting like we always did when one of us arrived at the other's home. We would have a glass of wine or cocktail and talk about our day, the drive, what was new with work, and so on. I loved this time; it was the best, and I would look forward to it as much as my Captain coming in. Unbeknownst to me, he had spoken to my dad a few months earlier. I do not know how the conversation went, and I don't need to—although I'm sure there wasn't any hesitation from Dad. He probably said, "You don't need to ask me!"

Paul got down on one knee. "*Carol, will you spend the rest of your life with me?*"

I looked down in joyous shock and saw a perfect diamond ring.

My first words were, "*It's so big.*"

My second sentence was, "*Are you asking me to marry you?*"

I know, it should have been implied, haha, but I didn't want to make any assumptions.

Captain laughed and said, "Yes."

As embarrassing as this is to admit, I asked if he would say the words, "Will you marry me"? I guess I was just so shocked; I needed to make sure we weren't just carrying on the way it had been.

The resounding "Yes!" made it official. We hugged, kissed, and I kept admiring the gorgeous ring. We toasted, and I sat in amazement, thinking, *After all these years, is this really happening?* At this point, I had to make phone calls and let everyone know we were engaged! Captain then gave me the Valentine's Day card. He had written in it:

I Love Our Life, To My Soon To Be Wife!

Love Your Captain,

Forever and A Day

We woke up the next day, and Captain had a leg Doppler scheduled. It seemed that his leg pain could be caused from a blood clot…

Love Letter to My Captain
February 25, 2019

Lover,

Thank you for being the best fiancee ever! Not only did you buy me a beautiful ring, you always take care of me, physically, emotionally and financially. I look at you and my heart melts. I still get butterflies when I know I'm going to see you, and then I do, and I'm so happy! There's something about you that makes me fall in love with you over and over again each time we're together. I adore you Captain! I'm looking forward to seeing you next week and attending the KW awards ceremony with the two of my favorite guys! Saturday will be fun to with Russ and Cara. Sounds like she's making some interesting plans! I hope you have a good week and I pray your blood pressure stays low :-) love you more today than yesterday. And forever and a day and then some

XOXO
Your Princess

We had quite the weekend. On Friday evening, my real estate office celebrated the agent's production awards from the previous year. It was held at The Sound Board at the Motor City Casino. Charles went with us, as soon he would be licensed with Keller Williams Lakeside. I loved having my Captain with me at these events.

On Saturday, we headed downtown to Joe Muers with Russ and Cara. They wanted to celebrate our engagement. They had been part of "our" relationship from the very beginning, and they'd welcomed Captain into their lives. Russ and Captain hit it off right away. They are like "brothers from another mother," as the saying goes. We have shared many crazy nights together and endless bouts of laughter. They're like our friends Rob and Tina. You never know how things will unfold, but you can guarantee you're in for a fair amount of laughter and good times! They were also part of the infamous Table 8 at Madeline and Cody's wedding.

Take Away:

Friends make the journey more interesting. When life gets too busy, make the plans. Sometimes, we do not realize how much we need those connections.

CHAPTER SIXTY-FIVE

To Wed or not to Wed?

Love Letter to My Captain

March 3, 2019

Hey Love of My Life,

Thank you for the extended weekend. Thank you for switching doctors and taking care of your health. I know it's a bummer that we need to take pills, but the thought of losing you is awful. Please, please, please continue to take care of yourself. Thank you for leaving Sullivan with my dad. I'm sure it helped him get through this weekend of Autorama. I know he wanted to go and it must be so difficult to make the decision not to go.

Thank you for understanding my need for your support for my career and future business. I really need to have the "home court" advantage, knowing you're in my corner makes all the difference. I realize you're not interested in selling real estate,

and you feel you've been there done that with rentals, knowing
you still want me to pursue my dreams is all I need. You are
my heart and soul and I will always want to make you proud.

Loving you From Afar
Your Future Wife

Dad decided not to go to Autorama this year. With Mom passing away, he was having a tough time trying to be social. He felt safe at home, plus it was March. With his lung disease, the cold air was also challenging for his breathing. He loved Sully, though, so Paul let him stay with my dad for the weekend while he was in. For a few years during our relationship, I had this dream of Paul and I teaming up and selling real estate together downstate or purchasing a rental or two, since he was going to retire. We still had not spoken of a date or place to get married, only that we knew it would happen. So much was happening with tax season, Madeline's baby shower, my dad's illness, Erica planning her wedding, and Charles finishing up his senior year. One thing was for sure: I didn't want to interfere with whatever Erica and Isaiah were planning!

Love Letter to My Captain
March 9, 2019

Hey Lover - My Future Husband

My Anniversary Lover

I know it was a quick conjugal visit… Lol… Thank God this
doesn't happen often, the short visit part, not the conjugal
part lol I want lots of that. I hate leaving you so soon, I know
I'm supposed to be just fine and be a big girl, that's tough to

do since I love being together, or at least knowing we're in the same ZIP Code :-)

I can't believe it's already March, pretty soon tax season will be over where did the last two months go amazing! I'm sorry it's been so expensive lately it's not always going to be this way, I promise. I appreciate all that you do and continue to do. I know no one else would ever do what you have done. I hope you don't ever regret asking me to marry you? There are so many avenues of my life and obligations right now, sometimes I feel so overwhelmed. I feel I'm pulled in so many directions. I try to get new business and then I worry I'll be out of town and I won't be able to service them. So at times feel like I am a horse at the gate waiting to be let out, and then I stop and say I can't finish it so I better not start it. I know that when we're in one town and hoping that will be downstate, I'll be able to actively work, sit in open houses, be in the office more, and be more aggressive in my real estate life.

I know I can do more, and I know I can bring in more money. Please believe me. That way you'll feel I'm carrying my weight for my family.

I love you greatly and will always love you.
Your Princess

Let's unpack this love note. When one sells real estate, unless it is during a pandemic, and you cannot physically get into show homes and take listing appointments, you need to be local. This is a face-to-face business. Prospective buyers need to tour homes physically, or at least want to, for the most part, before making an offer. Sellers need to know you are around if a buyer calls you and wants to see their home. I had resources and friends that helped when I was away. One of the reasons I decided to become a realtor was for the opportunity to work with people and help them during these monumental times in their lives. It was not to pay someone to do it for me. I was excited to be able to "get back at it," as I did prior to meeting Captain. I have to say, though, that the clients I had through these years were very understanding and worked with me if they knew me personally.

The other part of the love note was the money part. This seems to be a recurring theme in my letters, along with that other recurring theme of insecurity. Actually, now that I think about it, they could go hand in hand in certain aspects. Let me again tell you how fabulous Paul was and how he didn't need to do what he did for myself and my family. He basically took on another family in the financial sense up to this point, at least my share of expenses. I was making money, but not enough—and not as often as I would like. A kind of storm was brewing, and I didn't know if I was going to make it out on the other side as a wife. We still had no date, no location, and no plans for our nuptials.

Burying this would not do any good; we needed to talk, and we did. The results of our conversation were sent out in a group email.

Email sent out to the kids on March 15, 2019

Hi Everyone!

We're trying to figure out timing for our nuptials. The most important part of this is all of you. We know all of you are busy- work, school, having babies, planning weddings, building empires, writing books, other family obligations and so on.

Email back what dates/months are good for you and what dates/months will not work for you through the end of the year.

We're flexible- right now we're thinking anywhere from 4-7 days - somewhere tropical.:) I don›t want to take any of you girls to Zika infested areas though.

Be sure to reply all.

Let's get this on the calendar. :)

Papa Bear says hi to all:)

xoxo

There it was, out in an email, officially. When Captain and I talked, I mentioned how important it was for us to have our children there. In lieu of a larger gathering with our family and friends, I wanted to go away with all of them and stay under one roof. Our kids and their spouses/significant others are so fun, and I love being with them. I knew my dad would not be able to travel anywhere, and I thought if he could not go, then really, no one else should. My heart was breaking thinking about my immediate family and our dear friends; however, I kept telling myself not to be silly since this wasn't my first time getting married, and we were older—at least in comparison to many first-time weddings. My choice was to go far away enough so that no one could "surprise" us, and I wanted this time to be spent with all our babies.

It took some emails back and forth, but six days later, we picked a date that would work for everyone.

Email sent out from My Captain to the email chain

I will Marry you in August Princess!

Let's block off August 8 to August 15. As plans progress I will keep you all posted. Once I get past April 15 Princess and I will have more time to plan the exciting details.

It's going to be a PARTY.....family wedding party!

It meant so much to me knowing we could get all the kids' schedules lined up to meet for a week in August. It would not be the same if any of them couldn't make it, and I was not going to settle for that. Anyone who knows me personally knows how much family means to me. Actually, even if you do not know me, I am sure you have gathered that already from this book thus far.

Take Away:

If something means the world to you, be authentic and speak your truth. Yes, this is also a recurring theme here.

CHAPTER SIXTY-SIX

One Step Closer

Love Letter to My Captain

April 1, 2019

Hello Love of My Life -

I'm sorry you're sleeping alone tonight and better be lol- before the duration till I get back here! What a fun couple of days. I know how tired you are and how this is wearing on you. It will be over soon. I know it doesn't make it any better, but it makes me happy knowing the countdown is on, and the countdown to us getting MARRIED!

I am so looking forward to becoming Mrs. Murray. I love you so much and our journey has been so exciting. I've done and experienced events and places and food and drink and all things exciting and fabulous – with you! We've shared sad times also, I think that makes us grow stronger and closer to each other. I pray we continue to grow deeper in love and share continued intimacy, physical and emotional. I love you baby!

Forever today And always

XOXO
Your Princess

Captain was busy, and I was, too. Between real estate, appointments, my dad's visits to Ann Arbor for his lung issues, and the impending baby shower, life felt like it would never slow down.

Love Letter to My Captain
April 6, 2019

Dear Captain -

May your stress be little

May your cocktail be full

May you get through the upcoming days

With Finality.....and a lift of the haze!

Lol

Sorry, just a bit of tax season humor. I'm hoping you had a productive day and are able to get a good nights sleep tonight. May be a little golf watching today and a nice dinner. I love you sunshine. Soon this craziness will end and then we can make a decision on our wedding in August! Yippee! Yes, there's no getting out of it Captain... At least, I hope that's not the case.

It'll be a number of sleeps till I'm in bed next to you again. Enjoy the other blonde. Sleep well my very hot, handsome Captain!

Love you bunches and bunches!

XOXOXO

We were waiting for the final tax season to be over, and then we would start researching where to go to get married—or should I say start discussing. I had been doing some research on my own, hoping to go somewhere we had never been or maybe somewhere we'd never been together. The baby shower was the following weekend, and then tax season wrapped up before Easter the following weekend.

There was exciting news at the baby shower—a gender reveal! Grandbaby #1 would be a boy. Madeline and Cody had picked a name but were keeping that a secret until birth. And yes, if you have thought about the timeline, this new little bundle would take his first airplane ride at approximately two months old!

Love Letter FROM My Captain
April 21, 2019

Dear Princess,

Happy Easter! Thanks for being my Princess. I love you more and more everyday. We may have our little bumps in the road but we'll always enjoy this journey together.

I look forward to our marriage in Hawaii and all goes smoothly with our large group of families. It will be interesting to see how we all interact together for a week. You are the glue that keeps everyone together… I love you

Happy Easter

Love your Captain

We had decided on where to go, and I was so excited. I had always wanted to visit Hawaii. It seemed like the perfect location for us to wed. Far away, yet still part of the U.S.—as a mom, I worried about the group's proximity to hospitals and health care if someone should need it.

Love Letter to My Captain
April 22, 2019

My Sweetheart,

Thank you for coming downstate to share the Easter holiday with my family. It was a busy weekend, thanks for hanging in there. I'm so happy tax season is over for you I know you're in recovery phase of post tax season and de-stressing. So many exciting events coming up! Our journey continues to be adventurous.

It was great to have you back in our Ridgeway bed. It's so comforting knowing you're laying there next to me. I regret we didn't get more alone time, what we did get was fun!

I Love you Sunshine so very much. I am so excited for our nuptials in Hawaii. It's going to be fun planning this! I know you didn't need more on your plate, I'll try not to keep bugging you. I know this isn't your first rodeo, but let it be just as special please.

OK lover sleep well and know that I am always there in the background supporting you and loving you even if we're in different counties.

Counting down the sleeps-

XOXO

Love you BIG time!

You have a BIG one!

Big things on the horizon

Your Princess

4Ever and a day!

Take Away:

Make the plans, but be flexible. Life has a way of throwing curve balls.

CHAPTER SIXTY-SEVEN

A Beautiful Summer and a Beautiful Baby

Love Letter to My Captain
May 6, 2019

Sunshine –

Thank you for the great weekend! What I loved about it? Hot tub time, snuggles, the red wig appearance, and the succeeding event 😜 I could go on and on. ....The best part-us planning our wedding!! The wedding bands search and decisions made!! I love them and I'm glad Steve was there to assist. I'm feeling better that we're clicking along. I know you're stressed. It's all going to fall into place. And thank you again for allowing the beautiful wedding location with all our kids.

And then after we're married don't stress, I'm not going to put on like a bazillion pounds or anything, and we will still have things to look forward to. We just have to look at life differently and try some different things. There's always going to be something new to do. We'll enjoy life Captain, don't worry

lover, close your eyes and go to sleep. I love you forever and a
day

XOXO

While Captain was still playing golf, his lower back and legs had been bothering him, so it was more challenging. He spent some time with a chiropractor, and it was determined he should see a spine surgeon.

Love Letter to My Captain
May 13, 2019

Goodnight Sweetheart,

Love you with all my heart. Thank you for making Mother's Day special for me. Thank you for spending time at Madeline and Cody's new house and putting up with all the craziness my family brings. This is such an exciting time for us. I can't wait to be Mrs. Murray! Even better having all our babies with us for the big event. I am the luckiest girl in the world and I know it, and tell others. You were a gift dropped down from heaven, and I value you so much, we fit! I love you Captain so so much- sleep tight and I hope you have beautiful dreams of beaches, cocktails and bikinis!

I love you forever and a day

XOXO

Madeline and Cody had just closed on their house with basically no time to spare; she was due to have our first grandbaby two weeks later! Cindy and Leon had brought Dad over to their new home the evening of the closing. I was happy he could see it; however, within a little while, they had to leave because he was not feeling well. This was truly the beginning of the end for my dad. Shortly afterward, he decided to stop the clinical trial meds. The cure was worse than the disease. He knew that, in doing this, the fibrosis would take over and hasten his death. It must have been a relief not having to take something you know makes you ill, only to realize you are probably past the point of it providing any long-term success. He had given it a good shot, and I am sure the data the University of Michigan collected helped in some way for the trial. Dad had said in the beginning he was glad to be a part of this study, since he knew could possibly help others.

Love Letter to my Captain
May 19, 2019

Hey Lover,

Thank you for the beautiful birthday weekend! Thank you for my beautiful birthday card and plant, and the walking around cash:)

You treat me so well and you make me feel so good! You know what I mean :-) I'm so excited about our future, and have loved our journey this far. I know I'll make a great wife. If the past is any indication the future which I believe it is we will be a great team! Thank you for letting my dad keep Sully again these past couple of days. Erica will be so excited to see him next week. We've had a great couple of weeks and more excitement to come! I'm looking forward to a great summer with my lover!

Sleep tight handsome

Your Princess forever in a day

XOXO

Captain gave me a card themed from a husband to a wife. Where it stated "wife," he had inserted the word "almost" above it. It was so endearing. He also wrote in it, *Dear Princess, Everyday I love you more than the last. I'll Love you Forever and a Day!*

The following weekend, Erica and Isaiah came to Michigan. They were staying downtown for a wedding. We met up with them on Friday evening and had some fun.

On Saturday, Madeline and I went wedding dress shopping. I felt odd purchasing a true wedding dress, the traditional white gown, but time was of the essence, and I couldn't order one as the wedding was less than three months away. I tried on a few, and most of them looked silly on an "older bride." I know, I was beating myself up for no reason—plenty of people get married later in life. Among the dresses, one had just come in as a floor sample, and no one had tried it on yet. As soon as I tried it on, I knew it was the one! Madeline loved it, too; however, I laughed because she was ready to have the baby any day. I said, "Are you sure you like it? Or do you just want to get home and rest that bump of yours?" I believe this might have been karma for when my sister, Cindy, found her wedding dress back in 1988. Cindy's wedding timeline was tighter, only six weeks away, no it wasn't a shot-gun wedding! My mom, my mom's girl-friend, Janice, Cindy, and I went dress shopping. We had only been shopping in Birmingham, at Jacobsens, for thirty minutes, and they had one dress that fit Cindy perfectly. She looked beautiful in it. We all said, "Great, that's it! Ok, let's go to Peabody's now for dinner." I remember Cindy looking a little pale and saying to us, "Are you sure this looks OK? I haven't tried any other dresses on?" Truthfully, though, it really did look amazing on her. I know it sounds awful, but we chuckle about it now.

Love Letter to My Captain,
May 28, 2019

> *Thank you for being so cool, thank you for being so fine, thank you for being mine. Another great weekend in the books. Crazy, fun, a bit of alcohol, and lots of family love! We are so blessed in our lives, I am the luckiest girl to have met you and have you all to myself. Our lives are changing, but we'll figure it out. I know you're concerned about where, when and what... It will work out. You are extremely smart and always make the right decisions, you chose me! Golf is fun. I'd like to spend more time doing that with you. Do you think I'll get any better?*
>
> *OK lover - as baby watch continues maybe that little bugger will show up next weekend when you're back in town. I guess we shall see*
>
> *I love you bunches and bunches*
>
> *XOXO*

The baby did not arrive the following weekend, either. The wait was tough. I had to draw the line between wanting to know everything and respecting Madeline and Cody's privacy during this special time.

Love Letter to My Captain
June 3, 2019

Happy June My Lover,

Amazing how quickly May flew by! I can't believe we're still on baby watch. I thought by now we'd have a little cutie pie to hold. I'm especially bummed you're not going to be here to join in the excitement of the birth. I mean if it arrives this week or weekend I can't imagine it going on any longer. Poor Madeline!

I hope if you decide to go on your golf outing that you take care of yourself. I love you so much and worry about your health. I know I can't be there with you all the time so I pray you don't neglect any signs or issues. I know you're smart and won't push it just remember we have a wonderful future ahead of us. We have an exciting summer and I'm so happy to be your soon to be wife!

It will be way too many sleeps without you, I'll miss you, I'll be happy you're having fun though.

Please be careful

XOXO

I love you forever and a day
Your future wife
Mrs. Princess Murray

Captain ended up going on the golf trip with Russ and his friends. I knew they would have fun— sometimes too much fun. Again, I will say that I always felt responsible for Captain, as his daughters were not in the same state. I would say, "What would I tell the girls if something happened to you?" It was a cross between a wife and a mom. Men do not want moms, though. Captain lived life on the edge; at least, he did up until this point. When you love someone so much, I believe you try to protect them as much as you can. The hysterical point of this is that Paul never listened to anyone. He still walks to the beat of his own drum, and if you told him to be careful, you never felt one-hundred percent sure he would. Captain is unpredictable; however, thankfully, nothing has ever gone awry. And this, too, is one of the reasons I love him and get frustrated with him at the same time.

The baby is here! Baby David arrived on June 6. Charles, his buddy Zack, Ludovico, and I sat in the labor and delivery waiting room at Beaumont Troy all night. This was, of course, after waiting in the parking lot for the first hour. Zack said that if we do not get a text soon, "let's storm the place." We all laughed, and that is exactly what we did. Madeline told us to wait at home, but we couldn't; the FOMO was too much. We received a few text messages throughout the night, and in the morning, a request from Cody to get my dad to the hospital seemed odd. Then, we were notified that Madeline had indeed given birth. Dad drove himself to Beaumont Troy, and we all went in to meet the precious little bundle. Becoming a grandparent is life-changing. I now understand how my parents felt. The love I felt instantly for this tiny human I cannot put into words.

Love Letter to my Captain

June 10, 2019

Hi Lover, My Sweet Lover –

Hot, handsome, and dashing lover – I'm so thankful that I was able to spend a few hours with you last night and this morning. I love you so much and I am so happy you came home alive and well from your trip! Glad you enjoyed yourself and had the some boy time.

Now, I can't wait for you to meet the baby! I know you'll love him as much as I do. He's so precious and so so cute. I'm looking forward to spending some extended time with you this weekend, snuggling and whatever else may happen, are tops on my list of things to do with you. You are my everything and I'm so fortunate to be your future wife.

I love you Captain

XOXO

Three sleeps till I see you again

XOXO love you forever and a day

Your Future Wife

Captain returned in one piece. He was initially on the fence about golfing due to his pain issues, which were exacerbated when he was golfing.

Love Letter to My Captain

June 17, 2019

Sunshine, my sunshine, my lover, my husband to be!

What a fabulous weekend! I sure hope you're not getting tired of coming downstate so much lately! I mean, I know I'm down here, and now we have a super cute grandbaby to snuggle.

I'm so glad you were able to meet the little guy when he was so alert. I really think he digs you, who wouldn't? We are so blessed to share such a wonderful life together with our kids, who are doing so well and are great people, fun to be with, loving, successful and accomplished, each in their own way. I can't wait for us all to be together in August. What fun it will be!

So many changes on the horizon, one love that endures, you have always been my forever and a day and will always be, and then some. I hope you have a great week, productive and relaxing.

I love you Babe –

Your Princess

We had celebrated Father's Day at Ridgeway. I had that same feeling from when it was my mom's last Mother's Day to celebrate as a family. Dad was declining, but he kept pushing himself. He was ever so grateful to hold his great-grandson and share the day with his family. My heart was full. My family was growing, and at the same time, we were on the path to loss yet again.

Love Letter to My Captain

June 24, 2019

Hey there Love of My Life –

Can you believe June is almost over! OMG! Where did the time go? It really goes by fast when you're happy and in love. We have so much greatness and blessings in our life. I still can't believe I am living this life. Who knew? Thank you! Thank you! Thank you!

I apologize for ambushing you with this house on the lake.... Royal Lake, that is. I have a really good feeling about this home. I think it will be good for us, and for you in the transition phase. If it's meant to be it will work out. If not... We just keep on keeping on... One thing is for sure, we have a beautiful life and love story. I am so excited to become Mrs. Murray! The celebration will be such a special time. I'm so glad we can have our children witness our marriage and share our honeymoon. I know it's unconventional, we can always go on vacations by ourselves, which we've done so much of and will do together as husband and wife in the future.

OK sunshine have a great sleep and know that I carry you in my heart always.

Counting down the sleeps again...

Love, love, love you always and forever

Forever and a Day

Your Princess

XOXO

By this time, we had settled on an island, Oahu, and made plans to stay at a VRBO—a vacation rental through an online travel company—on the water outside of Honolulu in Waianae. The setting looked beautiful in the pictures. After some research—thank you, Diana and Madeline—we decided to get married on the property and have a chef come to the house for our celebratory dinner. It would make things easier for everyone, and the location we were staying at was just as gorgeous as any other.

We had not really figured out where we would go after we were married, and I was not concerned. If I had to stay at Ridgeway while Captain finished his year at Robert F. Murray and stayed in Mt Pleasant, we would make it work. As a realtor, though, I am in the business of homes, finding and selling them, and I noticed there was going to be an open house on a place that looked good and checked most of the boxes. It was a ranch with a three-car garage, a basement walkout, and, as a bonus, was on a small body of water surrounded by other homes. We stopped by the first day of the open house and then went back on the second day. Funnily enough, this was a for sale by owner property. By the end of that second viewing, Paul and I were talking about making an offer. By the following weekend, our offer accepted and we were doing a home inspection.

Take Away:

Sometimes, if one is patient and does not push, every-thing can eventually fall into place as it was meant to be.

CHAPTER SIXTY-EIGHT

Hawaii or Bust

July, 2019

The doctor had Captain take some routine tests and scans to be proactive in his healthcare. These tests were taken on July eighteenth. Two days later, we received a call from the doctor alerting us to some elevated levels of calcium that were detected during the heart scan. We were booked to fly out to Hawaii in less than three weeks. He told us that it would be best to see a cardiologist before leaving. We were able to get into the cardiologist that my parents went to on the following Tuesday. What a long weekend that was.

That visit crushed me. The doctor had the test results and started talking about three tests he wanted to have done. We told him we were scheduled to get on a plane in a little over two weeks with all our kids to get married. He said, "I'll tell you when you can get on a plane." Captain and I looked at each other in disbelief. Then, I said we'll get these tests done ASAP.

I was numb when we walked out. I couldn't believe it. I know the heart is nothing to mess around with, but why was this happening right now? It took so long to line up a week where all the kids could make it. However, Captain's health was first and foremost, and if we had to delay the wedding or have it happen elsewhere—somewhere within a short drive—we would.

Email to the Family From My Captain
July 23, 2019

> *Hi All,*
>
> *For the past 3 months I've had various medical tests/exams. The doctors are all pretty optimistic that my conditions are treatable. Today's visit was with a Cardiologist. He suspects that I may have a blood clot. He's adamant that I do no flying until this is resolved. In this metropolitan area seeing a doctor on short notice is next to impossible. Thanks to Carol's help we were able to schedule a blood draw (done today), lower extremity arterial doppler test (blood flow in the legs) for tomorrow, 2D Echo of the heart to check the arteries, stress test (both set up for Thursday) and a return visit to the Cardiologist this Friday.*
>
> *We are hoping that all tests come back fine and we'll all be in the air on our way to Hawaii on August 8. We'll be sure to keep you posted.*

It was a crazy week. We went to whatever facility or hospital in the tri-county area that could fit us in for the required testing. I basically told every scheduler I called our story, usually tearing up. We ended with the final visit to the cardiologist on Friday, late afternoon. I cried again, this time tears of happiness.

Email to the Family From My Captain

July 26, 2019

*Hello Hawaii Fans. After a week of prodding and poking I
got the go ahead to make the trip to Hawaii* 😊

*No Clots, no heart issues and no other debilitating condi-
tions to "ground" Papa Bear. I'm healthy as a horse (old gray
Mare). So we'll have a great time and wonderful wedding
with my Princess. She was a huge support arranging last
minute appointments with difficult care providers.*

*I do go in Monday for an epidural shot for the pain in my
legs. The Orthopedic doctor determined that I have arthritis
in the lower spine which causes the leg pain. It's not a minor
condition but more likely moderate causing pinching of the
spine. Further treatments for this condition will be required
but is not life threatening.*

*So pack your bags, sun screen and Hawaii attire and get
ready to PARTY!*

Love P-Bear

Love Letter to My Captain

July 30, 2019

Lover –

*What a whirlwind of the past week! Talk about shocking…
and then the darkness was lifted and we were able to get
past it and look forward to our future. Boy, I was really
scared. I tried not to show it. You were such a trooper and did*

*everything you needed to do for us. Thank you sweetheart.
Now we can enjoy the next week and get excited about our
wedding and the trip! I've waited a long time to marry my
Captain. Life is good and we are really blessed. Thank you
for being my rock, even in times of your distress. What would
I do without you? I'm so excited for our future. I hope your L's
in your spinal column continue to heal from this injection and
your pain disappears.*

I love you sunshine

Bunches and bunches

XOXO

Pretty soon I will be Mrs. Murray!

Good night lover sleep tight

Love you forever and a day and then some

Captain was still dealing with the leg pain, hoping the injections would help. It was a tough week for him. The week ahead was going to be busy picking up the pace, or should I say where I left off, preparing for the trip. The baby was being baptized that Sunday, with the party following at Maddy & Cody's, expecting close to 100 family members. I was busy helping her, helping with the baby, helping with my dad, and I didn't care one bit if I was tired, exhausted, hungry, or anything. Captain was given the ok to fly, the pain injection was working, and we were getting married! I was loving every minute of the craziness!

Love Letter to My Captain

August 5, 2019

Sleeptight my Lover,

This is your last week as a single man. I sure am excited to marry my captain. I know we're going to have a great trip. I'm especially happy that all of our babies are coming with us! You've been such a good man to my family, thank you for being such a sport yesterday at the baptism and always acknowledging how I spend extra time with my kids and family. I pray you always are understanding and enjoy being with the family. OK lover, I pray you have a great week and next time I see you we will be off to get married

XOXOXO

Your Princess forever and a day

The baptism and ensuing party went off without a hitch. I remember the excitement of that day. My dad was in good spirits; he was talkative and feeling well. After a week of the unknown, this is exactly what we needed: to unite as a family, express pure gratefulness, and watch our grandbaby get christened.

Take Away:

True wealth is having your health.

CHAPTER SIXTY-NINE

The End of One Journey and the Start of Another

Trip #42 to Hawaii was the one that trumped them all… it was Captain and I's wedding! The day was so incredible; it was really an awesome vacation with all the kids. The "Hawaii Crew" had their own email thread, and, as Diana put it, they were "planning some extra shenanigans" in addition to the grocery list for the VRBO. The kids made the trip even more special than I had anticipated. They planned meals and took turns cooking. Everything was delicious— an extra shout out to Margie for her organic pancakes; they were amazing, as the others would attest!

Paul and I not only appreciated the cooking but also those extra shenanigans scheduled for us. Madeline organized a surprise bachelor/bachelorette party the night before the nuptials. She enlisted Charles and Sara to help with the games. It was so fun and silly; I loved every minute of it. As a group activity, they surprised us with a catamaran snorkeling tour where we could swim with the sea turtles. Diana, Kevin, Sara, and Cody are certified divers, so they also got a couple of early morning dives in. Of course, I wanted to attend a Luau. Although it was very touristy, it was very enjoyable. We all spent quality family time together, which is what I had really hoped for, and the kids also went off on their own to explore.

The wedding day itself was magical. I spent part of the day preparing thoughts I would share that evening at dinner with everyone. I felt an overwhelming sense of gratitude just in writing it and putting it on paper. I knew how special each one of our kids and their significant others were, so it was important to tell them. They each played a big part in our journey.

Captain and I were married at sunset on the water's edge. We had a traditional Hawaiian ceremony, complete with the conch shell blowing, ukelele player, leis, and combining our separate sand bowls, signifying our oneness. We stood for the entire ceremony, probably not the best idea, considering it was ninety degrees with seventy-six percent humidity, and Captain was in a suit jacket and I in heels. The kids had the right idea: the gals had cute sundresses, and the guys were in short-sleeve Hawaiian attire—most of the kids also didn't wear shoes.

The catered dinner was on the upper back deck, with a long table set with linens, candles, cases of stunning pink roses, ribbons, and elegant golden Mr. & Mrs. tags tied around our chairs with Navy blue (my favorite color) tulle—all courtesy of my loving Madeline. Captain and I sat beside each other at the head, with everyone around us. The chef worked in the nearby on-site kitchen, and we were served course by course. All the kids were instrumental in making that day unforgettable. Since the long kitchen table had been moved outside for our dinner, a space was created inside for a dance floor. Kevin and Isaiah handled the music, as my Captain—I mean, husband—and I danced to "Two is Better Than One" by Boys Like Girls and Taylor Swift. This had been my ringtone for Paul for many years. I remember that dance vividly and the fun we all had dancing after that. Now, remember the part about wanting to stay in the States in case anyone needed medical attention… well, I'm glad we did. Diana turned in early on the wedding night, and Kevin took her to a clinic the following morning. It turned out that she was battling pneumonia. She was such a good sport throughout the wedding and the days leading up to it, bearing in mind she was ill. Thankfully, she still enjoyed the rest of the trip while taking it a bit easier.

While we were on Oahu, I visited Pearl Harbor, which was such a moving experience. I was so grateful to see and experience it with my children. Thank you to all those who served and currently serve in the military. I do not take it for granted; I enjoy my freedom because of you.

Like any great vacation, the days go by too fast, and the next thing you know, you are packing up to head home. I knew we had a long flight ahead of us, nine and a half hours. I want to thank Sara again for the upgrade to first class by gifting us her air miles. Captain could stretch his legs for the long flight, and even though the cardiologist had cleared us, I was concerned. I made it a bit more fun and purchased matching pineapple compression socks for those of us who left Michigan together. Yes, it is a bit corny, but hey, if I'm doing it for one, why not do it for all? Besides, it made for a helluva cute picture. Aloha, Hawaii!

Love Letter to My Husband
August 17, 2019

WOW!

We did it! We actually did it! What a whirlwind of a wedding/family trip/honeymoon. It was so fantastic Captain. Thank you so very much for loving me so and taking the whole family to Hawaii! Aloha! What a great time and the best part is that we married with all our children there with us. Sorry it was so hot. – Not sorry that you're SO hot!

You are as handsome as the day I met you. Thank you match. com for making my dreams come true. I love you and we are on to our next adventure, buying a home together!

Love you Captain

Mrs. Murray

Final Take Away:

It has been said that you cannot help who you fall in love with. I agree; however, you can't find love if you do not put yourself on the path to it or mentally open yourself up. I surely didn't imagine meeting my Captain and embarking on such an incredible journey. I am forever grateful for the "wink" through Match.com, and I know in my heart that our story evolved the way it was meant to be.

The End

www.ingramcontent.com/pod-product-compliance
Lightning Source LLC
Chambersburg PA
CBHW060849120626
46553CB00001B/23